The Secret Cemetery

with a Foreword by Sir Raymond Firth

The Secret Cemetery

Doris Francis, Leonie Kellaher and
Georgina Neophytou

with a Foreword by Sir Raymond Firth

Oxford • New York

English edition
First published in 2005 by
Berg
Editorial offices:
1st Floor, Angel Court, 81 St Clements Street, Oxford OX4 1AW, UK
175 Fifth Avenue, New York, NY 10010, USA

Berg is the imprint of Oxford International Publishers Ltd.

Library of Congress Cataloging-in-Publication Data

Francis, Doris, 1940-
     The secret cemetery / Doris Francis, Leonie Kellaher, and Georgina
Neophytou ; with a foreword by Sir Raymond Firth.— English ed.
          p. cm.
     Includes bibliographical references and index.
     ISBN 1-85973-592-4 (cloth) — ISBN 1-85973-597-5 (pbk.)
  1. Cemeteries—Social aspects. 2. Cemeteries—Psychological aspects.
3. Mourning customs. 4. Bereavement. I. Kellaher, Leonie A. II.
Neophytou, Georgina. III. Title.

     GT3320.F73 2005
     363.7'5—dc22
                                                      2005002341

British Library Cataloguing-in-Publication Data

A catalogue record for this book is available from the British Library.

ISBN-13   978 1 85973 592 3 (Cloth)
            978 1 85973 597 8 (Paper)

ISBN-10   1 85973 592 4 (Cloth)
            1 85973 597 5 (Paper)

Typeset by JS Typesetting Ltd, Porthcawl, Mid Glamorgan.
Printed in the United Kingdom by Biddles Ltd, King's Lynn.

www.bergpublishers.com

For all those who generously shared their cemetery
experiences with us

Contents

Contents

List of Figures

Acknowledgements

Many people helped to make this book possible. We begin by thanking Peter Jupp and the late Lord Michael Young of Dartington, as well as Professors Peter Loizos and Eileen Barker, Tony Kendle and Ann Dill, for their early encouragement that we study the then relatively uncharted realm of English cemetery behaviour. We offer our appreciation to the Economic and Social Research Council and to the University of North London for generously providing funding for field research. We are especially grateful to colleagues Jenny Hockey, Julie Rugg and Tony Walter for their ongoing support, many good conversations and challenging ideas, and to Brent Elliott, Jan Woudstra, Robert Clifford and Giles Dolphin for generously sharing with us their extensive knowledge of cemeteries.

We owe tremendous thanks to our research assistants: Claire Lee, who helped with survey work at the City of London and Bushey Cemeteries, and Simon Pulman-Jones and Fred Galooba, who conducted field research at Woodgrange Park Cemetery. Renee Miller generously assisted with correlating survey data and gave friendship and encouragement, and Janet Bohrer shared with us the methodology developed for survey research on the royal parks and helped us to adapt it for use in cemeteries. Early in the period of writing up our research data (and after the first author had returned to the United States), a one-day discussion at the University of California, Berkeley, generously organized by Tom Laqueur and also attended by Sharon Kaufman and Beth Dungan, produced many helpful critical comments and overall direction.

It is to the many people – our study participants – who shared their cemetery experiences with us that we owe our greatest gratitude. To the late Sir Raymond Firth, who wrote the foreword to this book during his later years, are due much honour and appreciation.

We thank the following people for their assistance in suggesting specific cemeteries as research sites. Hugh Meller and Julie Dunk urged us to study the City of London Cemetery. Kate Towers offered Richmond and East Sheen Cemetery and provided much helpful assistance during the research period. Marlena Schmool recommended that we contact the United Synagogue, and Jonathan Lew generously gave permission for research at Bushey, as well as at other United Synagogue cemeteries. Ian Hussein urged us to include London's Muslims in our research, and Sam Weller kindly facilitated our research at Woodgrange. Finally, it was Jan Woudstra who told us about the Greek sections at New Southgate as an appropriate study site.

At each cemetery we received the helpful support of management and staff and we would like to acknowledge their assistance. At the City of London Cemetery, the present manager, Ian Hussein, and past superintendents Ian (Ernie) Turner and Jon Luby graciously explained many aspects of cemetery management. The members of the office staff – Dave, Alan, Clive, Roy, Pam, Pat, Jackie, Lynn and Pam – patiently answered our many questions. Dennis and Gary Burke walked us around the grounds, giving the history of the site and discussing their visions and designs for the landscape; and Bernard Heath and the grounds staff explained their daily schedule of activities, which enable the cemetery to function. The 'men on the front gate' – Michael, Bryan, John, Colin and Kevin – gave us a warm welcome every morning, took us along on their daily rounds and offered many a warming cup of tea and good humour on a cold, rainy weekend afternoon.

The United Synagogue president, Elkan Levy, was most welcoming and supportive of our research and shared his deep knowledge of London's Anglo-Jewish community and its rich history. His guided tour of Willesden and our conversations at Bushey remain high points of the project. Charles Tucker, Stephen Garcia, Reuben Exekiel, Reverend Alan Greenbat, Michael Harris, Barry Kosmin and Sharman Kadish gently guided us to a greater understanding of Jewish cemetery behaviour. Ron Edwards at Willesden and Norman Myers, Mark

Williams and Shirley Weiner at Bushey explained so much to us about the cemetery landscape and its customs. Our appreciation goes also to Mr Hirsch of the Adath Yisroel Chevrah Kadisha and to Mr Calo, cemetery superintendent for the West London Synagogue of British Jews.

At New Southgate Cemetery, we appreciated the help provided by the members of the Evans family, as well as by the cemetery staff, particularly office manager Madeline Antoniazzi. We would also like to thank His Eminence The Archbishop of Thyateira and Great Britain, Peter Demetriou, Panos Arvanitakis and The Right Reverend Bishop Timotheos of Militoupolis.

For Woodgrange Park Cemetery, we would like to thank Mr Budge for giving us permission to study the cemetery, and its managers and staff – Clive Mansfield and Wayne – for providing illuminating information about ongoing developments there. We are also indebted to the Friends of Woodgrange Park Cemetery for their insights into the changing meanings and landscapes of that cemetery.

Throughout the research period, the Institute of Burial and Cremation Administration (IBCA) and its leadership – Ken West, Bob Coates (and his wife Sheri), Ken Elliott, Peter Gitsham, Peter Mitchell, Angela Dunn and Ian Hussein – extended a warm invitation to make our study available to their members, who provided a wise forum for our research findings and generously made available their understanding of cemetery behaviour from years of accumulated experience. Ken West deserves special mention for generously facilitating our survey of attitudes toward woodland burial at Carlisle Cemetery. Our thanks go also to Theresa Quinn of the Memorial Masons for her support.

We appreciated the insightful comments of our anonymous outside reader, and we thank Brent Elliott, Dave McCarthy and Melvyn Hartog for carefully reading sections of the manuscript and making helpful suggestions. Our particular thanks go to editor Jane Kepp for skillfully weaving together our different writing styles, and to Ken Bruce and Kathryn Earle at Berg for their generous patience, guidance and support.

Doris Francis would like specifically to thank Curator John Simmons, John Londsdale and Ian Leese of the Royal Botanic Gardens, Kew, for their confidence and encouragement. A thank you also goes to her Kew classmates for their generous acceptance of her as a fellow student and to Jane Reynolds and Mark Poswillo for their continuing friendship. To Louis Erhard, her appreciation is boundless.

Foreword

The Body in the Sacred Garden

Sir Raymond Firth

Are cemeteries a curious, even macabre subject of discussion? The authors of this volume do not think so, and they are right. Cemeteries offer a rich field for anthropological study, because they illustrate the emotional and symbolic meaning attached to material objects in human culture, including even the bodies of the dead. They show, too, how diverse can be the treatment of what is basically a very simple process, the disposal of a lifeless human body in the ground.

Death as the inevitable end of life has been a matter of much reflection by philosophers, theologians and poets, as well as of much concern to ordinary people. Such reflection has often been more on the fate of the soul than on the fate of the body. Yet the practical aspects of action following the demise of a person demand attention. In English society, disposal of a corpse is usually a matter for professional craftsmen known as undertakers. *Undertaker* in general means simply one who performs or agrees to perform a task or mission. It is presumably a term of Anglo-Saxon origin. But since its appearance in Middle English it has taken on some special meanings. In referring to those who arrange a funeral, the word *undertaker* contrasts with the American term *mortician,* a nineteenth-century word of Latin origin which means frankly one who has to deal with death. There is here a strong hint of the alleged reticence of the English toward private matters.

Social anthropologists have long considered death and its implications in a broad way for many diverse cultures. They have studied not only the technical practices of disposal of the dead body and the associated funeral rites and beliefs about the dead, but also the complex social reactions of the persons affected by the death. Regarding treatment of the body itself, they have shown how great is the variation of practices. These include inhumation (burial in the ground), cremation (destruction by fire), exposure (lodging in caves or treetops or setting adrift in a canoe) and mummification (preservation of the body by special treatment of the tissues with oils, etc). Anthropologists have also noted the habit among some communities of first burying the body and then exhuming the bones to be placed in a more permanent shelter.

Such different ways of disposing of the dead are not casual. They tend to be deeply embedded in cultural tradition, with strong sentimental and often religious associations. Disintegration is the ultimate end for a dead human body, whether it be exposed to predatory birds and animals or discretely covered over with earth. Parsees who set out the bodies of their dead in so-called Towers of Silence to be disposed of by vultures defend this custom as appropriate to their faith. Yet other Eastern and Western people think that to leave a dead body unburied is improper, even indecent or insulting. Kinsfolk and friends feel that a soldier who has fallen in battle or a road accident victim by the roadside should be given a 'proper' burial, often in consecrated ground. An analogous opinion was expressed by a character in a famous eighteenth-century Chinese novel, who said, in repentance for his bad deeds, that he would not 'deserve' burial when he was dead. Traditionally, in parts of China the burial of the head of the family was a matter of careful attention to the geomantic signs of good fortune. There was no bustle for internment; lucky days had to be chosen for putting the body into the coffin, nailing it up, starting to dig the grave and getting the coffin into the ground. By contrast, Hindu custom has long been to cremate a dead body, often with great ceremony and display of emotion.

Yet custom can change. Western burial practice, commonly in ground dedicated for that purpose by religious rites, has given way in many sectors of modern society to use of the crematorium and disposal of the ashes in a garden of remembrance. If there was ever any notion that cremation was reminiscent of the flames of hell consuming sinners, it has now disappeared. Yet other sections of society, in part because of religious belief, still adhere to the age-old practice of laying the body to rest in the ground.

The range of terms available in English to describe the earthen rest-ing place of a dead human body illustrates the many distinctive themes that may be involved in the complexity of thought and feeling about the placing of the dead. Some terms, such as *grave, burying ground, burial place* and *sepulchre,* of various linguistic origins, refer simply to the disposal of the corpse in the earth and covering it over. Others indicate places specially prepared, such as *mortuary,* for the temporary reception of a corpse, and *ossuary,* a storage place for the bones, implying their retention for a period. The terms *graveyard, cemetery* and *necropolis* etymologically indicate places specifically set apart for collective reception of the dead. The linguistic emphases in these three words are different. *Graveyard* refers to the enclosure containing graves; *necropolis* refers to the dead as buried in or near a city, or perhaps as constituting a city in themselves. *Cemetery* does not refer to the dead at all. In classical Greek the equivalent word meant simply a dormitory, and the English term then seems to imply a resting place or a sleeping place. In a Christian English community the old expres-sion 'God's acre', meaning God's seed-field, used from the seventeenth century, connotes a religious belief that the bodies of the dead are at the discretion of the Almighty, being 'sown' to produce a harvest of souls, or perhaps even of resurrected creatures, in due time. Still in relation to the disposal of the dead are terms such as *barrow* and *tumulus,* ancient sepulchral monuments. A *mausoleum* is a stately burial structure, reminiscent of the classical, perhaps legendary, tomb of the king Mausolus, erected by his sorrowing widow.

In Western society a cemetery is usually a place for collective burials set apart from the ordinary living and working places of the folk. But a dead human body is commonly looked upon with ambivalent feelings by kin. Aversion to a corpse as such, the 'lifeless clay' which was once so animate, is a general reaction. For hygienic reasons it must be removed from the company of the living. In many societies a dead human body is also regarded as polluting in the sense of involving ritual danger, which must be removed by cleansing performances. Yet some sorrow is usually felt at the loss of a person formerly well known. The mourning at the funeral may be quite genuine, and the memory of the person may lead to the wish to have the remains of the dead still near.

But to keep the remains of the dead in close association with the living may mean more complicated ideas, especially when a concept of a spirit of the dead may be involved. Some seventy years ago, doing anthropological research in the Solomon Islands, I lived among a small isolated community, the Tikopia. I occupied a leaf-thatched house with a sandy floor covered with mats plaited from coconut fronds. On one part of the floor the mats covered the graves of the father and grandfather of the owner of the house. When I took up residence I was asked by the owner to tread as little as possible upon those mats, out of respect for the men buried below. But the mats were not particularly taboo and could be sat upon by men in any serious gathering.

Traditionally on this small island, a Tikopia dwelling house was usually near the sea. Its floor was divided rather vaguely – not physically but socially – into three spheres. The 'eye of the house', usually facing seawards, was reserved as a seating place for men and was the site of any ritual procedures such as offerings to the dead. Because of its general ceremonial significance, the area was treated with respect. Women and children did not ordinarily go there, and when people slept they were careful to orient their heads, not their feet, toward it. By contrast, the opposite side of the house, figuratively called the 'back of the oven' because it looked out upon the cooking place at the rear of the house, was the area usually occupied by the women and children; often a small fire served for minor cooking tasks. The 'middle of the house' was common ground for social occasions and domestic jobs.

In family houses of some age, according to custom, elders and senior men were buried in the soil beneath the 'eye of the house', their graves marked by mats plaited from coconut fronds, which were carefully arranged with the head of each mat pointing outwards to the eave of the house. Each mat was personally known as 'the mat of our father', 'the mat of our grandfather' and so on. Junior members of the family were usually buried outside the house, but close by, as under the eaves. The grave area in the house, indicated by mats, was not treated as sacred but was respected and, especially where dead chiefs lay, regarded with reverence. Ancestor worship and spirit mediumship were part of traditional Tikopia religion, and spirits of the dead were regularly invoked to give health and prosperity to their descendants.

The spirits of dead ancestors could be appealed to no matter where their mortal remains might be. But the mixture of sentiment and self-interest in having these remains close at hand would seem to give a rationale to this somewhat unusual practice of in-house burial. There is no doubt that Tikopia of former times felt strongly that their kinsfolk who were near to them in life should lie near to them in death. The patterns of the grave could still reflect the patterns of domestic life. Many Tikopia then were pagan, and others, though Christian, still held to the worship of their ancestors. The common sentiment was that it was proper for the dead to lie close to the living. But by thirty years later, when all Tikopia had embraced Christianity, though there was still no common public cemetery, burials no longer took place within the house, though the graves were still close by.

In the West, burial usually takes place in the conventional cemetery. But sometimes an individual resting place is chosen, with the idea of having a loved one close at hand or associated with the scene of his past labours. In 1998 the world-famous violinist and patron of music Yehudi Menuhin, who died in Berlin, was brought back to England and buried at the foot of a tree he had planted on the grounds of the music school he had founded – a token of the deep sentiment felt by his family for him and his work.

Continued association of the dead with the living may be demonstrated by memorials. When the dead have been removed to cemeteries they may still be visited by relatives. Grief and mourning may abate with time, but it is common for flowers to be periodically placed on a grave in memory of the deceased for years after the burial. A more lasting memorial is secured when a tree is planted or a simple stone set over the grave. In literate communities a gravestone may be inscribed with the name and virtues of the deceased, in conventional form. In many cultures there has been a tradition of erecting tombs over the dead, structures of some architectural quality, sometimes with elaborate sculpture such as statues of the dead or more symbolic figures. While these really or ostensibly are intended to honour the dead, they often also glorify the living. A family's wealth, social status and aesthetic taste may all be displayed in a spectacular memorial. Association of the dead with the living is also manifested in many communities by periodic assemblage of kin at the tomb of a dead forebear. Ceremonial acts, offerings and prayers of worship show how the grave serves as a rallying point for members of the group, a focus for their solidarity.

This leads to the question, Who may be interred in a cemetery? In the West there are many public cemeteries the populations of which are almost random. Local people of all kinds are buried there, together with strangers who die in the vicinity and are not borne off to a natal or other resting place. But other cemeteries may be more restrictive, to the dead of a specific religious faith or a select ethnic minority. Travel writers have noted, for example, the Protestant cemetery in Rome, centre of a predominantly Catholic country. The burying grounds of Jesuit missionaries to China some three centuries ago near Peking (Beijing) have also been described. Such historical cases have many modern analogies. A special category of limited cemetery is that for soldiers killed in one or other of the two world wars. Because of the masses of men so interred, especially from 1914 to 1918, such cemeteries have been known as 'silent cities'. From various points of view a grouping of the dead may reflect their grouping in life.

Cemeteries may also be reservoirs of history. Some are sites to which people go to be reminded of a significant past, to show their interest in or respect for the heroic, famous or notorious dead and to demonstrate their own allegiance to an idea or value with which the dead person was associated. In walking the streets of north London near my home I have often been asked by foreign strangers how to find Highgate Cemetery. I have usually replied simply 'Karl Marx?' and received a beaming smile in return, before I gave the requisite directions. And on one occasion, on a visit of my own for other purposes, I saw a line of solemn Chinese men bowing before the massive looming statue of the great man. But this was before Marx fell from favour. In the same cemetery, more modest but more attractive to some literary enthusiasts, are the resting places of George Elliot and Margaret Radclyffe Hall. For the archaeologist the cemeteries of the pre-documented past have provided rich sources of information on the cultural life of their time. Even where a form of writing has existed, as with the Etruscans of central Italy, excavation of their ancient cemeteries has yielded a treasure of mural paintings, plaques and bronze and terracotta figures in tombs from about the eighth to the fourth century BC, which have thrown great light on the social and political organization, the domestic life and the art of this otherwise long-forgotten, mysterious civilization. Treasure in gold, jade and terracotta from ancient Chinese tombs has also vastly increased our knowledge of oriental history.

Disposal of the dead by burial in the West tends to conform to what may be termed the concept of appropriate places. Living people inhabit houses, dead people lie in cemeteries. But notions of appropriateness can vary. In the course of the last two centuries the idea has been put forward and gained wide acceptance that the last resting place of the dead should be in a pleasing environment, less forbidding than the formal stonework of a churchyard. Hence arose the idea of a cemetery as a kind of garden, arousing thoughts about the beauty of living things as well as reminiscences of the dead person. The thinking behind the concept of the garden cemetery has been complex, presumably owing something originally to the Romantic movement at the end of the eighteenth and beginning of the nineteenth century. As part of its attempt to bring nature as landscape into service to soften the keener emotions of the mourners, this concept focuses on the image of the cemetery as an entity in itself, not merely as a repository for dead bodies. The result is a paradox: corruption below ground matched by new life above ground. Death is not conquered but denied victory.

But mingled with the idea of cemetery as a place of memory for the dead, a witness to history and a beautiful landscape of a special order

are other considerations. There are problems of upkeep and management, of legal rights and obligations, of financial, even commercial
interests. Cemeteries occupy land. Some years ago there were said to
be over 100 cemeteries within a short distance of central London,
totalling 3,000 acres. (Land shortage may have been one of the factors
leading to the promotion of cremation.) To deal with such administrative and financial matters, a variety of organisations has developed.
In the Christian West, the church traditionally controlled the consecrated ground devoted to burial of those deemed suitable for interment
there, but public authorities have also had charge of areas for more
eclectic reception of the dead. Some cemeteries have come to be run
by charitable organizations – for example, Highgate Cemetery, where
the Friends of Highgate Cemetery and the Highgate Cemetery Trust
share control of this famous burial place. Nowadays commercial
cemetery companies have arisen, especially in North America, and
their combination of aesthetics and advertisement in the effort to make
a profit from the dead have stimulated some ironic literary comments.

Concern for the embellishment and care of cemeteries has led to
the creation of professional associations of those interested. In Britain,
for example, the National Association of Memorial Masons oversees
the making, installation and use of grave markers such as tombstones,
sometimes called lawn memorials. The Church of England has sponsored a handbook giving guidelines for the size and quality of headstones and the nature of other memorial objects such as flower
containers; it also discourages photographs of the dead, as are common
in some European graveyards. In France, the International Council of
Funeral Architecture and Furniture, representing about 300 modern
artists, it is said, recently took action to meet a growing French taste
for more colourful contemporary design in coffins and tomb materials,
avoiding the stiffness and sadness of the traditional *pompes funebres*.

The complex interlinked factors involved in the conception, creation
and use of modern cemeteries are examined by the authors of this
book. They state their main focus as the arrangement of death and
bereavement through ritual practices. They have given their subject a
great deal of analytic thought and a rich body of illustrative material.
In doing so they have made a double contribution to our knowledge
of contemporary society. Other books dealing with cemeteries have
been published, usually as guides and gazetteers or historical accounts;
the anthropology of cemeteries in their full social context has been
largely untouched until now. This is one merit of the book. The other
is that much of it is founded on fieldwork – close personal investigation
on site. So this work is a significant demonstration of the value of an
anthropological approach to the institutions of our modern Western

society. Social anthropology has long since given up the notion that it is concerned only with the life of exotic, 'primitive' peoples or even those whose culture is different from our own. Cross-cultural comparisons and the collection of data from alien types of society are still important parts of anthropologists' study. But they are properly supplemented by systematic, firsthand, day-to-day research in our own type of society. This book is a notable, perceptive addition to the growing number of anthropological studies of modern Western institutions.

1

Studying the Living in Cemeteries

This is her first garden. It's a memorial garden. It is a place to visit her still, and have a chat. The garden is another way of keeping in touch. I come every week on Thursday since she died. To tidy up, trim, cut the grass, put fresh water in, change the flowers that others bring. I feel she's still with me. I used to see her every day when she was living. I worked where she lived and I would see her and have a cup of tea and a chat. Although Mum's no longer alive, I still have a chat – for five minutes after I tidy up; I tell her what's going on.

> Thirty-eight-year-old East End resident whose mother
> had died two years previously and was buried at the
> City of London Cemetery

This book, a study of what people do when they visit cemeteries, began with Class 29 at London's Royal Botanic Gardens, Kew, where one of us – Doris Francis – was studying landscape design in the School of Horticulture in 1995. The instructors gave the class an assignment: prepare a planting plan for an older cemetery in the English Midlands that was sponsoring a national competition to refurbish its grounds. When the students reviewed the site, they found no visitors tending graves, and none was invited to speak with the class about visitors' needs and wants. When Francis told Leonie Kellaher, a fellow anthropologist and social gerontologist, about the assignment, they agreed that they wished to know more about what English mourners did when they went to cemeteries – about their activities, purposes and reflections.

Many scholars had previously studied burial sites, funeral rituals and mortuary behaviour among non-Western people, but few had made similar studies in their own contemporary Western industrial societies.[1] Furthermore, books on English gravestones and cemetery design existed, but none was written from the perspective of those who used cemeteries.[2] Here was new, useful research that needed to be done; as anthropologists, we would do our fieldwork at home, in England, in order to understand the cemetery experience from the viewpoint of the bereaved and to make our findings available to a wide public and professional audience. Although nearly every adult in London had some familiarity with cemeteries and what went on in them, these gardenlike places remained at once very public and very secret. We would study the unique culture that existed behind the cemetery gates to try to better understand these special spaces.

In 1996, the two of us – along with our sociologist colleague Georgina Neophytou – began to study London cemetery behaviour. We cautiously approached people and asked whether they would be willing to talk about why they visited the cemetery, what they did during their visits and what the visits meant to them.

Most people, we discovered, were willing to talk to us. We interviewed and observed the actions of long-time English residents of the East End at the City of London Cemetery, where a well-kept, post– Second World War 'lawn section', featuring straight rows of graves with stone markers and small gardens (Fig. 1.1), adjoins older Victorian areas of elaborate monuments and tree-lined avenues. For comparison with other religious and ethnic groups, we talked to Orthodox Jews at Bushey United Jewish Cemetery, where grounds landscaped with ornamental pools, trees and flowers surround more austere, unplanted burial areas with expanses of white marble stones marking graves in long rows (Fig. 1.2). At New Southgate Cemetery, we spoke with the families of Greek Orthodox immigrants from Cyprus, who have turned sections of the 150-year-old cemetery into an exuberant garden by surrounding large white memorials with carnations, roses and plantings of rosemary and miniature cypress trees (Fig. 1.3).[3] To extend our cross-cultural sample to London's Muslim population, we interviewed Bangladeshi and Gujarati immigrants at

Figure 1.1.
The lawn section of the City of London Cemetery, with its small grave gardens, 1998.

Woodgrange Park Cemetery, where new Muslim graves were located in small clearings amid the thick overgrowth that covered older Christian memorials (Fig. 1.4) and where broken headstones lay gathered into piles near the derelict Gothic chapel. Behind the gates, each site seemed to hold its own secrets.

As the three of us crossed these cemetery thresholds, we entered a space 'set aside',[4] a world that most people perceive as distinct from the everyday. As mourners themselves explained: 'When you go through the cemetery gate, it's another world.' What we discovered there was that for the bereaved who visit cemeteries, these burial grounds are special, sacred spaces of personal, emotional and spiritual reclamation where the shattered self can be 'put back in place'. Many mourners reported a sense of satisfaction, almost of sufficiency, at the end of a visit. They told of a charge of unrest that built up between visits and could be managed only through a return visit to the grave. Many actively resisted the push of the outside world to 'move on' and rejected the frequently asked question, 'Why go to the cemetery, there's nothing there?' Many cemetery visitors relied on their own resources and the support of friends and family; they gave themselves time to mourn without self-judgement and measured their present ability to cope against the standard of the self two or three years earlier. Few

Figure 1.2.
White marble
graves at Bushey
United Jewish
Cemetery, 1997.

allowed themselves to sink into total despair and monitored the amount of pain they could endure. Mourners reflected upon their own experiences to challenge popular homilies: 'Time doesn't really heal, but it does help to make the loss more bearable.'

The words, actions and reflections of these people also revealed the ways many of them used the resources of nature – the cemetery landscape and the flowers and plants they brought to the grave – and how they employed images of the grave as 'home' to put 'flesh' back on the bones of the deceased, to remember them and not to forget. Many users of City of London and New Southgate Cemeteries took part in a cemetery culture of gardeners whose embellishments of the grave with plants and flowers helped them to cope with grief, to keep the deceased's identity alive and to regenerate their relationships even after death. The observations and reflections of all these study participants revealed something of the public yet hidden and secret cemetery as a place that connects the world of the living with the world of life after death.

To think about a grave and its cemetery as being like a garden appeared to help many mourners make sense of the incomprehensibility of death and the experience of loss. Although the rural churchyard has historically dominated the English popular imagination

Figure 1.3.
Orthodox Greek
Cypriot graves
surrounded by
roses, carnations
and miniature
cypress trees at
New Southgate
Cemetery, 1998.

and iconography of death, the bereaved in our research study chose
instead to call upon the image of the garden when speaking about death
and burial.[5] It was the spiritual and regenerative aspect of the garden
that seemed to inform this association between cemeteries and gardens,
drawing on deep religious and historical roots. The imagery of paradise
and the Garden of Eden in the Jewish, Christian and Islamic traditions,
for example, suggested a beautiful, secluded park, ornamented with
water, trees and flowers.[6] Enclosed within this walled garden was the

Figure 1.4.
New Muslim
graves at
Woodgrange Park
Cemetery, 2002.

sacred tree of life; it was a place without death. In the teachings of
Christianity, the garden remains religiously significant – a reminder
both of the Garden of Eden and Christ's agony at Gethsemane.[7] As
Adam was required to 'dress and keep' the sacred space of Eden before
the Fall, so, too, the cultivation of the soil (and possibly the tending
of a grave) became work ordained by God, and horticulture and burial
in a garden offered a promise of paradise regained.[8] Throughout
English history, the enclosed garden has been seen as engendering
repose and promoting harmony, its flowers and trees emblematic of
spiritual truths, beauty and order. As an outdoor cloister, the garden
has also been depicted as a religious house, offering retreat for spiritual
and moral reflection, solitary meditation and communion with nature.[9]
Perhaps it was this ideal of the garden as a spiritual and palliative
resource that led to its being privileged as an ideal accompaniment
for burial.

As a place of contemplation, however, the English garden with its
fading flowers also confronts people with the transitoriness of life, the
certainty of death and the vanity of earthly pursuits – even while the
cycles of decay and renovation of nature offer consolation and solace.[10]
But in what other ways does the image of the garden inform mourners'
understanding of the cemetery? Both cemeteries and gardens are
bounded places set apart from the rigid regularity of daily schedules
and calendars; they are 'timeless' spaces of generational and accumulated time. Nature's powers of rebirth and regeneration, as experienced
in gardens and cemeteries, offer resources that confound and obscure
an irreversible linear vision of the human life course and suggest,
instead, a cyclical, repetitive and eternal view of existence that holds
hope for immortality. Through the creation of the cemetery in the form

of a landscaped garden, a harmony with nature was sought in death – a return to the lost Garden of Eden.

By entering the contemporary cemetery and viewing that world from the perspectives of the bereaved, we learned that while many mourners identified the cemetery with a garden, they also associated the ideas of home and tomb as another resource for dealing with death and loss. Dictionaries indicate an analogy between tomb and home ('one's abode after death';[11] and the 'last' home[12]) and many bereaved align these meanings when speaking about the grave plot and its marker.

Since ancient times, the architecture of the grave has mirrored society's thoughts about the dwellings of the living.[13] In writing about tombs as houses for the dead, the archaeologist Ian Hodder found that tombs in prehistoric Europe corresponded in shape, construction, orientation, position of entrance and decoration to houses of the same period.[14] The tomb has also reflected a culture's ideas about death and the afterlife.[15] The ancient Egyptians, for example, believed that the dead lived on in the after-world. The tombs of the elites replicated the houses the deceased had enjoyed while alive and were intentionally built with rooms, corridors and false doors and windows, thereby extending the home boundary into eternity.[16] The ancient Greeks, with a different view of the afterlife, feared death, and their gravestones often depicted and evoked the yearned-for humble home occupied in this life.[17] From the Middle Ages onward, the Christian tomb, often located in the churchyard or church nave, represented a sleeping place from which death would be overcome at resurrection.

In ancient Mediterranean societies, as well as among some traditional cultures in Africa and the South Pacific such as the Tikopia of the Solomon Islands studied some seventy-five years ago by Raymond Firth, the custom was to bury the senior men of the household under the floor of the residential dwelling.[18] This choice of burial location reflected the roles the deceased had played in life as well as those expected of them in death,[19] and so acknowledged their ongoing participation in the life of the family and community. The dead were believed to influence the lives of their surviving kin, and their spirits were regularly invoked to give health and prosperity to their descendants. In-house burial demonstrated the close, ongoing ties between the living and the dead and a degree of willingness to keep the dead 'at home'. These ancient, cross-cultural ideas linking home, garden, burial and the afterlife – still used by mourners today – provided us with a research opportunity for exploring the cultural meanings of cemeteries in contemporary, metropolitan London.

Six Cemeteries and Their Users

We elected to study such cultural meanings and the cemetery behaviour of the living at six burial grounds in or close to the greater London area (Fig. 1.5). At each site we concentrated on earth burial of the intact body rather than on cremation.[20] The City of London Cemetery was our primary field site, where we conducted research throughout the study period. At Bushey United Jewish, New Southgate and Wood-grange Park Cemeteries we concentrated our fieldwork mainly during annual commemoration activities, and we carried out intermittent research at the other two, East Sheen and Richmond Cemetery and historic Abney Park Cemetery. We also did supplementary fieldwork at older, now closed cemeteries where there were few new burials but where participants in our study continued to visit graves. The United Synagogue's Willesden and East Ham Cemeteries, the Greek Orthodox section at Hendon Cemetery and St Patrick's Catholic Cemetery were all sites of additional research.

We selected London for study because of its ethnic, religious and socio-economic diversity and its range of cemeteries of varying ages, contrasting landscapes and diverse management styles and structures. Current policy issues with which cemetery owners and managers are faced, particularly those concerning constraints on land available for full-body burial, appear to feature most acutely in the capital,[21] but are increasingly reflected regionally and in other metropolitan centres in the United Kingdom. In most urban locations, the need for immigrant groups to find burial space is also pressing. But London is not representative of England, and although some research conclusions from this study may apply to all cemeteries, other findings should be generalized to regional cemeteries only with caution.

Significantly, the 2001 Parliamentary Committee on Cemeteries and Burial Policy in the United Kingdom concluded that 'there is a lack of basic information on the number, condition and operational viability of the country's cemeteries', including those in London.[22] Thus, central government has acknowledged the need to steer legislation and practices that will preserve and enhance the conditions and use-management of English cemeteries, so that all groups have viable burial and cremation options well into the future. We hope this study will contribute toward these goals.[23]

We chose our six cemeteries for research according to the criteria of current status (active, semi-active or closed), ownership, population served (denominational or secular), location, date of establishment, size and landscape.[24] Our twofold intention was to concentrate on active municipal cemeteries used by non-denominational populations

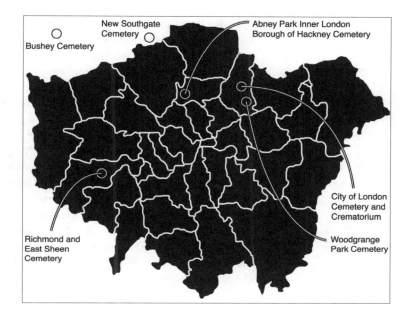

New Southgate Cemetery

Bushey Cemetery

Abney Park Inner London Borough of Hackney Cemetery

City of London Cemetery and Crematorium

Richmond and East Sheen Cemetery

Woodgrange Park Cemetery

Figure 1.5.
Cemeteries in the greater London area.

and on cemeteries serving cultural groups that formed significant segments of London's ethnic population and whose members had distinct burial practices and mourning rituals.[25] For the latter purpose, we included three different burial sites that catered, respectively, to the Orthodox Jewish, Greek Orthodox and Bangladeshi and Gujarati Muslim communities.[26] We did not select a specific cemetery for research on London's large Catholic population because the two nineteenth-century London Catholic cemeteries are very full, and many Catholics now bury their dead in the municipal cemeteries. Nonetheless, we carried out limited fieldwork at St Patrick's Catholic Cemetery in the borough of Waltham Forest, in conjunction with research on Catholics who used the main municipal study site, City of London Cemetery, located nearby.

The City of London Cemetery and Crematorium

As our principal research site we selected the non-denominational City of London Cemetery and Crematorium (CLCC), located at Manor Park in the London borough of Newham. It is among the largest municipal cemeteries in Europe and on a winter's day may schedule fifty funerals, ten of which will be earth burials. A steady stream of visitors attends graves in many sections of the cemetery, and many of these mourner-visitors were willing to be part of our study. Opened in 1856, the City of London Cemetery remains a model cemetery that is operated by a professionally trained management team and is used as a training site for accreditation of cemetery personnel.[27] It is the main burial and cremation facility for East London, serving the boroughs of Hackney, Tower Hamlets, Newham, Waltham Forest, Barking and Dagenham, and Redbridge.

The East End of London has been the first home to a succession of immigrant groups over the centuries. Huguenot silk weavers, Jews from Eastern Europe and working people from the countryside and Ireland were all drawn to the area's clothing trades, local markets, docks and building industries.[28] Immigrants from Bangladesh and Gujarat are the most recent arrivals.[29] Always an area of economic hardship, the East End has suffered from overcrowding, pockets of extreme poverty, sweatshop factories and, for many, the uncertainties of a casual labour market. During the Second World War, the East End was heavily bombed, with consequent evacuation and relocation of entire communities. With the closing of the docks in the 1960s, such changes in the social fabric of the area were further intensified by

Table 1.1 Principal Characteristics of Cemeteries Selected as Main Sites for Research

Cemetery	Location	Size (acres)	Date Opened	Denomination	Ownership	Status
City of London Cemetery and Crematorium	Outer London borough of Newham	200	1856	All and none	Corporation of City of London (municipal/public)	Active and in-filling spaces
Bushey United Jewish Cemetery	Home County of Hertfordshire		1947	Orthodox Jewish	United Synagogue Burial Society (not-for-profit)	Active, seeking more space
New Southgate Cemetery and Crematorium	Outer London borough of Barnet	60	1861	Greek Orthodox and others	Private, limited company	Active and diversifying to other groups
Woodgrange Park Cemetery	Outer London borough of Newham	16	1889	Muslim and Nonconformist	Private, limited company	Active, mainly for Muslims
East Sheen and Richmond Cemetery	Outer London borough of Richmond upon Thames	75	1839	All and none	London borough of Richmond (municipal/public)	Active, 'green', ecological sites
Abney Park Cemetery	Central-inner London borough of Hackney	14	1840	Nonconformist	London borough of Hackney (municipal/public)	Historic, a few family burials

economic dislocation. Socio-economic shifts continue to reshape the area today.[30]

Bushey United Jewish Cemetery

Bushey United Jewish Cemetery, located north of London in Hertford-shire, was consecrated in 1947 to meet the burial needs of United Synagogue members who lived in the north-west suburbs of London. Owned by the United Synagogue itself, the cemetery contains two prayer halls where funerals are held and also a *taharah* house, a facility for the ritually prescribed washing of the body before burial. The United Synagogue is a centrist Orthodox Jewish institution established under an act of Parliament in 1871.[31] The majority of London syna-gogues are grouped together into synagogal bodies, of which the United Synagogue is the largest. Interments only take place at one of these restricted cemeteries through the burial societies affiliated with these synagogal groups.[32]

The Jewish population of Great Britain is the second largest outside Israel and the United States. Jews were expelled from England in 1290, and the history of London's Anglo-Jewry began with resettlement in 1656 during Cromwell's Protectorate.[33] The earliest Jewish settlers were from Spain, Portugal and the Netherlands; they were followed by Ashkenazi immigrants, largely from Germany, in the eighteenth cen-tury. Today, the majority of British Jews are descendants of people who fled the Russian Empire between 1881 and 1914 or who arrived as refugees from Germany, Austria and Czechoslovakia just before the Second World War.[34] The successive waves of immigrants have dis-persed from the East End to suburbs in north-east and north-west London.[35]

New Southgate Cemetery

The Great Northern Cemetery, now known as New Southgate, was consecrated in 1861 by the Bishop of Rochester.[36] Located in today's outer London borough of Barnet, the cemetery has Reform Jewish, Roman Catholic and Baha'i sections, but we selected it for study because of its strong link with the north London Greek Cypriot community, which has helped shape the character and style of the cemetery since the 1950s.[37] The neighbouring boroughs of Haringey and Enfield are home to the largest Greek Cypriot population outside Cyprus. Today, the cemetery is owned by the New Southgate Cemetery and Crematorium Company, Ltd, a private British firm established in 1933. According to management, a proportion of profits are now being reinvested 'to improve the formerly low level of maintenance'.

As a colonial power, Britain ruled Cyprus from 1878 to 1960, establishing a long colonial connection between the two countries. The first wave of Cypriot immigrants reached England in the 1920s, mainly from rural settlements. Cypriot immigration peaked in the 1950s and 1960s but was followed by a final wave of displaced Cypriot refugees after the 1974 Turkish military invasion and occupation of northern Cyprus. Greek Cypriots are to be differentiated from mainland Greeks, some of whom migrated to England as professionals or entrepreneurs and whose family members purchased a Greek section of Norwood Cemetery in 1840. In our research at New Southgate, we concentrated mainly on the Greek Orthodox areas, including the two acres purchased from the cemetery by the Greek Orthodox Cathedral, Hagia Sophia.[38]

Woodgrange Park Cemetery

We selected Woodgrange Park Cemetery for study because of the rapidly increasing numbers of recent Muslim immigrants from Bangladesh and the Indian state of Gujarat who use this burial ground because management permits them to practise some of their traditional burial rituals here. They do so alongside a declining population of English mourners. The latter are concerned with the mortal remains of East Enders who once lived in the neighbourhoods now occupied by the newly settled Muslims. The earlier English-born group moved upwards in socio-economic status and outwards to the suburbs, a trajectory the newer Asian groups are likely to follow.

Woodgrange Park Cemetery is located in the Manor Park area of the London borough of Newham, on the A13 arterial route, which runs eastwards and out of London from the Whitechapel area. South Asian men came to this part of the capital, settling there and elsewhere in England, in the 1950s and 1960s.[39] From the mid- to late 1970s, families were reunited as Bangladeshi and Gujarati wives and children arrived. The older, now dependent generation – the parents of the first immigrants – also arrived in the 1980s and continues to do so. Coming from rural communities with few, if any, capital assets, these Bangladeshis and Gujaratis occupy lower socio-economic categories and register low on many indices of health and material well-being, particularly infant mortality.

Woodgrange Park Cemetery was opened in 1880 by a joint stock company and has remained privately owned, changing hands several times over the past fifty years. The present owner's operations and alterations to the landscape offered us a unique opportunity to observe the details and dynamics of cemetery change. We saw shifts in clientele, the original English users' rearguard battle to protect their graves from being turned over to single-depth Muslim burial, and the sale of four acres of cemetery land for the development of new housing after it had been cleared through exhumations. The community associated with the burials of the earlier English population opposed the clearing and land sale. Through an organization called Friends of Woodgrange Cemetery, their protest led to an act of Parliament in the House of Lords that specified the broad limits of alteration to the cemetery and laid down markers for its management until the early twenty-first century.[40] The dynamic among management, the Friends group and the new immigrant Muslim population thus became a focus of research.

East Sheen and Richmond Cemetery

We chose East Sheen and Richmond Cemetery, a municipal burial ground run by the London borough of Richmond, because it offers a range of burial options, including a special section for babies, the choice of a simple, upright slab of regulated size in the lawn section and the option of a fully kerbed grave in a variety of landscape settings. It also has an 'ecological' area that is maintained in a 'more natural' state. The choices people make when they have a range of burial options available for the same fee gave an indication of user preferences and provided research data that was not always available at other cemeteries in the mid-1990s. This site was originally two cemeteries, the first of which was opened in 1836 and amalgamated with the second in 1903. The cemetery is immediately adjacent to the great space of Richmond Park and serves populations in the south and towards the west of London. The socio-economic profile of this local authority describes one of the most advantaged populations in greater London, though it also contains small pockets of deprivation.

Abney Park Cemetery

Abney Park was one of a ring of private Victorian cemeteries located around inner London in the nineteenth century. Today, this historic site provides few burial spaces but represents both the enduring and the changing meanings that inactive cemeteries hold over time. Located in Stoke Newington, a part of the densely populated inner London borough of Hackney, Abney Park Cemetery was founded in 1840 for Nonconformists who had settled in the area in the seventeenth and eighteenth centuries.[41] It was laid out on the site of the Abney Estate, the chapel being built where the old house had stood. The main east entrance lodge, office and gate piers, which now open onto a busy high street, were designed in a funereal Egyptian style.[42] The grounds and trees provided the nucleus for the much praised Arboretum, which boasted 25,000 named varieties of trees and shrubs and 1,029 rose bushes planted by George Loddiges, a celebrated Victorian nursery-man.[43]

The cemetery quickly filled, income declined and, after 1939, maintenance was minimal. Deterioration and dereliction followed until a rescue plan was formulated in the 1970s to stave off redevelopment for housing. Today, the cemetery is owned by the local authority of Hackney but is managed by the Abney Park Cemetery Trust. The trust has initiated clearance of the prolific vegetation and sought funding for restoring buildings and monuments. Although Hackney is a borough with socio-economic indicators of poverty and deprivation, the area immediately around the cemetery is one of accelerating gentrification where house prices approach those in adjoining Islington. Professionals are repopulating this part of London, sometimes labelled the 'eastern artistic and cultural corridor'. The place of Abney Park Cemetery in these changes has undoubtedly been significant.

Studying People at Cemeteries

To observe the actions and learn about the perceptions and observations of visitors to these selected London cemeteries, the three of us – two anthropologists and a sociologist – made daily and weekend visits to our study sites over an eighteen-month period spanning the years 1996 to 1998. Later, we conducted additional short periods of research to update our data. The accessible, public settings of these cemeteries made it possible for us to study the diverse experiences and behaviour of some 1,500 visitors who talked with us about their reasons for coming to 'their' cemetery. Study participants included men and women of all ages and all socio-economic backgrounds (some from marginalized and some from disadvantaged groups), members of both established and newer immigrant communities, living close by and distant.

Our shared method of study was to talk with people on the cemetery grounds, most often directly at the gravesite as they engaged in their customary activities. In making initial contact, we approached visitors tentatively. We usually circumvented those attending new graves; the superintendent of the City of London Cemetery initially denied us permission to speak with the newly bereaved and – deciding to concentrate our research on long-term visitors – we voluntarily followed this restriction at all the other sites. In a short introduction, we explained the project (and offered a one-page information leaflet), guaranteed confidentiality and assured people that they did not have to respond to any questions they did not wish to answer and could terminate the conversation at any point. Most visitors then expressed a willingness to talk. The direct refusal rate was very low.

Each discussion was initiated with the question, 'May I ask you . . . ?' or 'Would it be intrusive if I asked you . . . why have you come to the cemetery today?' The conversation then took its own shape from the response, generally continuing along an informant-led pathway. We also invited people to ask us questions. A decision was made at the start, partly in consultation with the cemetery authorities with whom we had negotiated permission, that the use of recording equipment would be inappropriate in such a setting. Visitors agreed to let us take notes, which we expanded upon soon after the interview so that their comments and statements could be quoted verbatim, although all names have been changed to maintain confidentiality. We designed and used an *aide-mémoire* to help us standardize and record information (see Appendix 1).

When we began this research, cemetery behaviour in Great Britain was largely uncharted territory. Although the ethnographic approaches just outlined were adopted from the outset, additional methodological innovations were called for as the fieldwork progressed. We quickly learned, for example, that cemetery visitors usually preferred to complete the interview at the time of the initial contact rather than at a later date. Thus we generally had only one opportunity to interview each informant. Study participants tended to terminate the discussion when they felt that enough had been said, although all were generous with their time and observations. Subsequent conversations, when they occurred, were often circumscribed and limited, but some were willing to talk for a few hours and others agreed to further meetings. The body of material we collected, therefore, is not entirely typical of ethnographic fieldwork. Instead of the more traditional detailed conversations with a small number of key persons over an extended period of time, we made contact with well over a thousand individuals, couples and groups at the study cemeteries. Although some of the short exchanges may indicate reluctance to engage very fully, basic information could be gained from even a few minutes' conversation.

In the end, our contacts with the very large number of people who contributed to our findings fell into three levels of intensity (numbers are approximate for each category):

- Level 1 (28 per cent of 1,500): Limited observation of people's activities at a grave, with some conversation
- Level 2 (47 per cent of 1,500): Relatively brief interviews in which information was obtained about visitor-mourner practices at the grave; *aide-mémoire* completed

- Level 3 (25 per cent of 1,500): In-depth interviews in which additional information was obtained about feelings, reflections and disposition on the meaning of grave visiting and cemeteries; observation of activities at the grave, with conversation and discussion.

Although not all of the 1,500 encounters yielded extended commentary and observation, more than 300 people were willing to speak at considerable length, sometimes on repeated occasions and occasionally in their own homes and gardens.[44]

The extended cemetery discussions (Level 3) were often intense, immediate and intimate, with information and explanation being imparted and elicited in concentrated and sometimes emotionally demanding ways. The nature of people's comments, many of which are quoted verbatim throughout the book, suggests that study participants were often ready to reflect deeply and were disposed to do so because of the focused setting and circumstances of the grave visit. It was relatively straightforward, though often emotionally challenging, for mourner and researcher to engage through the powerful presence of the grave, from which cues for conversation could be taken. As their words illustrate, many study participants were already speaking inner thoughts 'in their heads' and, not infrequently, out loud. To direct these thoughts towards another person at the graveside appeared to give the mourner an occasion for further reflection on inner and external worlds. Although most people agreed in the first instance to talk for 'just a few minutes', many conversations continued for much longer. In addition to talking, we carefully observed what people were doing and asked questions about their activities. On occasion we would stand to the side and remain silent until the informant diverted from his or her task to make an observation, to continue the conversation, or to indicate that it was time to finish the interview.

Each researcher generally worked alone. Doris Francis initiated the study and worked at all the sites, later concentrating her efforts at the City of London Cemetery, Bushey United Jewish Cemetery and East Sheen and Richmond Cemetery.[45] Leonie Kellaher spent time at Woodgrange Park and Abney Park Cemeteries; and Georgina Neophytou[46] was occupied at New Southgate Cemetery. However, on special occasions when more extensive, comparative work was undertaken at the main CLCC site, the three of us worked together, sometimes with additional help from assistants.

We also combined forces to conduct survey work at each site, on both ritually significant and 'average' days, using a methodology adapted from that developed for research in the royal parks.[47] For such work we designed 'visitor count recording sheets' on which we could record the date, ritual occasion, cemetery site, day of week, weather, temperature and time period of observation. On research days we positioned ourselves at each of the cemetery entrances and, using the recording sheets, documented the time of entry, means of transport, number of persons in each group, their approximate ages (under 25, 25–44, 45–64, 65 and older) and the gender of all visitors. On special occasions when hundreds of people entered the cemetery within a short time, we could not approach cars directly and so relied on visual estimates, particularly concerning the approximate ages of visitors.

We also devised research strategies specific to each site. In order to investigate the multiple uses of old cemeteries such as Abney Park, we gave visitors maps of the site and asked them to trace their routes through the grounds, to mark each place where they stopped and to indicate what activities they engaged in at each location. At CLCC, we invited large family groups visiting at Christmas to map their 'pilgrimage routes' and to indicate each grave they visited. In the residential areas bordering Abney Park and Woodgrange, we conducted household surveys (through direct interviews and question-naires – see Appendix 2) to find out people's responses to these overgrown urban cemetery environments. Finally, through Carlisle Cemetery in Cumbria, we conducted a postal survey about woodland burial (see Appendix 3) and sent out a questionnaire (under a cover letter from Carlisle Bereavement Services) to all users who had preselected this form of disposal.

Because of the sensitive nature of cemetery activity, it was unrealistic to think that we might systematically sample research participants, possibly from lists held by the cemetery itself. However, we periodically reviewed the characteristics of our study participants and attempted to adjust our 'samples' to compensate for deficits and biases. That is, we drew on our survey findings to ensure that the individuals, families and groups interviewed, as well as the ages and genders of study participants, were aligned with those of the visitor statistics we gathered for each site. We also kept in view the different sections of each cemetery as frames for approaching potential participants, especially in cemeteries where certain areas were associated with distinct cohorts of deceased and mourners, different burial costs and various forms and types of memorialization.

The question of bias in our entire universe of informants is also important. The population of potential study participants was, of course, skewed towards those who chose to visit cemeteries rather than avoid them and towards those who had chosen full-body earth burial rather than cremation for their deceased. In order to contextualize the cemetery visiting experience, we devised a variety of strategies to contact non-visitors. For instance, at the City of London Cemetery, in three sampled areas representing shorter and longer periods since burial, we identified graves that appeared to be untended and that were not decorated at either Christmas or Easter.[48] As confirmation of our objectivity, we asked both a cemetery groundskeeper and another visitor to the same section to make a determination about whether the sampled graves had been visited or not. We then identified the owners of the unvisited graves through the cemetery office, which approached them by post with a brief questionnaire on general cemetery issues. The response rate was low, but it appeared that many of these owners were elderly, lived away from the area, or both. Such data suggest that age, health and absence of living relatives are probable factors in non-visiting. Accompanying partners, who either remained in the car or reported not visiting the graves of their own kin, were also in a position to shed light on the dispositions of those who did not visit graves and were interviewed using an *aide-mémoire* devised for non-visitors.[49] For some, there was a family culture of non-visiting; in other instances, remembrance rituals were carried out at home, often by placing fresh flowers or candles by the deceased's photograph. For still others, family ties had been severed years before.

To contextualize our findings further, we conducted limited research at the City of London Cemetery on rituals surrounding cremation. The researcher would occasionally speak with relatives who had come to tend the grave of a family member whose cremated remains had been interred or would accompany family members on their visits to both the graves of relatives who had been buried and to the memorial gardens, where rose bushes and brass plaques marked the ashes of the deceased. Occasionally the researcher also attended funeral services preceding cremations. Although such fieldwork was opportunistic, carried out as possibilities presented themselves in the course of the research, these occasions allowed comparative analysis of a broad range of memorial practices of remembrance and offered us the opportunity to question people about their preferences for earth burial or cremation. We found, for example, that young people whose families previously had chosen cremation and the dispersal of remains may now reject this option as an inadequate focus for grief. Instead, they select burial, have cremated remains interred and erect a memorial, or take ashes home and do not use the cemetery at all.

Each of the three of us came with a different cultural and religious background and inevitably brought our own approach to our mutual research tasks. We also brought a range of scholarly, emotional and psychological dispositions to the project,[50] along with a spectrum of interests and motivations that had drawn each of us to the subject of cemeteries. In the course of the work, each of us established contacts of varying intensities with groups of study participants. Although traditionally in anthropology the fieldworker was positioned as the 'objective outsider',[51] we readily acknowledge that in our case, the observer was not so distant or different from the observed – the mourner, the visitor (these terms are neither coterminous nor mutually exclusive) – though the times and places in which participants delivered their observations might have been less than familiar to us.

Our analyses are grounded in the data of these mourners' experiences, which are, paradoxically, both mundane and extraordinary. It is through their perceptions, reflections, observations and behaviour that understandings about the bereaved themselves and the liminal, betwixt-and-between worlds they come to inhabit can be approached. In linking the memorial landscape with the expressed emotions and behaviour of the bereaved, we have begun to analyse how the cemetery enables the living to remember the dead and to construct meaning through social action and the materiality of the grave. England is often described as a death-denying society in which two-thirds of the population select cremation and the eventual dispersal of ashes. By studying the public mourning practices of the significant minority who choose earth burial rather than cremation, our research on London cemeteries contributes a more balanced understanding of a wider range of contemporary mortuary behaviours in a Western industrial metropolis.

We wrote this book to tell both the general public and other researchers about cemeteries, but we hope it will also serve to inform planners, policymakers, managers and others involved in the mortuary trades about cemeteries' meanings from the perspectives of the bereaved. We emphasize the cemetery as an unexplored, non-clinical setting in which the roles and policies of managers as they negotiate with the needs of mourners can create a memorial landscape where the expression of grief is guided and supported.

Three Interlocking Themes: Body, Home and Garden

Our primary goal at the outset of research was to collect baseline data about what people did in London cemeteries, because such information was practically non-existent.[52] We formulated our initial questions to ask: Who visits cemeteries? When and how often do they go there? Whose graves do they visit, and what do they do and think while there? We also questioned whether elderly widows were the predominant group of visitors. Moreover, did cemetery landscapes and grave-tending activities reflect current trends in horticulture that favoured native species, perennials and more 'natural' environments? If so, were mourners' psychological needs and cultural expectations met through the established protocols and practices?

As subsequent chapters reveal, we learned that men, women and children of all ages, religions, ethnicities and income levels visit cemeteries, at frequencies ranging from every day to once a year, with short and expanded intervals of not visiting. During these visits they tend the grave, clean the memorial stone, arrange flowers, talk with the deceased and with other visitors, and reflect on profound issues. Their behaviour, including their private, individual mourning rituals, is shaped in part by the existing cemetery landscape, itself a product of the cemetery's history, the practices of previous and present generations of mourners and the current management's policies (chapter 2). Mourners may accommodate management's regulations, finding small ways in which to distinguish 'their' grave and its occupant, or they may resist management by persisting with personalized grave accoutrements not permitted by formal rules. In the first year after a death, they begin to adjust personal needs and preferences to culturally or religiously prescribed mourning practices in order to cope with the anguish of loss and to maintain in some form a relationship with the deceased (chapter 3).

In the years that pass after the first anniversary of a death, some survivors find it emotionally important to keep the deceased's memory alive, to conduct a relationship with the departed that evolves as part of the survivor's present life and to teach the value of family ties with the deceased to the next generation. To accomplish these goals, they develop culturally shaped but personal rituals that may revolve around investing the memorial stone with the deceased's identity, creating a garden at the gravesite that expresses the individuality of both deceased and mourner, or visiting the gravesite to maintain the memorial stone, to pray for the deceased's soul, or just to spend time in the deceased's 'presence' (chapter 5). Throughout all these rituals, an overriding goal is to perpetuate kinship ties with the deceased and among family members both living and dead (chapter 6).

For members of minority and immigrant ethnic groups, cemeteries can play a role in preserving a sense of cultural identity and creating a sense of community beyond the strictly familial. In today's world of movement and global interconnectedness, the decision of migrants to bury their kin in the new country of residence, rather than to repatriate the dead, can be interpreted as an initial step in grounding a new situated identity and in establishing a new 'home' for the deceased, the living and their future descendants. To illustrate, an Afro-Caribbean woman who was a research participant for this book reflected on how both movement and fixity had become fundamental to definitions of home and identity when she explained that her son's London grave was his 'halfway home', a place she saw as midway between Jamaica and heaven. As members of such groups establish burial grounds in their new places of settlement, they invest the cemetery with a sense of 'homeland': it both evokes the territory of origin and reflects the genesis of a new identity in a new place of settlement (chapter 7).

Sometimes the character of an older cemetery may change dramatically when it becomes the burial site for a new group of users such as the Greek Orthodox and Asian Muslims we interviewed. But even old cemeteries where burials no longer take place can be given added meanings and purposes by contemporary visitors – as sites of cultural heritage and historic interest, for example, as providing a focus, sense of place and of the past for new local residents, or as special, 'out of the ordinary' settings for retreat and meditation (chapter 8). (Many old cemeteries are also places for sexual liaisons, drugs and drink, but we did only limited research on these alternative uses.) Many older sites have amenity value, offering a diversified green landscape in an urban environment, and thereby suggest models for new cemetery designs. Old cemeteries encourage the living to examine the meaning of the ancestral past, and they summon the present generation to honour its contract and connections with the past dead and those yet to be born.[53]

Permeating all of these uses of cemeteries and all of the wide range of behaviours we observed in them were three essential themes: the concept of the tomb as the deceased's 'home', the idea of the cemetery – and sometimes the gravesite itself – as a 'garden' (chapter 4) and the importance of the physical presence of the body in the grave. Just as a person's literal home is a material symbol of the self and family, so, too, does the tomb, as home, embody the 'personhood' and meaning of the deceased. When a person dies, his or her social identity will not perish so long as it can be reconstructed through the memories and actions of the living. Marking the burial site helps to maintain the deceased's reality for those who wish to continue the connection.[54] As the final home of the departed, the funerary monument provides an enduring physical presence on which to focus memories of past interactions and thus to help keep alive the memory of the dead.

Home is also identified with other family co-residents and is the setting where significant social interaction takes place. The establishment of a grave, like the building of a home, reflects and is a medium for the reconstruction of domestic relationships.[55] This meshing of the social and the material can express a range of familial connections –

from those of positive meaning, affection and belonging to those suggesting disappointment, conflict or negative memories. The marking of the grave thus reveals complex interrelations between the public rituals of mourning and more private emotions and feelings. A forty-year-old man sitting beside his mother's grave in the Greek Orthodox section of New Southgate Cemetery, for example, told us: 'I'm here looking for advice . . . I'm at a loose end, that's why I'm spending time here, thinking . . . On Sundays we would visit our mother's house to see her, now we come to the cemetery to see her.' Another Greek Orthodox man, visiting the grave of his wife and other family members at New Southgate, said, 'There are five of us here. This place is like our family residence.'

By talking with such people directly at the gravesite and by observing their activities, we gained insights into how mourners drew on the silent, symbolic language of flowers, gardens and stones to express private emotions and to maintain their relationships with the departed. Their public, though coded, statements provided clues to inner processes and feelings not always easily verbalized but made physically present through mourners' memorial practices. As one visitor put it, 'Flowers are the only gift we can give them.' In the cemetery, the 'ordinariness' of planting, tending and ordering the grave allows the extraordinariness of death to be transposed to a more mundane level. The domestic setting of home and garden is translated to the grave site and is reinforced through the performance of many everyday activities associated with these places.

For many mourners, cultivated flowers are associated with specific ways of thinking about the deceased and about relationships towards the dead. Flowers are the traditional gifts of love, remembrance and mourning and are used to establish contact with the departed, as well as with the living.[56] Customarily, flowers (which are the reproductive part of plants) may be placed on the hearse and later on the grave as images of regeneration, and before burial, petals may be strewn into an open grave.

Flowers have symbolic meaning in practices surrounding death and mourning because they symbolize the human life course. The descriptive terms applied to human development parallel a plant's progress: 'to put down roots', 'to blossom', 'to flower', 'to come to fruition', 'to unfold'.[57] Both humans and flowers grow, mature, age and die, flourish or wither in the particular environment upon which each depends for sustenance and support.

For mourners, gardens and the cultivation of flowers are often sources of personal and aesthetic satisfaction. Attending to plants in a memorial garden, either at home or in the cemetery, provides an opportunity for contemplative connection with the self and with nature and is often healing and restorative.[58] A beautiful garden may represent the beloved deceased and express the mourning process. The investment of time, effort and care required to maintain a memorial garden may also be a part of the idea of 'saving' the personhood and memory of the departed from decay and extinction.[59] Memorial gardens are personal statements and creative acts of the survivor – frequently acts of defiance and resistance, but also acts of accommodation and acceptance.[60]

Every garden is a balancing point between human control and wild nature. A garden is nature under control and domesticated, free from weeds and other 'matter' out of place.[61] When extended to the cemetery, this symbolism is often invoked by mourners to mystify and camouflage the gap between life and death. Cemetery and garden are places 'apart' where the cycles of nature and time are not only clearly evident but also manipulated. Both are specialized spaces of contradictory and ambiguous meanings that allow clarification and obfuscation through ritual action. Both cemeteries and gardens display, contest and invert social relationships; both represent, reinterpret and re-model the relationship of person to nature. As places betwixt and between the ordinary and the extraordinary, cemeteries and gardens mystify, conceal, mediate, bridge and transform the unresolved opposition between nature and culture, the private and the public, the natural and the supernatural. Metaphorically, the grave, by being planted as a garden, aligns human death with the natural, vegetative world of growth, decay and renewal.[62] Thus the gardener's ability to keep cultivated plants alive at the grave garden may offer consolation. As one 65-year-old man who made a weekly three-hour bus trip to tend the grave of his partner at the City of London Cemetery said:

> I'm no gardener, but the person who is buried here was a professional gardener all his life. This is Burton's personal garden. I'm sure he makes everything grow. I said, 'You look after it and I'll do out here what has to be done practically.' . . . Coming to the cemetery does help. When I come here I say, 'I've been to see Burton,' not 'I've been to the cemetery.' You don't let go, but do you have to?

So central were these complementary metaphors of home and garden to study participants' explanations of their cemetery activities that we have devoted chapter 4 to exploring their many meanings. Participants' ideas about the physical body of the deceased, however, run like a thread throughout this book, and we wish to emphasize the

importance cemetery visitors attached to the presence of the body both
in the ground in a particular place and as 'embodied' in the memorial
stone and sometimes the grave garden.

Lying beneath the ordered surface of the typical English cemetery,
the body is the unspoken, if not secret, component of the funerary
landscape and, arguably, the prime motivating force for all who engage
with the cemetery. Normative ideas about the corpse, along with active
or residual, theologically founded beliefs concerning the body and its
link to the soul, influence the ritual actions of bereaved survivors and
thus the enduring 'personhood' of the deceased.[63] Although secular
ideas permeate much of British society, and although only some of the
bereaved we interviewed claimed any theologically informed beliefs
about body, soul and the afterlife, most of our study participants
indicated a concern for the deceased's bodily remains.

In religious ideologies, the body in both its animated and expired
states is never just an organic, biophysical entity, although it is that
also. Within the Christian theological tradition, the human body is a
physical, mystical and spiritual entity; it is both immortal soul and
mortal flesh. Created in the image of God, the person is both matter
and anima. Through bodily suffering and ascetic control, salvation is
made possible, and on the day of judgement the soul will be reunited
with its 'body' and rise to heaven for eternal life.[64] The Christian
view of the body is thus presented in a neo-Platonist, dualist form,
as both soul and flesh. The importance of the body in Christian
belief is manifested in both life and death; the body is the vessel of the
soul, so its treatment after death is theologically central to Christian
eschatology and to that of other religions. Catholic prohibition on
cremation until the 1960s, and the continued rejection of this method
of disposal by the Greek Orthodox and Orthodox Jewish communities, reflects this set of beliefs. Islam, too, forbids cremation.[65]
For the Greek Orthodox, the presence of Orthodox bodily remains
consecrates the earth in which they are buried. This belief is also held
by Muslims, who do not perform formal consecration ceremonies of
burial grounds. Burial – particularly of those who have accumulated
merit through pilgrimage to Mecca – adds to the sacred capital of the
land.[66]

In Judaism, there is no official, monolithic doctrine on the relationship between body and soul, and ideas of the afterlife and the possibility of resurrection remain ambiguous.[67] It can be argued, for
example, that biblical authors may have held the holistic notion of
the living person as a single entity, a 'living soul', and that only later
did Talmudic and Rabbinic writings suggest the dichotomous concept
of body and soul as two distinct entities that have become conjoined,

such that at the death of the body, the spirit separates from the body and returns to God. In later writings, it was further explained that there were three aspects of the soul. Interestingly, one aspect, the *nefesh*, remains constantly hovering over the place where the body is buried. To honour the *nefesh* and to give it a defined place to dwell, a monument is erected over the grave; the word *nefesh* (lit., 'soul') is still used to refer to the memorial stone.[68]

In traditional Jewish communities, a deceased human being is compared with an impaired Torah scroll, which is religiously disqualified but still revered for the exalted function it once served. This symbolism is occasionally made materially manifest when a bag of worn prayer books is put into the grave with the coffin at an Orthodox Jewish funeral.[69] A human being is believed to be created in the divine image; the corpse retains its holiness and must be treated with respect for the character and personality it housed. For the physical resurrection of the Orthodox Jewish body, its remains must be buried in consecrated soil. In Orthodox Judaism, autopsies and dissection are forbidden. While the law overrules it when necessary, this prohibition is similarly applied by Islam and the Greek Orthodox Church, which also disallow embalming. For the Muslim, interment must take place as quickly as possible, because the soul cannot leave the body until then, and it is thought that the body continues to experience pain up to the point of burial. The separation of body and soul thus starts at burial. Such ideologically based views about the body that inform mortuary practices – the ritual preparation of the body and the rites of burial – are discussed in chapter 3.

The basic funerary practices of those who are the focus of this book, such as cleaning the memorial stone and refreshing the flowers, draw on and elaborate connections between body, home and garden to negate or resolve the paradox of death as a part of life.[70] Our research suggests that these transformative ritual acts resurrect and symbolically 'reconstruct' the body, control nature and, by implication, 'control' death, and so keep the departed 'present' and 'alive'. In today's cemeteries, as in those of dynastic Egypt and in the early Christian cult of the saints,[71] the body remains the symbol of the self, and even in death ideas of embodiment persist. Concepts of the person are linked to the corporeal self and to its material extension through the tomb, made up of memorial stone and sometimes garden.[72] In this book we explore the interrelated themes of home, garden and body to reveal how the materiality of the corpse, bodily being and personal identity and biography are linked through commemorative acts that transcend the dualistic separation of body and soul.[73] This exploration of deeply embedded and embodied cemetery practices aims to illuminate the ongoing engagement and – to use religious terminology – communion between the living and the dead.

Conclusion

In the sequestered setting of the cemetery, we were able to observe a great variety of individual and private mourning practices and to discuss questions of meaning with a range of people who generally did not seek bereavement counselling. Repeatedly, the bereaved gave consistent explanations for visiting the cemetery and carrying out their particular tasks at the grave. Few offered religious or spiritual expectations or requirements as an overriding explanation for visiting the burial grounds. For most, their actions were engendered by strong emotions – of loyalty, loss, memory and a continued attachment, literally and figuratively, to the body, identity and memory of the deceased.

For analysis of our cross-cultural findings, we have taken account of the diverse experiences of the thousand or more visitors of different ages and various religious, ethnic and socio-economic backgrounds who shared with us their reasons for coming to the cemetery.[74] Survivors are often changed by the experience of death, and many become involved in a continuous process of meaning making, which can be enacted and observed in the cemetery as well as at home. This book is a study of what such memorial practices tell us about Londoners' present attitudes towards death, nature and culture, religion, society and the individual at the end of modernity.

Memorial behaviour seems to be culturally learned. It is often in the cemetery that mourners are taught how to enact the bonds that continue to attach them to the deceased, and it is there that the lives of both become inscribed upon the individual grave and then on the wider funerary landscape. The cemetery, with its conventions of stone memorials and bereavement practices, thereby encodes emotional responses, producing and reproducing cultures of grief. Our research focused on the material manifestations of such cognitive and emotional processes as they were performed and written upon the cemetery landscape. Throughout this book we explore the complex twin symbols of home and garden to reveal how people engage with and act upon the sacred, sculptural space of the cemetery, generating rituals of mourning that express loss and perpetuate memory.

To lead in this direction, the following chapter on the historical evolution of English cemetery landscapes reveals how the varied uses of nature in the design of the grounds help to shape memorial behaviour and are, as a consequence, altered by that same behaviour. By entering the territory – physical and emotional – of different London cemeteries and spending time with mourners at the gravesite, we have begun to view this sequestered, secret world from the perspectives of insiders.

2

The Dynamics
of Cemetery
Landscapes

Shaded by trees and beautified by shrubbery, where each grave
may be made a flower-garden and each tomb a shrine . . .

John Strang, *Necropolis Glasguensis*, 1831

Large, public cemeteries in London are a modern phenomenon, the
outcome of radical burial reform in mid-nineteenth-century Britain.[1]
Since that time, the aesthetic evolution of cemetery design has both
prompted and mirrored people's changing views of death and customs
of memorialization. The appearance and structure of the funerary
landscape provides visual and experiential cues for those who visit and
use the cemetery.[2] These clues both shape mourners' actions and emotions and constrain them, as well as convey the meanings of customs
and practices in a particular cemetery setting. Individual and collective
memorial behaviour, in turn, leads to changes in the evolving cemetery
landscape: even as familiar traditions endure, people and groups
innovate with new practices and meanings that in time may be accepted.

Over the past 150 years, the appearance and structure of London
cemeteries have been continually re-created, reconfigured and reinterpreted as attitudes and values linking death, nature and environmental

imagery evolve. The changing memorial landscape, composed of monuments, architectural buildings, trees, shrubs and flowers, has worked as a metaphor guiding people's dispositions and experiences as they think and act in response to death, bereavement and memorialization. Responses to individual bereavement, enacted at a particular grave, continue to be influenced by and to influence the broader picture – the landscape of the cemetery. Victorian burial grounds, for example, were renowned for their rich plantings and elaborate monuments – appropriate arenas for the 'celebration of death'.[3] In the post-war years, manicured lawns and uniform, back-to-back graves corresponded to a more rational, controlled management of death.[4] Contemporary 'green' burials in a woodland of native trees commemorate life and death as partners with nature.[5]

Origins of the Modern Cemetery

From the eighth century until the nineteenth, most people in England were buried in the few acres around a church; the prerogative and duty for interring the dead lay with the established Church.[6] In urban areas, parish residence conferred the right to burial. Churchyard landscapes followed old traditions of graveyard arrangements: the spot safest from ghouls, vampires and evil spirits, for example, was the ground next to the east wall of the church, nearest the altar.[7] For added precaution, nobles and wealthy commoners were buried beneath the church floor or in the structure's wall. Paupers' graves, meanwhile, were repeatedly reused or over-buried. In some places the poor were laid in unmarked, mass graves, ten to seventeen corpses together.

Unwilling to submit to Church of England rites for burial in consecrated soil, Jews leased their own separate grounds. Dissenters and other non-Anglicans interred their dead in unconsecrated burial grounds such as London's Bunhill Fields, which had been in existence since 1665. It was this desire to be independent from the control of the Church of England, as well as the growing concern that overcrowded graveyards posed a threat to public health, that accounted for the origin of modern cemeteries in Britain.[8]

By the nineteenth century, with heavy migration to industrial cities, urban churchyards were suffering tremendous strain. During the first forty years of that century, London's population doubled, from 985,000 to nearly 2 million.[9] Housing and sanitary facilities proved inadequate, and death rates in overcrowded areas increased rapidly, creating ever-growing numbers of dead to be buried. After centuries of interments, existing inner-city burial land was already inadequate.

The limited grounds were, nonetheless, chronically used well beyond their maximum capacity, with coffins stacked or corpses only partially buried. For the working classes and lower classes, that made up 70 per cent of the urban population, interment became a squalid and insecure affair.[10] The activities of resurrection men and body snatchers, who provided disinterred cadavers to the medical community for dissection, added to fear of the desecration of corpses for all social classes.

People also began to perceive overcrowded, unsanitary parish churchyards, close to densely populated areas, as causes of epidemic diseases such as cholera and typhus. Fluids, gases and smells from human decomposition ('miasmas') were postulated to be sources of contagion. Crusading reformers such as Dr George Walker depicted the burial crisis as part of a larger debate about urban sanitation, poverty and health.[11] They urged the banning of burials inside city limits. Others, such as George Milner and John Strang, called for more aesthetic and appropriately sympathetic surroundings in which feelings of grief could be privately expressed.[12]

In the second quarter of the nineteenth century, joint stock companies began to offer a radical alternative to churchyard burial by laying out cemeteries on the outskirts of cities and towns.[13] In London, entrepreneurial companies saw the opportunity for profit and sold private, suburban, secure, permanent burial to the wealthier mercantile, professional and ethnic communities. Mirroring their commercial and industrial strategies, mourners chose monuments of varied styles, materials, motifs and colours to give positive identity to themselves and their families, in the same creative ways in which the entrepreneurs had used advertising to differentiate their products in a field of similar commodities.[14] The attractively designed ornamental grounds and elegant architecture of Kensal Green and Highgate Cemetery, for example, became famous London attractions that 'invited the living and celebrated the dead'.[15] At the fashionable Norwood Cemetery, members of the wealthy Greek Orthodox community established a separate section with a Doric entrance, classical statues of the Virtues and a neo-classical mortuary chapel resembling an ancient Hellenistic temple.[16]

Only a few cemetery companies, however, sought profits by catering mainly to the moneyed minority.[17] The Nonconformist founders of Abney Park Cemetery were more typical in their religious and social motivations. These Congregationalist forefathers laid out a non-denominational cemetery for all social classes that served as the replacement for the then full Bunhill Fields.[18] Concerns about public health and the wish to provide burial to the poor lay behind the establishment of cemetery companies at mid-century. Other private schemes, such as the Great Northern Cemetery at New Southgate and Woodgrange Park in Newham, were opened toward the end of the century, but their full design intentions were never realized because of lack of financing.

Thomas Laqueur suggests that these private burial grounds, removed from historic, sacred spots in overcrowded cities, were significant in providing a 'radical innovation in the spatial geography of the dead in relation to the living and of dead bodies in relation to each other'.[19] In contrast to urban churchyards, where many corpses were crammed together, private cemeteries offered every deceased person a separate, identifiable grave with a unique memorial of individual choice, a focus for romantic contemplation and commemoration. There, money and freehold, not inherited privilege or the vested power of the Anglican clergy, provided the middle classes with membership in a new democracy of the dead and a 'symbolic geography' for a new community of the living.[20]

The private cemetery companies helped inspire the 1850 and 1852 Burial Acts, which prohibited churchyard burial within London city boundaries and empowered local vestries to set up burial boards as the principal agencies for establishing municipal cemeteries. In 1853, the arrangements for London were extended to the rest of England and Wales, and later to Scotland and Ireland, thereby founding a national system of public cemeteries. With passage of the Local Government Act of 1894, the functions of the former burial boards devolved to the local authorities, who were empowered to lay out cemeteries.[21]

One such modern burial ground was the City of London Cemetery, on which we focus in the following pages.[22] Its history exemplifies much of the evolution of London cemeteries from the mid-nineteenth century to the present. Since its establishment, the City of London Cemetery has served as a model for cemetery design and management, both in England and abroad. Its managers have taken a leading role in the development and provision of services, including London's first municipal crematorium, memorial gardens, lawn graves and woodland burial. This cemetery offers a largely intact historical landscape and an accompanying written chronology from the perspectives of its founders, directors, superintendents, engineers and gardeners.[23] These people transformed abstract concepts of death and mourning into physical reality and drew upon images from nature to convey ideals and attitudes about grief and commemoration. The following account, based on archival research and interviews with present and retired administrators and landscape personnel, suggests that the funerary landscape is the outcome of relationships of power and economics between the manager as 'retailer' and the user as 'customer'.

Case Study: The City of London Cemetery

By an act of Parliament in 1852, the commissioners of sewers – men responsible for public hygiene and sanitation – were constituted as a burial board for the City of London and empowered to create a cemetery for the city's 106 parishes. The commissioners directed William Haywood, surveyor and engineer for the Department of Sewers, and Dr John Simon, the city's medical officer of health, to develop an 'open and spacious cemetery distant from the City to be substituted for intramural interment'. The two men shared a concern with issues of urban health and a desire to end the invidious burial distinctions between rich and poor that 'honored the successful and obscured the failed'.[24] Simon, for example, opposed the customary mass burial of paupers. He advocated, instead, an individual grave for each interment, with tenure of twenty years, which would have greatly extended the time most bodies remained in the ground.[25]

In 1853, the commissioners followed the recommendation of Simon and Haywood and purchased a 200-acre site in Little Ilford (now Manor Park). This parcel had been part of the Earl of Mornington's Wanstead estate in Epping Lower Forest and lay seven miles from the centre of London. The accessible location, attractive planting and porous, well-drained, gravelly soil met Haywood and Simon's selection criteria. The factors guiding the choice of a site suitable for a cemetery were similar to the 'qualities of a place that create the promise of a garden': the layout of the land and sources of water, the established vegetation, the location relative to surrounding human settlement and the orientation of the site to the wind and sun.[26] Similarly, the creative acts that formed the cemetery landscape were akin to those that shape a garden: 'molding the earth; defining and connecting spaces with walls, paths and monuments; planting and tending and giving the place meaning through such purposeful actions and sacred rituals'.[27]

In designing the City of London Cemetery, Haywood designated an 89-acre section for the original cemetery. His calculation was based on the number of burials per year in the parishes (3,000), the approximate size of each grave (28 square feet) and the number of years (20) before reuse. Land was also earmarked for plots sold in perpetuity, as well as for buildings, landscaping and roads. The city's improvement committee recorded its pleasure with the purchase and re-emphasized its multiple aims: that this new cemetery be appropriate for the sober task of sepulchre, that it be worthy of the eminence of the city and that it be provident in its expenses. The report stated that the committee members:

> regarded the City of London Cemetery as a work for posterity as well as the present generation; and that the required buildings and other works should be substantial, appropriate for the solemn purposes to which they are to be applied, and at the same time, remembering they are for the use of this important City, as elegant in structure as a due regard to economy would admit.

In following the committee's brief, Haywood and Simon were guided by John Claudius Loudon's *On the Laying Out, Planting, and Managing of Cemeteries*,[28] the major nineteenth-century treatise on the aesthetics and rationale of cemetery design. Loudon wished to end the abuses of the dead being perpetrated in churchyards. He wrote: 'The *main object* of a burial-ground is the disposal of the remains of the dead in such a manner as that their decomposition, and return to the earth . . . shall not prove injurious to the living; either by affecting health, or by shocking their feelings.'[29] Loudon's efficient, rational canons of cemetery design were incorporated into Haywood's plans. These principles still apply to the City of London Cemetery and define the characteristic features of many English cemeteries.

The Cemetery as Garden Landscape

Surrounding the City of London Cemetery is a high boundary wall intended to secure the graves from disturbance. Border plantings enhance the sense of enclosure and provide sheltered privacy for contemplation at the gravesite.[30] Loudon also advocated one main entrance to the cemetery. Haywood followed this principle and designed a gated archway that links the porter's lodge with the superintendent's office to form an imposing front façade. Symbolically and materially, the main gate and boundary wall distinguish the cemetery as a privileged place, separate in time, space and emotion from the everyday routine of its surroundings'.[31] But although the secular world of the living and the consecrated realm of the dead are set apart, they are also linked by the unending stream of daily funerals and rituals and annual rites of memorialization.[32] Such rituals transform the walled space of death into a sacred place with special rules governing behaviour.

Although Loudon opposed catacombs as a health hazard, Haywood designed a semicircle of catacombs as a way to attract a wealthy clientele and to compete with the private cemetery companies.[33] These catacombs were built on the sunken, oval site of a drained lake and formed a focal point visible from each of two chapels. The catacombs, however, were never fully subscribed. Part of the structure was redesigned in 1930 as a columbarium (a vault for urns of cremated remains), and another section was recently remodelled to accommodate the Books of Remembrance, ornate memorial books that are opened once a year on the day selected for commemoration.

Following Loudon's principles, Haywood laid out a system of drains and main roads to permit hearse access to every part of the cemetery, and gravel walks that allowed visitors to get to an individual plot without walking over other graves. Straight carriage drives radiated from the main entrance to the Anglican and Nonconformist chapels and, by way of a central circle, to the catacombs (Fig. 2.1). These wide, direct routes signalled efficiency and functional convenience – values of the urban, mercantile world.[34] In contrast, Haywood designed the peripheral routes as curving drives, which encouraged a more leisured, intimate pace that prompted contemplation and evoked the rural experience of a park or landed estate.

In Victorian England, cemeteries and parks developed in parallel as central features of nineteenth-century city planning and as sources of urban pride and civic adornment.[35] These shared public places were underpinned by popular theories about the benefits of fresh air, nature and education for physical and moral well-being.[36] Both institutions were described as 'the lungs of the city', and their designs had similarities. For example, Regent's Park was the prototype for Kensal Green Cemetery, and evidence suggests that Loudon's Derby Arboretum provided the model for Haywood's cemetery design.[37] In this regard, it is interesting to note that in his early lithographs of the City of London Cemetery, Haywood suggested the amenity value of the designed landscape by depicting couples promenading in front of the catacombs, which were attractively planted with arbor vitae. He also promoted the solemn dignity of the grounds, appropriate for interment, with drawings of the elegant, inspiring architecture of the two chapels.

The City of London Cemetery has two religious buildings: an Anglican chapel situated on consecrated ground and another for Dissenters in an unconsecrated area. Both chapels were placed in central positions, visible along uninterrupted vistas from all prominent points. By providing funeral chapels, the secular municipal cemetery proclaimed its new role, appropriated from the Church of England,

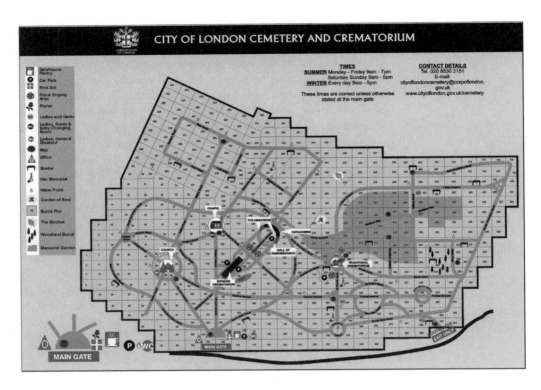

Figure 2.1.
City of London
Cemetery and
Crematorium.

of burying and maintaining the dead. These powers and duties of sepulchre were part of a new municipal social order. The choice of Gothic architecture[38] for both chapels implied that equal honour would be given to all forms of Christian religious and cultural sentiment. Gothic architecture was a suitable statement for the corporation's cemetery inasmuch as this style had accrued additional public status and civic authority as the recent choice for the Houses of Parliament and other prominent public buildings in London and the provinces. In the 1860s, the cemetery's new role in caring for the dead was reinforced, symbolically and materially, when it became the repository for bodily remains exhumed from the city's demolished churchyards.[39] Monuments, often incorporating architectural features removed from these churches, were erected over the reinterred bones.

In contrast to the crowding and spatial confusion of urban graveyards, the layouts of modern cemeteries were rational and ordered. The interior of the City of London Cemetery, for example, was divided into squares, which were further subdivided to record the precise location of each interment (Fig. 2.2). With the implementation of an efficient grid system, mourners had a specific, accessible, marked burial plot on which to focus their grief.[40] From the outset, cemetery records

Figure 2.2.
Loudon advocated a marked, accessible grave as a focus of grief, a characteristic of the modern cemetery seen in this Victorian section of the City of London Cemetery.

chronicled the name, date, location on the grid and depth of each burial. For private burials, Victorian mourners were permitted to select any location within their price category, because graves were not dug in rotation as later became the case.

In 1855, Haywood prepared a diagram of the City of London Cemetery showing 'the proposed mode of appropriating the ground for the different classes of interred, depending on position, access and cost'. This landscape design provided an opportunity for private customers to replicate or manipulate their socio-economic standing after death. Graves situated along avenues and roads were first class (Loudon had advocated that impressive monuments be located along roads and main walkways), and the more costly vaults and large family mausoleums usually occupied these desirable positions. In 1875, for example, Haywood designed his own Gothic-style mausoleum, which was to be located in a prime place near the cemetery entrance. The next row back from the road was second class, and those behind, third class.[41] Although the sponsors of most private burials selected a full grave with upright memorial and kerb surrounds, individual variations in style, height and types of materials were permitted in all three classes, creating a somewhat 'ecumenical' atmosphere, particularly in the central part of the cemetery. Monuments and epitaphs, which expressed individual taste, conveyed moral sentiments and projected a desired public identity, were also allowed, subject to approval by the cemetery management. Mourners were permitted to plant flowers on the graves, and cemetery gardeners were available to maintain plots.

Loudon and Haywood both opposed large, exclusive areas for common grave interments, a practice followed in some private cemeteries, such as Kensal Green. Instead, Haywood hoped to 'separate and disperse this class of graves, by placing them in the rear of the reserved ground or in the general area'. Haywood argued that an area segregated for common interments would be both uninviting and unsanitary, with large accumulations of human remains (six to twenty coffins per grave) in one location. Dispersion of common graves was also intended to improve the general appearance of the cemetery by avoiding the dense packing of tombs and monuments together. Haywood noted that this solution 'avoided the broad distinction between rich and poor'. He further advocated that a slab be placed in the vicinity of the common graves and, upon payment of a fee, the details of the deceased be inscribed. 'This enables those persons who from circumstances cannot afford to purchase ground, the opportunity of putting up some memento of their deceased relatives.' It is impossible to determine whether this practice was ever followed informally; official cemetery records reveal that not until 1921 was a charge made for the right to erect and place a tablet on a common grave.

Loudon suggested that trees and shrubs with dark, evergreen foliage and narrow conical shapes be planted in rows parallel to the main avenues. Yew and cypress, historically associated with places of sepulchre, would underscore the sense of propriety in disposing of the remains of the deceased and would signify the cemetery as a special site distinguished from a pleasure park. Loudon further stipulated that there should be only a moderate number of trees, in order not to take up grave space, impede the circulation of fresh air, or make the cemetery untidy when they dropped their autumn foliage. Here Loudon, following Strang, recognized that the special attributes of trees contributed to making the cemetery 'a locus for memory'.[42] As Keith Thomas and, more recently, Laura Rival have suggested, trees are potent, life-reaffirming and death-denying symbols that express ideas of trans-generational continuity and renewal.[43] Trees grow over time and change with the seasons and so are also metaphors for the human life cycle. As we discuss later, the many and varied meanings of trees within an evolving memorial landscape were subject to interpretation and reinterpretation by different groups with different sets of interests.

Like Loudon, the founders of the City of London Cemetery perceived that they would further the city's image by 'supplying . . . tasteful decoration of the grounds, and by healthful accomplishment of the purposes of the cemetery'. As John Simon stated in his introductory report:

> Further, I daresay you would think it inexpedient that your Cemetery should be entirely without decoration and elegance. Fifty-four acres of head- and footstones, or the same extent of bare mounds, might vulgarise even the aspect of death. By the judicious introduction of trees and turf and shrubs, of bends and undulations, you would probably seek to interrupt the long perspective of so many tombs, and, by these artificial resources of planning and planting, to enhance the native solemnity of the spot.

William Davidson, the landscape designer and gardener for country villas, was hired in 1855 to supervise the initial planting of the cemetery grounds. Following Simon's introductory report, Davidson designed the area inside the front gates as an open lawn, clear of interments. This open lawn section, the first area visitors saw, was evocative of a villa, a country estate, or a landscape park and underscored the cemetery as a place of ordered nature, wealth and permanence. The carefully designed ornamental beds, with their emphasis on seasonal colour and artistic groupings of evergreen and broad-leaved specimen trees along major carriage routes, provided decorative elegance and aesthetic appeal to the middle classes, who espoused Victorian ideas of nature as best managed and organized for the benefit of man. The planting of 'old-fashioned' flowers suggested a rural atmosphere reminiscent of country churchyards and cottage gardens.[44]

Davidson's design thus creatively integrated three contrasting garden images: the eighteenth-century landscape park or villa; nature, subordinate to man's rationality and artifice; and the rural country garden.[45] Each of these symbol sets would later be adopted by management and the emphasis shifted to convey the then current image of death and the corresponding cultural mode of bereavement. One such shift was revealed in the Bishop of London's consecration of the cemetery, in which he praised the rationally planned and 'elegant necropolis, which correctly separated the resting place of the dead from the dwelling space of the living'. The Church of England thereby acknowledged interment outside the city and accepted the transfer of direct authority for burial from the Anglican Church to the secular municipality – in other words, from a religious world-view to a utilitarian and functional concern with issues of health and disease control. The aims of the cemetery's founders, however, extended beyond a concern for public health and set the standard for municipal cemeteries. The City of London Cemetery's impressive funerary landscape and unifying Gothic architecture mirrored its vision of a new community based on corporate identity, religious equality and the equal treatment of all classes.[46]

By 1905, design principles and articulated goals of equality had given way to organizational and administrative realities. Half a century after the City of London Cemetery was founded, its ledgers revealed that 274,065 common burials had taken place but only 31,393 private grave interments. The cemetery was enlarged in 1861, 1875, 1887, 1906 and 1914 to accommodate the increasing number of 'pauper interments'. These newly enclosed sections – 'clandestine cemeteries' – were entirely devoted to communal burial.[47] Deciduous trees lined the new roads. The landscape was marked by piles of dirt surrounding the common graves, which remained open and 'hungry' until they had received their required ration of coffins. In an effort to control the bereavement activities of working-class mourners, the commissioners requested that these 'common graves be kept in better order'.

During this period of expansion to accommodate common burials, Davidson's original landscape designs matured and were over-planted in a more abundant and less formal style. The boundaries of art and nature appeared to shift, suggesting an alternative view of death and mourning that supported a more contemplative sensibility. The generously planted landscapes of rhododendrons, recently introduced to English parks and gardens, the attractively grouped flowering cherry, silver birch, ash and copper beech trees, the cedars and cypresses from many parts of the globe and the selection of limes, planes and horse chestnuts to line the avenues paralleled the richly developed expression of bereavement then practiced by the wealthier Victorians. 'Romanticists saw marriage as a communion of souls, a family as bonded in eternal love, and friendship as a lifetime commitment. . . . To grieve was to signal the significance of the relationship, and the depth of one's own spirit.'[48] Nature and emotions were allowed even fuller expression in the cemetery, symbolically ornamented with purple-leaf beeches. Romantic emotions of mourning contrasted markedly with Loudon's earlier functional, evergreen plantings and their intended association with rational, sanitary disposal and fear of contagion. Nature, however, was still managed and controlled: at the end of the nineteenth century, the cemetery landscape did not yet challenge the glories of middle- and upper-class commercial and political ascendancy. Rather, it continued to celebrate them.

Throughout the twentieth century, the planted landscape remained an outstanding promotional feature of the City of London Cemetery. Nature was a significant component of its marketing strategy and was periodically reinterpreted and reconstituted in accordance with prevailing mortuary practices. For example, the 1929 advertising brochure 'The Cemetery in a Garden' reconfigured the symbolic imagery of the funerary landscape, arguably to address the post-war bereavement mood of the nation,[49] while attending to the more personal needs and aspirations of its clientele. The brochure began by placing the cemetery in a verdant, landscape park setting, a place where mourners could find comfort in the transcendent beauty of nature. It described the rural beauty of the 'endless and countless trees, flowers and lawns' of the cemetery, in quiet contrast to the 'life of its industrial surroundings and all the busy town land just beyond and all around it'. This idealized image was intended to appeal to those who craved a rural retreat of calm and tranquility and to those of increasing income and aspiration who could afford private burial, if not a villa in the country.

Importantly, death and disposal are only vaguely suggested in this 1929 brochure; they are never directly discussed. Soothing nature is offered as a palliative for painful, unspoken grief; the seasonal mutability of arboretum and garden is recommended as suitable for a cemetery.[50] The restorative character of living trees and plants was thus to provide a vehicle for transforming the turbulent emotions of loss into a more fixed hope in renewal and regeneration:

> Here are no trees of mourning – cypress nor yew nor weeping willow; only seemly beauty as of some great park adorned. In such a place it seems easier to leave those we have loved – surrounded by the charm of Nature, which, season after season, spreads its own tribute of leaves and flowers about them and whose perpetual renewal is a refutation of human grief.

The text of the pamphlet further emphasized the 'historic memories' of the cemetery site and referred to its past use as the landscape park of the Earl of Mornington. Thus, it subtly implied that title to a plot in the City of London Cemetery was part ownership of a country estate and that to visit a family member or to be buried in the cemetery was to participate in that ideal.

This depiction of the cemetery as a peaceful garden estate undoubtedly appealed to the post-war emotions and socio-economic aspirations of the middle classes and some of the working classes; it also coincided with a change in burial patterns within the cemetery itself.

By 1925, the differential between communal and private interments had evened out – in that year, 1,319 private burials and 1,354 common burials were recorded. Two possibilities account for this reversal: increased incomes enabled more families to choose a private grave, and acceptance of cremation was beginning to grow.[51] The City of London was the first municipality in London to erect a crematorium. This new building, 'situated in a secluded part of the Cemetery', was designed in the Gothic style to harmonize with the existing chapels and to convey the same religious authorization as burial. A 'garden of remembrance' for the strewing of ashes was designed near the crematorium.[52]

Memorial Gardens

Although the City of London Cemetery was among the first to have a garden of remembrance where ashes could be scattered, some mourners wanted more tangible and lasting forms of memorialization for their cremated relatives and friends. In the late 1940s, a group approached the managers and offered to donate a commemorative sundial, garden seats, rose bushes and shrubs for the memorial garden. Some time later, the cemetery superintendents responded to this request with new ideas of their own, though they were careful not to abnegate power or control over the management of the landscape. Roses and shrubs, which would be purchased and planted by the cemetery staff, could now be dedicated, with a small plaque indicating the name of the deceased, for a renewable ten-year period. This scheme proved widely popular, so that today some 20,000 rose bushes have been planted and 32 of the cemetery's 200 acres are devoted to the gardens of remembrance. This reconfigured memorial landscape records the way management's cooperation with mourners in devising new forms of memorialization for growing numbers of customers choosing cremation also enhanced economic returns.

The expansion of the memorial garden and the development of a new lawn section for burial after the Second World War changed the design of the cemetery (war damage was minimal) in significant ways. Roses, particularly standard roses, were introduced by popular demand into both of these innovative landscapes. In an interview, John Mattock, the English specialist rose-grower, explained the rose's ready acceptance as the commemorative cemetery flower after the Second World War. Rose gardens had previously been widely planted in Victorian parks and remembrance gardens and already had a significant association with memorialization. Roses are fragrant and have religious and romantic meanings. They have a long flowering season, are expensive and are widely acknowledged as a special gift. That roses are linked strongly with sentiment may be read from their names – 'Remembrance', 'Loving Memory', 'Peace'. Significantly, roses are evocative of authentic country life, rural peace and familial security. These symbolic connections made a small stake in the country and a home with a garden (the popular metaphor for the grave plot) equally available to all cemetery users.[53]

In 1953, the cemetery employed Richard Sudell, the landscape designer and author of popular gardening books, to design a new series of memorial gardens. Sudell's designs reworked themes and images that echoed earlier eras of English garden history, thus further engendering a sense of rural tradition, security and rootedness following the war years. Among Sudell's revivals of older styles were separate garden 'rooms' with hedged walls and the planting of standard and shrub roses in small, geometric beds surrounded by brick paving. The beauty, tranquillity, professional execution and skilled maintenance of the memorial gardens drew increasing numbers of customers to the City of London Cemetery and Crematorium.

These gardens of remembrance were developed on terrain that had been used almost a century earlier for common graves: the burial grounds of the anonymous poor, cleared of markers after twenty years, were recycled for a new type of commemorative landscape. Perhaps it is paradoxical that common-grave interments and cremations each subsidized private burials, and the two were equally efficient in disposing of large numbers of corpses without taxing land resources. In the social geography of the cemetery, pauper interments and cremated remains were situated far from the prestigious chapels and main avenues lined with ornate monuments dedicated to named individuals.

After the Second World War, local authority funds were short and the costs of labour and maintenance were increasing. Cemetery expenditures exceeded income, and most local authorities perceived burial grounds as a 'wasting asset'. Each grave sold meant the permanent loss of finite burial space and added to long-term costs – for example, when family members were no longer alive to assume the cost of repairs on deteriorating, dangerous memorials. Cremation, in contrast, was not viewed as depleting capital assets. Rather, it maximized income to offset the growing financial deficits of maintenance and burial.

In 1965, a new crematorium was built, with an improved standard of facilities and an increased capacity for disposal.[54] The new building was not, however, constructed in the cemetery's traditional Gothic style. A low, single-level design with no spires rising above the trees presented the new metaphor for dying, death and disposal – an image of death as rational, sequestered, removed from home surroundings and handled by unseen, unfamiliar technicians and professionals – that emerged in Britain after the devastation of two world wars.[55] The appearance of this crematorium represented an efficient, unsentimental system that treated everyone as equal in death, a philosophy that mirrored the earlier principles of the Commonwealth War Graves Commission[56] as well as the country's post-war commitment to democratic socialism and a more equitable society. Significantly, too, it was in this post-war period that Lawson cypress and arbor vitae were planted to screen off the distinct landscapes of burial and cremation – two contrasting views of the meaning and practices of death and memory.

The Lawn Section

In the 1950s, this more cost-effective, rational approach to the management of disposal resulted in a further alteration of the ceme-tery's landscape. A new 'lawn section', inspired by the ideological designs of the War Graves Commission, was introduced. Two of the commission's aesthetic principles were adopted for this new burial area: first, a grid for similar-size monuments, uniform in height and width, again 'symbolizing equality of treatment in death', and second, the restful appearance of neatly mown grass and the brightness of flowers, advising that a cemetery 'need not be a place of gloom'. Although much of the new section was turfed, tree and shrub planting was reduced, creating a 'simple, harmonious and open landscape'. The efficient use of gang mowers and mechanized grave diggers and the assignment of plots on a strictly rotational basis, which gave users less choice regarding burial location, were instituted to save staff time and labour costs.

The cemetery's 1955 promotional booklet praised the new lawn section for 'its high standard of maintenance'.[57] Instead of the Vic-torian cult of romantic mourning expressed through 'large and ugly memorials'[58] and abundant plantings, the new lawn cemetery, along with the carefully manicured memorial gardens, reflected more rational control of both nature and emotion. The aesthetics of the orderly lawn design, echoed in the geometrically laid out avenues of uniformly sized red horse-chestnut trees, paralleled the then popular paradigm of grief where 'unresolved grief', like 'unbridled' monuments, was no longer acceptable. Death, like illness, was a loss from which one should recover and from which one should move on in order to form new relationships.[59]

This new lawn section had originally been planted as two separate parcels, one earmarked for private graves and the other for communal burials. In 1956, however, management eliminated the common graves option as uneconomic and disorderly.[60] Although the number of common interments had dwindled to 619 that year, 'the [common grave] area to be maintained had increased'. At the same time that he criticized the unkempt landscape of small memorials, the superintendent admitted to difficulties in reforming the mourning behaviour of the poor:

> There has also been an increase in the number of relatives who take advantage of the opportunity to place small memorials on common graves and the result has been that, in the areas devoted to these common graves, there has grown up a vast congestion of small memorials interspersed with flower vases, jam jars, etc. – ugly to look at and most difficult to keep tidy. Grass can only be cut with difficulty by hand and leaves and rubbish become trapped between the multitude of small memorials. Moreover, the area where burials are taking place is always unsightly and depressing by reason of the large heaps of soil which must always be present there. As the years go on, more ground has been used up.[61]

By the 1960s, many more families could afford burial in a private grave – often the first piece of property they had been able to purchase. The option of a private grave, in perpetuity, with the right to erect a memorial, was finally available to all. Equality in death, advocated by Haywood and Simons more than a hundred years earlier, was at last – in some measure – achieved at the City of London Cemetery. But in adopting the War Graves Commission's design of straight rows of kerb-free, uniformly sized stones, management ruled out the modern version of the large Victorian memorial. Many potential buyers objected to the new kerbless style, because it did not prevent traffic over the grave. This was viewed as disrespectful treatment of the deceased: 'I have an uneasy feeling with people standing on the graves; it is not correct.' Others felt they had no economic alternative but to purchase this new style of grave: 'Someone came home and said, "Now they're burying in a new way. You can't bury at the cemetery with the big stones no more, only headstones." They were selling plots of land off; there was no option, it was £200.' Today, people report the same reservations about the lawn section: 'I do not like to tread on the graves. You do it here but you do not realize it – they call it lawn.' 'No one walked on him while he was alive.' One cemetery official summed up the situation: 'Many people want a long grave, but financially they settle for the lawn.'

To induce acceptance of the lawn model with the kerb-free memorial, management offered family members the opportunity to tend the small border garden in front of each marker (Fig. 2.3). This proposal opened up new possibilities: the chance to continue the Victorian tradition of bringing and arranging cut flowers on the grave,[62] but also the opportunity to engage with 'Mother Earth', to plant a small memory garden and thereby to claim a personal stake in the ideal of 'country'. With previous common graves, opportunities for commemoration had been extremely limited, as this woman explained about her father's public grave: 'It had four headstones. It was a full-length grave; other people were in there. We just put flowers, there was no room to plant.' Although flowers and gardening were widely loved in the East End community,[63] it was only with the purchase of an individual grave – 'His stone has his name on it, and it's like he's here.' – that many grieving family members gained possession of their own garden plot.

Mourners seized the new opportunity, and using the resources of nature they created individualized and distinctive memorials within the expanding and uniform spread of homogeneous stones. This new sense of ownership, accompanied by notions of empowerment and self-determination, was further demonstrated when mourners contested management's control of the small space behind each memorial. Family members pulled out the shrubs the cemetery gardeners had planted there and replaced them with their own standard rose bushes. Just as the cemetery founders, designers and managers had reconfigured nature in the past to foster new types of mourning behaviour, so lawn section users assumed this role as they reordered the grave-garden plantings to convey how grief might be expressed in the 1970s, 1980s and to date.

As this case clearly illustrates, graves and cemeteries, like other domestic spaces, can also speak to relationships of power, ownership and agency.[64] In a parallel instructive example from post-war England, the functional architecture of inter-war council housing estates was often associated with feelings of alienation and stigma among the tenants. However, such negative emotions were reversed when renters were allowed to 'take possession' of their homes and to assert control and 'ownership' by making changes through decorating and maintenance work.[65] This example helps to explicate the corresponding response at the City of London Cemetery when the intentionally egalitarian type of lawn grave was introduced after the Second World War. There, too, families accepted this functional and minimalist form of memorial – the 'home' of the deceased – only when they were allowed to buy the private grave plots and were given permission to

Figure 2.3.
Small border gardens in front of each grave, a standard rose bush behind. City of London Cemetery, 1997.

use the little piece of land in front of each stone to plant their individual grave gardens. Cemetery landscapes, like other public spaces, are about the power and ownership of management, which frequently makes decisions based on economic realities, but they can also be shaped by the needs, wishes, actions and demands of consumers – by the families of the dead.

In discussing the introduction of the new lawn section with older study participants who recalled its methods, it became clear that other family members also felt positively about this new burial option, which reflected a level of economic achievement through private ownership of a 'family grave', and about the attendant opportunity to express grief personally through newly created planting rituals. For many, the lawn section represented an English ideal of private ownership of property and thus became a source of status, self-esteem and positive social identity. Such accounts also reveal the class-based nature of memory and the way it can operate to structure and legitimate past inequalities. One informant remarked, 'The lawn cemetery is a new way of life: Before, the old graves [public graves] were littler, now we have more money; the very big graves were for the wealthy.' Or as another said, 'As the family got better off we were able to buy plots dug for two, three, or four members; before they only had communal graves for six people, and strangers were buried on top of each other.' Another woman commented, 'Common graves were all right years ago, but if people have money, the lawn is the finest thing; it's smart.'

The same woman spoke proudly of her parents' grave – 'They're on the lawns' – suggesting emulation of the eighteenth-century ideal of a grassy landscape park designed by Capability Brown.[66] Other older visitors likened ownership of a private cemetery plot to rural life: 'Our dad loved the country and animals, and this was the nearest we could get for them; there were cows on the flats and swans on the water. This is the family grave – no one else can go in here, it's ours.' Tending a private grave also offered solace through intimate involvement with the grave:

> My family liked the new lawn section – it saved space and the cost of the memorial, and they were proud of being part of the new part. In the beginning, my mum came almost daily and got comfort from tending the two-foot-square garden, and used the donations from her neighbours to pay for the first year's maintenance.

Through development of the new lawn section, with its affordable burial options and acceptance of a housekeeping role, the cemetery management took account of the needs of the bereaved and developed a viable interface for future collaboration. The trust established between the superintendent and the users legitimized new, though restricted, bereavement activities that centred on the cultivation of the small grave-garden next to the monument. That this organizational concession was offset by the imposition of greater uniformity for memorials is perhaps affirmation of the inseparability of garden and stone for the significance of grave and cemetery design. It is also testimony to the role of management in the evolution of the larger memorial landscape, the dynamic of which reveals much about the interplay of nature, society and death and about changing expressions of grief.

By the late 1990s, when we undertook our study, the original appearance of the lawn cemetery had been transformed through the activities of mourners. A new cemetery culture, focused on practices relating to maintaining the memorial stone and tending the grave garden, had altered the burial landscape. Mourners likened the cemetery to a peaceful park with beautiful, well-kept gardens: 'It's like God's garden on earth, it gives me consolation.' The post-war design, with its natural light and open space, had been adopted by City of London Cemetery users and interpreted to portray their contemporary acceptance of death as a dimension of life and nature. 'Death today is acceptable; it is an open, natural part of life, just as it is in the cemetery with sunshine and colour.'[67]

The war-graves aesthetic has been reinterpreted by City of London Cemetery mourners to signify core values of East End culture, notably a lack of status distinctions: 'It's a classless cemetery now. . . . No one here looks poor or rich, no one is higher than the others.' Uniformity of design also expresses traditional neighbourhood standards of neatness and tidiness, extending to the cemetery the domestic ethic that people practiced to maintain dignity and self-respect in the face of overcrowded housing and limited economic resources. 'I love the lawn, it's neat and tidy. Here, it's tidy, the dead are respected, and they're taken care of.'

Three Contrasting Cemeteries

The City of London Cemetery illustrates how the garden metaphor has been employed to create many of the lasting features of the traditional English memorial landscape. At three other London cemeteries among our research sites, the English metaphor of cemetery as garden has been adopted in varying aesthetic forms, with different landscape outcomes. The Greek Orthodox, Orthodox Jews and Muslims have historically refused burial under Church of England rites on consecrated soil, so these groups have established their own separate burial grounds. Greek Orthodox mourners at New Southgate Cemetery, Jewish mourners at Bushey United Jewish Cemetery and Muslims at Woodgrange Park Cemetery have each made use, to greater or lesser degrees, of the metaphor of cemetery as garden in order to meet and express their religious, emotional and cultural needs to maintain a continuing relationship with the deceased. Although the same essential components of the memorial landscape – interred bodies, stone markers and their epitaphs, the postures and gestures of the bereaved and the surrounding landscape of trees and shrubbery, paths and contours – work together at each site, they have been configured differently to create distinct environments of memory specific to each cultural group.

At all of these sites, ongoing dialogue and negotiation between the requirements of mourners and the aims of administrators have also been registered, materially and symbolically, on the cemetery landscape. On different occasions and in multiple ways, the bereaved, with their distinct needs, wants and obligations, have resisted, subverted, contested, accepted or adopted as their own the stipulations and regulations of management.

The most striking feature of the landscape at New Southgate Cemetery, which is used by north London's growing Greek Cypriot community, is the exuberant appearance of its graves and monuments, which reflect an individual and eclectic aesthetic. The expanding Greek sections of the cemetery are crowded, colourful and elaborate. The landscape immediately signals the attention showered on these graves. The plantings – scented carnations and roses, rosemary and miniature cypress trees – the white marble monuments covered with potted plants and cut flowers in vases, the lighted *kandelia,* or votive lamps and the watered graves all mark the attitudes that the Greek Orthodox hold toward death and the dead. One might argue that the landscape at New Southgate is the material expression of the community's attempt to deny the stark reality of death and the dead bodies that lie in the place comfortingly named *kemederion,* 'the place of sleep'.[68] A multisensory memorial language of flowers, ornaments, photographs, icons, light and scent are all deployed in an attempt to achieve eternal life through memorial and memory.[69]

Just as mourners at the City of London Cemetery portray its lawn section through the metaphor of the garden, so, too, do Greek Orthodox users of New Southgate see their cemetery as a garden, an imagined and wished-for replication of an idealized Cypriot cemetery. The ground is covered with shingle, not grass, to re-create a 'Cypriot burial ground'. 'This is my idea of heaven and it's in this cemetery right here,' said one man. 'Like this peaceful beautiful garden, full of colour, trees and birds and the strong smell of incense in the air. I find this place to be the true place of religion – this is where God is, not in the church but in here with my wife and daughter, and the earth and trees and flowers and the birds.'

Unlike the Greek Orthodox section at New Southgate, where each grave is a garden, at Bushey United Jewish Cemetery the metaphor of cemetery as garden is used mainly to describe the larger memorial landscape. As one United Synagogue rabbi noted: 'At Bushey there is peace and tranquillity. It is like a garden and feels like a garden of rest. It is beautifully kept.' But although the cemetery entrance is landscaped with narrow borders of roses, hanging flower baskets, grass and a pedestrian bridge over ornamental ponds ('We want to make visiting as pleasant as possible'), the burial grounds themselves appear as a huge expanse of closely placed white marble stones (see Fig. 1.2). Tree planting is limited; ash and clinker (a gravel-like material) cover the ground, which is kept grass and weed free. Few graves are covered with flowers.[70]

This landscape reflects land constraints and changes in the ethnic composition of London's Jewish community. In 1873, when Willesden, the first United Synagogue cemetery, was founded to accommodate the burial needs of London's eminent Anglo-Jewish families, its design reflected the ethos of the times and the ideals of upper-class English society. Willesden was laid out with a broad carriage drive, its grounds were elaborately landscaped and tended by a full staff of grounds-keepers and many graves were planted with flowers in emulation of a well-kept Victorian garden cemetery. At the turn of the century, however, the make-up of the London Jewish community changed, and the United Synagogue came to represent a middle-of-the-road ortho-doxy. An influx of Eastern European immigrants, many of whom maintained their standards of religious observance, led to a strengthen-ing of the orthodox tenets of the Anglo-Jewish community and a pulling back from tendencies to assimilation.

The design of Bushey, consecrated in 1947, reflected this reaffirma-tion of traditional practices in its comparatively austere burying ground with an emphasis on the immortality of the soul and equality in death. Moreover, it had become difficult to purchase land for a cemetery by the twentieth century: suitable sites were limited, and many communities did not want a burial ground close by and so denied planning permission. To conserve space, Bushey was laid out using a grid design with gravel pedestrian paths between rows of single-depth graves marked by standing memorials of regulated size. Thus, ethnic and religious trends, together with limited land resources, led to a modification of the English aesthetic of cemetery as garden and a return to a more traditional layout free of amenity plantings.[71]

Today, many users accept Bushey as the standard of what an Anglo-Jewish cemetery looks like: 'Jewish cemeteries are functional and austere, not decorative.' Mourners interpret the landscape as reflecting Jewish spiritual beliefs about the separation of the soul from the body: 'It's clean and neat . . . there's just bones here now.' 'Only the body is in the ground, the soul goes back to the Creator.' Visitors focus on the individual stone rather than the ornamental features: 'To be honest, I wouldn't notice if they planted six more trees; I come for my mother's stone.' This comparatively solemn aesthetic encodes more orthodox burial traditions and also visually signifies the separateness of Jewish grounds and practices from those of Anglican society by not using flowers or wreaths at funerals. ('We do not flower our people.') The tidiness of the cemetery is praised as meeting psychological and religious priorities: 'The cemetery is nicely kept; it would upset me terribly if it were overgrown. I like to feel it's tended.'

This aesthetic of difference carries through to the external design. The main approach to Bushey is through a modest entrance in the high surrounding wall; no grand gates or space for long funeral cortèges distinguish the site as a burial ground. Many people view the cemetery entrance as a route back into Jewish history: 'We're rooted, but rootless at the end of the day. The grave is something to come back to. The cemetery is the whole Jewish context, content and continuity.'[72]

At Woodgrange Park Cemetery, rapid change can be read from the landscape as the cemetery becomes a predominantly Islamic place of burial. The expanding Muslim sections contrast with the original Nonconformist areas, once marked by monuments featuring Christian or classical symbols of death, mourning and resurrection but since buried under layers of vegetation or cleared for housing or reuse (Fig. 2.4). As these older graves are overlaid with new Muslim burials and memorials, the main beneficiaries of the changes are the local Bangladeshi and Gujarati Muslims, whose religion requires single-depth burial.

At Woodgrange, two different ritual calendars, contrasting sequences of mortuary practices and contrasting metaphors of cemetery as garden operate simultaneously but somewhat discordantly. This dynamic situation, related to the distinct customs, religions and economics separating these two cultural groups, has left its mark on the landscape. In the past few decades the cemetery has changed from the ordered, tidy ideal of landscaped garden put forward for the City of London Cemetery into a place of exposed, upturned earth with low, fairly simple kerbed monuments amid patches of litter and brambles – a disorder that earlier users tend to attribute to managerial practices rather than to the new Muslim users. One Church of England user of Woodgrange remarked, 'This cemetery used to be a good cemetery. . . . I was born in this area and used to see it when I was young . . . . It's because the cemetery is not consecrated that they can do what they like with people's graves.' However, the appearance of the cemetery may increasingly reflect the landscape of *coverstan,* the graveyards in the region of Sylhet, Bangladesh, described by Gardner as 'patches of "wild" land'.[73]

Muslims may tend towards an ideal of a garden cemetery in spiritual and mystical rather than material terms. At the same time, and especially over the last few years, some graves are increasingly being planted more elaborately as members of the community adopt English styles of grave tending. Significantly, too, one enclosed area owned privately by a group called the Patel Trust is surrounded by Leyland cypress trees, possibly suggesting the idea of a paradise garden as depicted in Islamic art – though perhaps just capitalizing upon the rapid growth and dense screening properties of these trees.

Conclusion

Today, despite land shortages and increasing maintenance costs, burial continues as a viable option at the City of London Cemetery, and a

Figure 2.4.
Old graves,
cleared of
brambles, in the
original Non-
conformist area of
Woodgrange Park
Cemetery, 1997.

wider range of burial choices, with a corresponding broader price differential, is now offered. Public and leased lawn graves, earlier options that were eliminated in the 1950s, have been revived, and a new style of 'classic' lawn grave is now available. Traditional Victorian graves with concrete landings, vault graves with standing memorials and above-ground burial in the catacombs are other options, as is 'woodland', or 'green', burial. Each burial choice determines the permitted style, wording and ownership of the monument, installation procedures and period of tenure.

Such regulations, as well as those dealing with floral tributes and grave planting, affect the ways mourners use the City of London Cemetery to commemorate their dead. At the same time that more burial options are being offered to a wider group of potential customers, the religious and ethnic makeup of the cemetery is also changing as London becomes more culturally diverse. This broadening of both the socio-economic and the cultural composition of the user population will inevitably affect the appearance of the cemetery as survivors choose different grave options as the new 'homes' of the deceased.

As our primary research site, the City of London Cemetery exemplifies the evolution of the cemetery landscape, including the creation of the grave garden, burial and memorialization practices and the dynamic push-pull relationship between users and management. Similar elements and issues are relevant at New Southgate Cemetery, Bushey United Jewish Cemetery and Woodgrange Park Cemetery, where distinct landscapes of memory have also been created. Though the idioms vary with the different cultures, it is into these distinct landscapes that the bereaved first enter the cemetery when, at the head of the funeral procession, they accompany the body to its place of rest. And as we examine in future chapters, it is in such public settings that mourners are guided in their expressions of grief. In London's cemeteries, through the language of stones and flowers, the passages of burial and both initial and ongoing bereavement become marked on the landscape.

3

Planting the Memory: The Cemetery in the First Year of Mourning

Death provides the opportunity to transmit traditional teachings.

United Synagogue Rabbi

During the days, weeks and months that culminate in the first anniversary of death, mourning practices, guided by cultural and religious beliefs as well as by cemetery staff, frame and constrain feelings of grief and disorder and help to direct their expression through acceptable idioms. In public settings such as cemeteries, the bereaved are educated in the public expression of private emotions. And it is through the language of stones and flowers that burial and the first year's bereavement become marked on the landscape. Each new grave transforms, reshapes and reaffirms the cemetery as a place of memory. A fresh burial is visually recognizable by the newly upturned earth and the cemetery's identifying burial marker and number. Over the first year, the appearance of the grave may be transformed as the bereaved, following a customary schedule of memorial visits and practices, become involved with and change the site. The grave may be elaborated, for example, through decoration with flowers, the placement of a temporary wooden marker or floral headstone and the setting of a permanent stone memorial. The cemetery landscape is built up through the commemorative activities of individual mourners who draw on traditional cultural aesthetics to reaffirm the personal identity and group membership of the deceased.

The four distinct landscapes at the City of London, Bushey United Jewish, New Southgate and Woodgrange Park Cemeteries reflect the different religious beliefs, cultural ideals, burial customs and economic resources of their respective users, as well as varying interrelationships between mourners and managers. The practices unique to each site can be classified into the following six stages: pre-mortem considerations, the death and delegation of the undertaking for burial, preparation of the corpse, the period of pre-burial mourning, interment and first-year post-burial mourning and its associated commemorative rites.[1] The duration of these stages varies according to each culture's customs, the practical schedules of the undertaker and cemetery staff, and individual needs.

During the first year's burial rituals, relations of trust and accommodation between cemetery administrators and mourners govern the passage of the body. By focusing on the negotiations initiated during the year of interment over possession of the body and control of the grave, we can begin to speculate about what conditions are necessary to give mourners the time and space to come to terms with their loss. The dynamic relations among all the parties who have an interest in the grave, including those affiliated with the cemetery, create an environment that may assist or impede the acceptance of the reality of death and the creation of memory. The individual's formal journey, the social transformation from a living person to a corpse – a body to be processed and disposed of – is subject to legal and bureaucratic procedures that apply to every English cemetery.[2] The practices and customs associated with the first year following burial lay the foundations for longer-term commemorative rites that consolidate in the landscape of the cemetery.

The first year is also the time when relationships between and the interdependency of mourners and management are negotiated and established – the time when administrative procedures and regulations, the customs of the cultural group and the needs and sentiments of the bereaved are in dynamic interplay. In the following accounts of the first year for each of our four study sites and their respective populations, we draw on official practices as well as cultural, ritual and religious rites as guides for exploring what individual mourners actually do when faced with loss, how existing cemetery practices may vary in content and form from the 'ideal' and how authorities respond to such variations. It is in this negotiated context that the behaviour and sentiments of the bereaved are expressed, moulded and registered on the cemetery landscape.

City of London Cemetery

At the City of London Cemetery, a calendar of memorial rites and practices of remembrance, all cemetery centred, mould the expression of loss in a newly created idiom of grave garden and stone. Various factors enter into the family's selection of a municipal cemetery: local custom and the deceased's preference to be buried with or near kin ('East Enders are buried here, it's the biggest; it's traditional and all her family is here.'), the fact that the favoured denominational cemetery is full, location, standard of upkeep, word of mouth and the suggestion of the funeral director. At CLCC, decisions on the type of grave selected among the available options are based primarily on price and aesthetic preference.[3] The passage of the body into the cemetery landscape begins when the appointed funeral director contacts the cemetery administration to arrange the burial.[4] The booking is arranged for about a week later.

Until the day of the funeral, cemetery officials refer to the deceased by his or her full name. On the day of the funeral and thereafter, he or she is referred to by both name and allocated burial number. Cemetery personnel write to the owner of each new grave just prior to the funeral, advising him or her of the number allocated and giving details of the grave registration. The letter also makes certain that the name of the owner and other pertinent information are correct. As with all details at the City of London Cemetery, a precise system ensures that mistakes are avoided. Cemetery rules and procedures, as well as obligations and restrictions relevant to the grave, are included in the letter. A deed (see Appendix 4) is sent to the owners approximately four weeks later.

With a week or more before the funeral, the place where the body awaits burial may affect the grieving process, particularly when local customs are changing and new practices may be less satisfying than those they are replacing. Many study participants recall (and a few still follow) the former East End convention of keeping the deceased at home before the funeral. Under this custom, the interval between death and interment was, with the guidance of the undertaker, determined by family members, who were in possession of the body. Medical and mortuary personnel now manage end-of-life practices; control of the corpse has been surrendered to outsiders. Traditional practices of caring for the dying and tending the deceased, once located in family and community, are being absorbed by professionals, including cemetery administrators. In an interview, an East End woman contrasted the old and new customs:

> It was usual to bring the dead back home and to keep them in the parlour until the day of the funeral . . . . We went into the parlour and we spoke to them, we walked in and looked at them . . . . The coffin was open; the body was embalmed. They were dressed in their good clothing. We were not frightened. We always used the local undertaker, he knows all the families . . . . The local doctor came in, and my neighbours came to pay their respects, and even the children were taken in to see the deceased, it was natural . . . . When my husband died, people came to my door to say their condolences, but only one friend went with me to see my husband at the undertaker's. My friends took me to the chapel in their cars, but they did not come in.

Today the public passage of the body into the cemetery follows traditional East End custom, but in a modified fashion: the funerary flowers may now substitute for the corpse in making the customary journey from home to the burial ground. In one observed case, an East End family chose the traditional Victorian glass-sided hearse with black-plumed horses to give their 85-year-old mother a 'good send-off'. On a back street near her former home, the coffin containing the body, which had been kept until then at the undertaker's, was transferred from a modern funeral car to the hearse. This Victorian vehicle then stopped in front of the deceased's former home, where the family members and floral tributes waited. After the flowers were arranged on the top and in the back of the hearse for maximum visual display, the funeral director, dressed in a morning coat and top hat, walked slowly in front of the horses as they pulled the hearse down the street, and again when they entered the cemetery.[5]

For both active and nominal members of the Church of England, in contrast to Orthodox Jews, the Greek Orthodox and Muslims, the formal schedule of activities expected of mourners in relation to the deceased concludes with burial.[6] The bereaved, as members of an increasingly secularized and individualistic English society, are 'on their own' to cope with loss.[7] The absence of public mourning customs in contemporary English society, the lack of religious rituals calling on survivors to aid the soul's passage and the abbreviated cemetery experiences of many visitors, from which they might model current practices, have left a vacuum but also an 'opportunity'[8] for the creation of new rites.

However, it is a relationship of trust between mourners and cemetery managers, we maintain, that is necessary for the formation of a cemetery culture that provides post-funeral guidance and support to the bereaved. One way in which the cemetery wins the confidence of new users is through its maintenance of the grounds. At the City of London Cemetery, for example, agreement has been established between management and the bereaved that both the cemetery and visitors will respect, honour and take care of the dead, and it is the upkeep of the landscape that symbolizes this unspoken understanding. A former superintendent articulated the cemetery's contribution to this tacit contract:

> We need to monitor the level of maintenance so that people feel proud to be buried here . . . . We also have to meet people's emotional needs and expectations, that this is a place which is safe, attractive and that their peers think is a good place to be; that they feel safe, content with the surroundings and that they can concentrate on what they have come for. We give the frame-work where they can express their emotions. This is the impor-tant thing, the framework, the environment.

Initiation into the culture of grave tending begins with the removal of the funeral flowers from the newly mounded grave. Survivors are given seven days after the funeral to clear the memorial flowers before the cemetery takes them away; signs are posted stating this. The bereaved describe this task as 'the worst job'. New mourners report that they feel most vulnerable and uneasy when the grave is new and the soil 'rough and raw'. The fresh earth of the new grave echoes the fresh grief over recent loss. To cope with their feelings as expressed so directly by the bare grave site, many bring potted plants and vases of cut flowers to create an immediate headstone. Others pour a bag of topsoil over the stony under-layer brought up by the mechanical grave digger and plant the grave with flowers. Like new homeowners, a few mark the plot's boundaries with stones to delineate the property lines and to protect the grave from being inadvertently walked over. Through these many activities, which are both expressive of grief and emotionally distracting from that very grief, survivors assert control over the grave and symbolically retake possession of the body. From the first week following burial, the activities of coming to the cemetery regularly and tending the grave are learned and practised and become for many one of a series of ways to express and cope with loss.

Whereas some bereaved people, 'not wanting to take liberties', restrict their initial gardening to the regulated dimensions, others plant the entire plot. 'This is a nice big garden; we have one year to do what we please. We're beginning the process of preparing for critical planting, when we'll plant with discipline and a plan and we'll be limited to fewer, but nicer flowers.' The fully planted grave begins to give material representation to the profound emotions of grief, which are seen as legitimate during the first year. Later, personal and social constraints will confine the expression of loss, just as the cemetery eventually imposes more stringent restrictions on the planting space.

For many, the absence of a gravestone only exacerbates an emotionally trying time. One recent widow articulated her anxiety and her belief that the memorial would better enable her to handle her loss, 'I can't relax till I get the headstone up. I'm uneasy; I can't get it together until I get the headstone.' Or as the parents of a deceased seven-year-old daughter explained, 'We wanted something quickly and could not bear it with a stake and number.' It is at some point within the first six months after burial that mourners at the City of London Cemetery usually erect the memorial.[9] The cemetery does not impose a time frame, nor is there a customary set of ritual practices surrounding the stone setting as there is for the Anglo-Jewish community. Some mourners aim to select a unique marker, which no one else has, whereas others are content to imitate their neighbours: 'The stonemason told us to take down the plot number of the stone we like, and he will come to look at it to get the same one.'

In contemporary, secular English culture, bereavement is often described as personal and private, without formal guidelines and customs. For those with no prior experience of death and who lack a model for handling the practicalities of bereavement, the cemetery becomes a resource, offering a suggested time frame and examples of how others cope. Indeed, at CLCC it is possible to observe the evolution of a subculture of mourning, a collective composed of a segment of the population who select burial and elect to visit the cemetery to remember their dead. The cemetery provides a unique public space where grieving behaviour, often marginalized by society, is both evoked and managed by cemetery procedures and peer practices. It is a place where conversations with and observations of other mourners provide a level of understanding, instruction and integration not found in everyday social interaction.

Although survivors may erect the memorial stone within a few months, the cemetery staff delays at least one year in order for the ground to settle before turfing the grave. Some mourners attempt to accelerate the process. They sow their own grass seed and may plant a few spring bulbs, which will not be permitted once the grave is permanently turfed. Such activities indicate a need to settle the physical aspects of the burial and to move beyond the betwixt-and-between stage of an unfinished grave. Bereaved survivors report feeling more settled, even pleased, when the grave is officially turfed. For many, it is a significant marker in the process of grieving. 'It's like having carpeting installed in a new house: now we can get down to putting things in order.' Once the grave is turfed, however, mourners must limit their garden planting to the allotted space of half a square metre. Their acquiescence to, if not total acceptance of, this rule signifies an adoption of the cemetery's cultural code of a more restrained expression of grief. After the first year, mourners must scale down their grave-tending activities, but they still find ways to adapt them to express a complex, shifting range of emotions that are scaled down dimensionally but may be intensified in other ways.

Although City of London Cemetery visitors are not guided by established rituals backed by religious or cultural ideologies, many mourners turn to the resources of nature to help mark their grieving process.[10] Here we argue that for both churched and unchurched mourners who have family members buried at CLCC, the cemetery is a location for a new, dynamic, collective culture of bereavement, engendered by the English love of gardens and the ready availability of plants and flowers in local markets and shops. Innovative funerary rituals are being built around the material artefact of the memorial stone coupled with the small grave-garden plot. Transformations in the appearance of the grave register grief on the landscape in customary ways. The clearing away of the funeral flowers, the establishment of a floral marker, the creation of the memorial garden, the erection of the stone marker, the turfing of the grave and the regathering of family to mark the first anniversary of death with the placement of floral offerings (which are seen to temporarily re-create the appearance of the grave following the funeral) all have symbolic import and reveal how the garden becomes an evolving memorial.

The first year following death is particularly difficult as mourners are forced to celebrate significant occasions without the presence of the departed. Many transfer these former celebrations to the cemetery and visit on Christmas, Easter, birthdays, anniversaries, and Mother's and Father's Days. In the past, visitors came to the burial ground less frequently than nowadays and with a different annual calendar. The following recollections of a flower vendor who sold bouquets from a van in front of the cemetery gates reveal how these shifts in cemetery visiting patterns have been accompanied by increased availability and choices in cut flowers:

Today, more people go to the cemetery; they are more conscious of Easter, Christmas and Mothering Sunday. Before, these days were not so widely thought of. Mother's Day only came in after the war. Now, flowers are more colourful. Before, with Easter, you could only buy yellow and white – daffs and narcissus were the flowers for spring. At Christmas, people chose bronze, dark reds; now they choose any colour flower. Mothering Sunday was originally celebrated in the US and it came here with the service-men after the war. On Father's Day, it was red and blue: red carnations and roses, blue iris. Father's Day only came in after Mother's Day, not until the sixties. People used to come on Whitsun, but now it has died away.

Thus, the cycle of the seasons and nature, the calendar of religious and secular holidays, and significant family dates such as birthdays and anniversaries are linked through careful, sustained attention to the grave garden.

As we describe further in chapter 5, in later years, after the plot is turfed, cemetery guidelines regarding the grave garden become more stringent. The designing of the garden, the tending of plants and the selecting and arranging of cut flowers may be given more attention and refinement. Conversely, these grave gardens may also display freer expression and experimentation as the meaning and memory of the deceased and the identity of self and other are renegotiated over time. The need to control grief also shapes and contains its expression and may thereby assist in maintaining an enduring tie with the deceased. Thus, although the tending of the grave plot has its roots in cultural expectations and practices, its meanings, experiences and interpreta-tions are variable over time and from individual to individual within the same cemetery community.

Bushey United Jewish Cemetery

At Bushey United Jewish Cemetery, a distinct set of religious and cultural rites marks the passage of the body and soul and the parallel journey of the mourners during the first year of bereavement.[11] Unlike the newly created practices linking nature and death at the City of London Cemetery, the prescribed Orthodox Jewish rituals of burial and mourning do not draw on the resources of nature to mediate, define and aid the individual grieving process.[12] Bushey is a distinctly Jewish cemetery, where Orthodox practices are reflected in its sacred landscape and where mourners are guided and supported by the burial society, their synagogue rabbis and their fellow congregants, family and friends.

In London, the Jewish encounter with death and disposal is experienced mainly within the confines of the religious community and is orchestrated by customary ideals and traditions. The interval between death and burial is marked as a special period (*aninut*) during which the bereaved, experiencing grief and despair, must deal with the reality of death and make immediate funeral arrangements. The United Synagogue, through its burial society, is responsible for the management of Bushey United Jewish Cemetery, and United Synagogue members pay 'funeral expenses scheme' as a part of their annual dues to cover their burial expenses. Thus, before death, a contract with the cemetery is already in place. When a congregant dies, the burial society is the undertaker and assumes responsibility for care of the body from death until interment, and thereafter.[13]

Orthodox Jews must be buried in the earth within twenty-four hours of death, so the digging and preparation of the single-depth grave – either a reserved space next to a close family member or a new grave – must be started immediately. A single telephone call to the London burial society office initiates the efficient process. Both British legislative procedures and Orthodox Jewish ritual requirements guide the burial society in the burial process.

In preparation for the funeral, the *taharah* (rites of purification) is carried out at Bushey by the volunteer members of the *Chevrah Kadisha* (Holy Association). Men and women work separately, each taking care of their own gender;[14] it is traditional that close family members are not involved with the ritual preparation of the corpse. After the body is washed,[15] the final rite of *taharah* is performed: approximately six gallons of water are poured over the entire body in a continuous stream. The body is then wrapped in clean sheets, dried and dressed in a white linen shroud,[16] which, as the head of the women's *Chevrah Kadisha* explained, 'protects the soul against evil and decomposes easily, allowing the soul to soar'. No knots are used, and there are no pockets in the garment – 'The body leaves with nothing, only good deeds and a good name.' The body is then placed in an unadorned wooden coffin, which is closed and sealed. 'No distinctions are made between rich and poor: all receive the same ritual care, the same plain linen shroud and a simple wooden box. In death, great and small are one.'

During the period from death until interment, the deceased is not left unattended. After the purification ritual, the body is watched over in a special room, the *vachin*, located in the *taharah* house. Before the funeral service, the immediate mourners' outer garments are torn, 'to express anguish and spiritual distress'.[17] One female study participant noted this ritual's emotional effectiveness: 'This gesture helps you. . . . By concentrating on tearing material, it brings things down to earth and gives perspective. It expresses the emotions of being overwhelmed by grief and being numb. It helps you to come to terms with reality. It makes it real.' As an outward symbol of grief, the rended clothing is worn throughout the first week of mourning.

Funerals are held at the cemetery's prayer hall, not in the synagogue. The coffin, traditionally covered with a black cloth but now with a blue velvet cloth embroidered with a Star of David, is wheeled in on a bier and placed in front of the podium, where it occupies the space between the men and women, who stand on opposite sides of the hall. The rabbi, who may have known the deceased as one of his congregation, delivers the eulogy, which describes the personality and character of the departed, sets his or her life in a religious context, offers the mourners comfort and hope and stresses the fragility of human existence.

The body is then drawn on the bier from the hall to the gravesite, followed by the family and the assembled people. This procession of mourners, visible across the landscape, signifies the sanctity of the grounds and forms a strong visual image reflecting the strength of religious custom. As the president of United Synagogue remarked, 'It is considered a righteous act to accompany the body to its final resting place and to send the soul on.' On the way to the grave the entourage stops seven times, pausing to reflect on the meaning of life and the vanity of earthly pursuits. The coffin is lowered into the ground, and the mourners, followed by relatives and close friends, fill the grave with earth. The shovel is never passed but rather replaced on the pile for the next person to take anew.

Interment is the ritual time when some Jewish mourners believe the soul is departing the body, whereas others trust that the corpse is still animated by the soul and that only when the dead flesh has returned to nature does the spirit soar. When the grave is filled with earth, the period of formal mourning begins. The emotional import of these burial rituals was explained by a female study participant: 'Mourning does not begin until you actually see the body go into the ground and hear the thud, and you do the shovelling of dirt onto the coffin. This is the reality. The sound of the thud, when the earth first hits the coffin to cover it, still makes me shiver.'

At the close of the burial ritual everyone washes his or her hands before returning to the prayer hall. The rabbi recites a memorial prayer, and then the chief mourner or mourners recite Kaddish.[18] At this point the focus is redirected from honouring the dead to comforting the mourners, who are now seated. As one mourner described it: 'Everyone files past, expressing their condolences and wishing you a long life. The last person in the line stands you up; this is the beginning of the mourning process, you are in limbo until then.'

Following the burial, the mourners return to the home of the deceased, where they are served a meal of condolence. Prayers are said, and friends and more distant relatives congregate to pay their respects to the dead and to comfort the mourners. The funeral day starts the week of intensive mourning, the *shivah*, when the surviving family members are confined to the house and must refrain from work and other normal activities. One reflection is especially telling: 'Time is a man-made thing. . . . The *shivah* period lasts for seven days, then there is the first month of mourning, and then the eleven months until the stone setting. It is like, and seems to parallel, the dead person moving on. Resting and going on again – perhaps it also parallels our own grief and grieving process.'

As people live to older ages, some families no longer sit *shivah* for seven days. One seventy-year-old son whose mother had died in her nineties explained, 'I decided that I would sit *shivah* for only two nights. The main reason was because mother was such an advanced age, all her contemporaries and advanced relatives had died; only my contemporaries knew of her.'

The first year of bereavement for Orthodox Jews in London is marked by a series of graduated ritual practices that guide the mourners in acknowledging and accepting loss and expressing grief.[19] For close relatives other than parents, a mourning period of thirty days (*sheloshim*) is the outward ritual mourning obligation. Traditionally, mourning for parents lasts twelve months, during which it is the expected duty of the son to attend synagogue daily to recite Kaddish.[20] One son described his practice and experience over the first year:

> I went daily to the synagogue, daily for the whole year. . . . It is a difficult time, but after a period of time, the reality of the death becomes clear. The prayers in the synagogue are about remembrance and not forgetting. They are not specifically about coming to terms with what happened and accepting the reality, but it happened in the course of time.

This ritual, if observed, has different levels of effectiveness, however. As one United Synagogue bereavement counsellor remarked: 'For men, going to the synagogue is a public expression of personal grief, but many bury the important part and do not deal with grief. Going to the synagogue takes up their time and fills their day.'

Figure 3.1.
Temporary frames
mark new graves
at Bushey United
Jewish Cemetery,
1997.

In the Anglo-Jewish community, it is customary to erect a tombstone approximately eleven months after the burial. In the meantime, a temporary frame – painted red and giving the name and burial number of the deceased – marks the plot (Fig. 3.1). Three to five months after the death, family members usually select a memorial. One stonemason described this visit as a significant time: 'It is hard for them to come here, but once they come, the burden is removed, something else is completed. . . . We encourage people to see the stone. . . . When they've seen it once, it is not such a shock in the cemetery.' The decisions to be made at this time about the permanent stone can be an occasion for family friction and negotiation, as the comments of two brothers who were visiting the cemetery suggest. One said, 'We've come to visit our mother's grave – this is the first time since she was buried six months ago – and to check the grave to see that it has not been defaced.' But after looking at the unsettled conditions of the grave plot – the temporary red frame surrounding the upturned, exposed earth – the more determined brother remarked, 'I'd say it's time to put the gravestone up; it looks a mess. We need to have a gravestone discussion and to settle an order. It is incomplete like this.'

Jewish custom does not advocate frequent cemetery visits during the first year of bereavement.[21] Rabbis encourage the family to restrict their visiting to once after the first week, again at the end of the first month and again at the stone setting, in order to encourage the soul to make its journey unimpeded. Some mourners, however, indicated that the religion was lenient and friends supportive in allowing them to come to the grounds when they felt so inclined – 'Do as your heart wishes.' Others stay away until the consecration of the stone, perhaps at the rabbi's guidance and perhaps for emotional reasons:

> For my sister, I did not go all that year as I did not want to see the grave without the stone on top. I felt relief when it was actually up. It was a focus of where she is. It's interesting – it was a definite physical and emotional feeling. I did not want to visit without the stone on top. I think a grave without a stone looks raw.

The consecration of the memorial as the first anniversary of the death approaches often marks the end of the mourning period. Friends and family gather at the graveside to dedicate the monument. At this time, the bereaved may re-experience their initial emotions of grief. For some, the ritual itself renews the loss and begins, rather than ends, intense mourning: 'It was an ordeal thinking about the consecration, worrying all those months in advance, the pain and emotions, that it would be like reopening a wound, meeting with people again, and in public.' For many, however, the stone setting is 'an excellent way to end the period of mourning, to actually mark the passage'. Another Jewish mourner explained:

> I found the stone setting to be hugely significant. Particularly the timing of it. It was appropriate, it marked the end of the year of mourning. . . . It was an acknowledgement, publicly, of the worth of my mother and an ending of one phase. It represented a moving on through the stages of grief and being in mourning, being bereaved. As a recently bereaved person, you are entitled to special understanding, and after the stone setting you are no longer to expect special treatment . . . you can no longer be seen as different, as special. You now can attend *simchas* [celebrations], buy new clothes, listen to music, dance. . . . During this period, I did not go outside to concerts, to the cinema, to dance. It was a full year of grief. But I was relieved not to dance, to have to be in public with a brave face.

Thus the Anglo-Jewish community marks the first year after death by a sequence of prescribed rituals intended to guide, support and contain mourners in their bereavement. They are expected to accept the reality of loss, to adjust to life without the deceased and to find a place for the deceased within a new reality. The ideal is for the memory of the departed to be held in a positive and helpful way.[22] 'The year is dictated by Jewish law; there is a pattern. You are supported through the process by these spaced times and in this cemetery environment.'

New Southgate Cemetery

The prescribed rites of the funeral, ritually scheduled visits to the grave and consecration of the memorial stone that publicly mark the Orthodox Jewish passage through the first year of mourning are experienced in the public space of the cemetery, not in the synagogue. The Orthodox Greek Cypriot community has also created a sacred place of remembrance at New Southgate Cemetery, but in this case, memorial rituals are linked to both cemetery and church.

For most bereaved families in London's Greek Cypriot population, information regarding funeral and burial arrangements is obtained from friends, relatives, one of the many Greek Orthodox churches in London, the advertising section of the London Cypriot press, or the London Greek radio. The main Greek funeral service takes place in church, and the final funeral prayers are said at the grave. Assistance in selecting a plot at New Southgate is usually given by the Greek funeral undertaker or the cemetery's staff, including the Greek-speaking office manager, who has experience in Orthodox funeral preparations 'to further ensure a good funeral at such a difficult time'. A New Southgate study participant commented:

> My son in-law phoned St Mary's Church . . . and the Cypriot funeral director. He came over to our house with some papers and a catalogue. He was very helpful because my English is not very good and he could speak some Greek. We chose the coffin. I gave him the shroud and my daughter's clothes so that he would dress her and told him to take care of her. My other daughters and me chose a white suit for her – she was young, she was like an angel. The priest told my son-in-law he could book us in the following week.

A number of visits and activities precede the arrival and interment of the body at New Southgate Cemetery. For some mourners these visits fulfil religious and traditional requirements; for others they are more personally and emotionally motivated. Because frequent visiting is expected after burial as well, an accessible location is the principal factor in choosing a cemetery site. Prayers for the repose of the departed are offered at the grave within the first year, as well as in the church.[23] Mourners also visit the grave to ensure that the *kandele*, the votive lamp, remains alight. During these commemorative acts and rituals, ethnicity and kin traditions and history are learned. Burial within the cultural community helps to maintain traditional customs and thus encourages reincorporation of the second and subsequent generations into the society of origin:

> New Southgate is like a Cypriot cemetery; they allow you to do all the Greek things here. I was told that there are cemeteries in London were you can't even put up an Orthodox cross, or they make you have a Catholic or an Anglican funeral service before you can bury your dead in their graveyards.[24]

> It was the undertaker who told us about the cemeteries, their facilities and all the costs. He came with us to New Southgate and they showed us what was on offer there. It looked peaceful, full of flowers and well maintained. I liked the idea of being with our own people. We looked around and chose a double-depth and double-width grave for my daughter and for me – when it's time for me to join her. There is also enough space for the others [the speaker's two other children] when their time comes. The four of us can be here together and it will be our place.

Once a date for the funeral has been arranged, the details are published in London's Greek community press. Such memorial announcements are customarily accompanied by a traditional funeral lament, *moirologi*. The second stage in the funerary journey begins when the Greek undertaker transfers the corpse to his premises. There it is ritually prepared and awaits burial.[25] One undertaker explained, 'I do these basic preparations for all Greek funerals, whether it is asked for or not, because this is what we do, it would not be an Orthodox funeral without it.' The body is washed, wrapped in a shroud and then dressed in new clothes and shoes, all in preparation for 'its journey to the other side'. The hands are crossed over the chest and tied as 'a symbol of the life-bearing cross'.[26]

Significantly fewer of the traditionally prescribed preparations of the body are practised by London's Greek Orthodox community nowadays than in the past. The actual handling of the body is said to be too painful and traumatic an experience, so many families delegate such 'intimacy' with death to the professionals. According to the funeral director: 'Very few clients ask to get involved in the ritual washing and dressing of the body; those who do are elderly women who tell me they want to do *psisigo* [performance of a charitable act that accrues grace].' Some of these old women prepare the body, wash it, cross the arms, put the shroud on it and dress it in new clothing and shoes. After the preparation of the body is complete, family and friends may come to pay their respects at the chapel of rest. Only a few families ask for the body to be taken home; in most Greek funerals, the body is taken directly to the church, and the hearse stops off at the deceased's home only to collect flowers and mourners.

Whereas burial in Cyprus usually takes place within twenty-four hours following death, in London, where many burials may be in process at once, it can take more than a week for the church funeral and the burial to be arranged. During the winter, when the mortality rates increase, burial may be delayed two weeks or more. Therefore, the length of time when the person is dead but still physically part of the living community is protracted. It is only once the body is sealed in the earth that the final separation between the world of the living and the world of the dead becomes reality. For the immigrant genera-tion, accustomed to a shorter funeral cycle, this waiting period is portrayed by some as one of silent despair, devoid of supportive religious or cultural rites. Two elderly study participants described this difficult time: 'These days seemed endless, waiting for the funeral and the whole thing to be over. Whilst he was at the undertaker's, it was so strange – I was in a haze, everything was so unreal.' 'I would go and see her, and felt good that she was still there and I could see her. But I also felt that the more I looked at her, the more pain I felt because it was not her, and she should have been put to rest much earlier. But December is a busy month; we had to get in line.'

Greek Orthodox funerals take place in the church. The main part of the service is concerned primarily with the 'forgiveness of the sins of the deceased, the purification of the soul and its ultimate incorpora-tion into the appropriate and desired location in the other world'.[27] In the past, the deceased would lie in an open coffin during the part of the service known as the *prostheses*. Doctrinally, viewing the body and giving it the final farewell kiss were regarded as necessary and beneficial for the deceased's relatives and also served to remind mourners of the 'fleetingness of life itself'.[28] Ostensibly, because of the overt expression of emotion shown by some relatives, which 'interfered with the liturgical drama and got in the way of the service', priests now prefer a closed coffin and a calmer, more orderly atmosphere.[29] Some see the newer prohibitions as denying an important aspect of Christian understanding: 'Out of touch with death itself, we have drifted away from the reality of death. We hold back and are encour-aged to hold back from seeing, touching, or holding a dead body.'

Following the church service, people go to the cemetery. When the hearse and the priest arrive, they form a procession to escort the deceased to the grave. Mourners gather around the grave as the coffin is lowered into the ground. The priest fills the air with incense and recites the final, brief funeral prayers: 'It is our duty to return the dead to the earth – we are following a divine command';[30] 'Dust thou art, and unto dust thou shalt return.'[31] Oil is poured over the coffin in the pattern of the cross – 'We proclaim also the resurrection by sealing the remains in the grave with the cross'[32] – and last, an earthen receptacle (usually the plate containing the *kollyva,* a traditional dish of boiled wheat) is broken and thrown onto the coffin. Using a special spade provided by the cemetery management, the priest tosses the first shovelful of soil onto the coffin, and others follow by throwing a handful of earth.

The management of New Southgate Cemetery is attuned to the needs of the Cypriot community: 'The Greek funeral is a very special occasion and we do all that we can to facilitate a smooth and dignified occasion.' In preparation for a burial, cemetery personnel line the grave with flowers, put out baskets of petals for the bereaved to scatter and set up tables for *bariyoria,* the funeral meal of consolation. Managers have also brought earth from Cyprus and offer it for placement in the grave for those who wished to be buried with soil from home.

The food provided – usually olives, pieces of bread, cheese and wine – is consumed in memory of the deceased and for consolation of the living. In partaking of this ritual, mourners ask that the deceased's sins be forgiven. From this point forward in the burial service, the deceased is given the appellation *makaridis,* meaning blessed, anointed, deceased. After the food is consumed, the mourners make their way to their cars, leaving the cemetery workers the task of filling the grave. Many study participants felt uncomfortable about leaving the grave open and exposed; they wanted it filled immediately:

> I didn't want to leave him there like that, but they have their rules and we had no choice. They told us the gravediggers would fill it up and it will all be taken care of very soon. You have to trust them, don't you? We have no choice. The grave is very important for us. I hope they don't disturb him ever. That's why we bought this plot here, so that we can have power over what happens to it. There are places, especially the council graves, where they throw the body out and put others into the grave. It's important that the body stays undisturbed. It's a special thing, not like just a bundle of flesh and bones; it is special, loved and remembered. We couldn't really afford to buy the plot here, but he is here now; the grave is ours and we have rights.

At New Southgate Cemetery the management sells wooden crosses and glass boxes (which hold the *kandele*), ready to be placed at the grave immediately after burial. The Orthodox cross and the *kandele* visually distinguish the Greek grave, even within the first week after burial. On leaving the cemetery, the principal mourners, accompanied by extended family members and close friends, return to the home of the deceased or another family member for the post-funeral meal.

The number of visits to the Orthodox grave is not rigidly prescribed but varies according to the 'type' of death and the mourner's relationship with the deceased. There are, however, a number of important religious memorial services and rituals that must be followed within the first year of an Orthodox burial. The cycle begins at the end of the first week with a memorial at the church and a visit to the gravesite. Some mourners may use the time in the first week or month to place the wooden cross and the *kandele*. 'We put up the cross and brought potted plants on the third day of [my sister's] memorial. My mother could not bear to see the cut flowers wilting. She was upset that for a few days there was no *kandele* at my sister's grave.'

The second significant memorial rite takes place on the fortieth day and is the most heavily attended, both at the church service and in the cemetery. Following the fortieth-day memorial, a wooden Greek Orthodox cross is placed on the grave, if one was not already in place. A glass-fronted container is attached to it for housing the *kandele*, icons, photographs and any other personal objects significant to the deceased. Shortly afterward, mourners bring potted flowers and plants as well as cut flowers to the grave. Many begin their gardening in earnest during this period. 'The first year of my mother's death we put a wooden surround on top of the grave. It became like a big giant window box for us. We planted everything and everything just grew. It was as though the flowers wanted to grow for her to please her.' When the stone memorial is erected, the temporary wooden cross, the box holding the *kandele* and the icons and photographs will be removed and replaced as part of the permanent memorial. There is no hard and fast rule about when the stone should be erected, but many study participants were guided by the cemetery officials or other cemetery users who suggested a year or longer after burial.

Each visit to the grave requires the burning of ritual incense and the lighting of the *kandele*, which can also be replicated in church. There are three other traditional memorials, which occur at three, six and nine months after the funeral. Thereafter, although personal visits may occur at any time, the main religious commemorative ritual is carried out yearly.

Throughout the entire period of mourning, survivors often experience a tension between fear of the person's ultimate oblivion and hope in ritual as a gesture against that oblivion. Religious custom, individual emotions and the cemetery experience itself may facilitate or restrain the resolution of these tensions. During the months of prescribed memorial practice, many mourners said they felt conflict between their concern for the safety and security of the grave and their need for individualized memorial practices. In burying the dead, the bereaved must take it on trust that the cemetery management will act as guardian over the interred. Even though rules, procedures and traditional rituals appear to provide stability and may help to restore a sense of order and control at a time of emotional upheaval, some mourners felt 'processed'. Some reacted negatively to the formal rules and structures both at the funeral and the grave and demanded that their individual needs be understood and acknowledged.

The grave, which becomes a small garden within a larger garden, is seen by mourners as a material sphere within a metaphysical spiritual realm. Management, however, find this concept problematic in that mourners 'see the grave as their own personal garden and want to make it look as individual as possible'. Study participants reported that New Southgate Cemetery had instituted new rules requiring family members to purchase memorial stones from masons approved by the management, and some felt that this restricted their freedom of choice. Others suggested that the cemetery facilities would be improved by the hiring of guards and the availability of seats where visitors could rest. Any rule or action on the part of the church, the funeral directors or the cemetery management that appeared to negate mourners' feelings of individuality had the potential to undermine the relationships among the principal actors involved in the 'business' of death.

Woodgrange Park Cemetery

All of those who attend funerals at Woodgrange Park Cemetery now are Muslims, chiefly from Bangladesh and Gujarat, which is not to say that mourning over longer periods is restricted to this new group (see chapter 5). Woodgrange Park Cemetery has emerged recently and rapidly as a Muslim burial ground, and its systems for accommodating this new population are far from seamless. Indeed, it may not have been the intention of traditional users or managers to achieve the regime that now characterizes the cemetery, unlike the 'more calculated' objectives for the other sites we studied.

The standard legislative requirements for burial apply at Woodgrange Park, but cemetery personnel say they sometimes have to advise their new Muslim clientele – first- and second-generation Asians coming to terms with burial procedures in a new country – on certain matters. The Muslim ideal of burial within twenty-four hours of death is the same as that for the Anglo-Jewish community, but the recently improvised arrangements at Woodgrange shape the experiences of those who use this privately owned cemetery rather differently from the experiences of those who bury their dead at Bushey United Jewish Cemetery. Because of the rapid changes, the pace of administrative and ritual activity up to the time of burial is more hectic than measured at Woodgrange. One exception can be seen at the enclosed section that has been purchased from the cemetery by a group called the Patel Trust. In this fenced part of the cemetery, where those buried and their families are 'shareholders in the freehold' who have already paid their dues and reserved grave plots, burial arrangements appear to be more closely regulated. The landscape of this small section gives a different and more ordered account of activity and dispositions at the time of burial.

Throughout all sections of Woodgrange, Muslim interment has eclipsed the old order of Christian burials. Though Christian burials no longer take place, memorialization does continue at established, though increasingly insecure, Christian graves. The tension generated by these developments is discussed in chapter 5, because it has implications for long-term mourning for both groups. Most of the new Muslim burials are undertaken by one Muslim family firm. From this firm's base next to the important Whitechapel Mosque, the several miles to the cemetery are bridged through ritual and administrative links. Long-standing contracts with the cemetery owners and their site manager and frequent communication appear to substitute for the more formal systems seen elsewhere, so that burial in an accelerated time frame can be managed. Only minimal leeway exists, however, should complications arise. For example, some users and the site manager remarked on instances in which the dimensions of the proposed grave were communicated incorrectly, thus creating a delay; the grave having to be enlarged while the mourners waited apprehensively for completion of the interment.

Increasingly, Muslim death takes place in hospital rather than at the family home, where prayers would have been recited and rituals observed as death approached. Gardner uses the terms 'compromise' and 'contestation' to characterize death in an institution.[33] Hasty or insensitive handling of the body by hospital staff, for instance, may inadvertently disrupt the ritual process that should attend and follow death – last rites such as placing drops of water in the mouth. Sooner rather than later after death, possibly after attendance at the deathbed by an imam, a respected male trained in the interpretation of Qur'anic scripture, and by family members, the body is taken to the funeral director's premises. Ritual preparation of the body by members of the community, still the norm in Bangladesh, is unlikely in London.

Gardner, describing the tension exerted upon Bangladeshi immigrants between *desh*, the homeland, and *bidesh*, the host location, suggests that with death, 'ambivalence seems to fall away, [and] *desh* becomes the place where one truly belongs, the locus of spirituality and the self.'[34] Very soon after death, any wishes or arrangements made for repatriation of the body to the 'homeland' for burial are addressed. The proportion of repatriations is in decline; and ties with *desh* loosen with the passing of generations.[35] For this particular community, which is not wealthy, financial planning for burial is unlikely. (Members of the Patel Trust, because they have paid in advance to reserve burial space, might be considered an exception.) The main preparation for death, it is believed, should be spiritual rather than material and follows the injunction, 'To die as a Muslim is to have had a lifelong disposition to prepare for death. It is necessary to contemplate death and be ready for it with good deeds.'[36] Study participants translated this ideal of perpetual preparedness into the vernacular:

> The cemetery reminds me of my death, so not to do anything bad. This car could be a Rolls Royce, but it is not. Why?! Because I come to the cemetery. If I didn't come here I would probably steal and cheat and then I could afford a Rolls Royce. If I steal from people and I die, then what will happen?

> The important thing is to remember our past, and if we come here [to the cemetery], it will remind us to lead good lives and not to do bad things, because tonight I could be here as well. This is a very strong feeling, I feel it when I come here.

The body is prepared, generally at the Muslim funeral director's, for imminent burial. The first ritual act is to turn the deceased's head toward Mecca.[37] The body is then washed, reflecting similar ablutions performed upon entering Mecca or before praying. It may be washed by a professional or by a family member, but always by a person of the same sex. Family may attend when a professional washes the body, whether at home or at the mortuary. The person who washes does so without special ritual but throughout the task recites the Qur'an to acknowledge God and Muhammad as his Prophet. The body is treated with respect and modesty is preserved; the task may take half an hour.

After the corpse has been washed, it is dressed in sections of unsewn cloth of cotton or calico, which cover the body and face. Prayers follow the washing and shrouding of the body, which is then placed in its simple coffin. Uncoffined, shrouded burial is traditional but is not always permitted in Britain and may be more costly. There have been some uncoffined burials at Woodgrange, requiring preparation of a grave of more complex structure and so incurring higher costs. Ideally, within twenty-four hours of death, the prepared body is moved to the mosque, where prayers are recited. The body is not admitted to the main part of the mosque but remains in an adjacent, curtained space, sheltered from the elements. While prayers are said for the deceased's soul, the curtain is drawn to reveal the shrouded or coffined body, though the person is not named. These rituals, presided over by an imam, are brief and are attended by male members of the community. Traditionally, the women remain sequestered at home, though a few of the women interviewed at Woodgrange said they had been present at the funerals of close relatives, sometimes justifying this by explaining that there were few others to attend.

With little delay, the male mourners follow the body, most travelling by car, to the cemetery. A single grave will have been dug, ideally oriented to the south-east and Mecca. Where the grave space consists of the upper level of an older Christian grave, orientation to the east may be impossible, because the original cemetery grid plan aligned the graves at right angles to the main paths. In some instances, where the kerbed graves are set at angles to the path, suggesting the correct orientation, compromises seem to have been managed. The Muslim community that uses Woodgrange is appreciative of the chance to observe some, if not all, of their rituals, and the 'cosmetic' nature of grave orientation provoked no comments from our study participants. It is likely that they accede to this along with the many other adjustments they are constrained to make, in and beyond the cemetery.

The vehicle carrying the body is driven close to the grave plot, and the coffin is carried by relays of men, apparently jostling to shoulder the weight. Following injunctions from scripture, the burial itself is speedy: 'The Prophet said, "Hurry up with the dead body, for if it was righteous, you are forwarding it to welfare, and if it was otherwise, then you are putting off an evil thing down your necks".'[38] The interment is always accompanied by prayers said by an imam or other respected male, and after five minutes or so, the grave is filled by those present. Commonly, mourners strew cut flowers on top of the grave and leave them to wither. Wreaths of flowers, unusual at Muslim burials in the past, are increasingly being adopted.

That the body be free of pressure and the heavy weight of earth, both within the grave and on the surface, is important for Muslim mourners. Soon after interment, the spirit must rise and respond to the angels who approach the soul. Weight pressing down on the corpse restricts this spiritual elevation and condemns the soul to a 'silence' that leads to exclusion from paradise. Muslims believe that if there is something on the grave then the angels cannot ask the questions after death: 'Who is Your God? What is your religion? Who is your prophet?'[39] The spirit of the deceased must be free from weight and pressure and able to 'exhale' the responses. The requirement that the surface of the grave should be clear of monuments or grave-slabs was said by several of our informants to relate to this injunction. Referring to the heavy Victorian monuments placed on the graves of earlier groups buried at Woodgrange, one participant commented, 'Large monuments act as hiding places for evil spirits that torment the dead. . . . The person buried there must be suffering.' Elaboration and wasteful expenditure were also cause for objection to the old memorials: 'Why waste money on meaningless monuments?' The Islamic ideal for burial is simplicity, an absence of either material or emotional extravagance – a rationale sometimes given for prohibiting women, who are thought likely to be distraught, from attending funerals.

Muslim study participants stressed the importance of not treading on a grave, and families typically erect fences or otherwise demarcate the body's position in order to prevent this. The need to protect the grave may be fulfilled in an impromptu, though traditional, way by collecting twigs and branches from nearby trees and shrubs and spiking these onto the newly turned earth to make a low barricade. Within days after burial, a marker will be placed on the grave. This may be a handwritten notice or a small brass plaque mounted on polished wood and staked into the soil at the top of the grave. The marker will give the deceased's name, date of birth or age and, if he or she was a first-generation immigrant, village of origin. The local London address may also be added. It will be removed if and when a permanent marker is set in place.

After burial, the male members of the family visit the grave frequently. Trips are made to the cemetery following prayers at the local mosque, especially on the Friday following burial and subsequent Fridays. The older men invariably wear prayer clothes, as do some of the younger men. Men visit alone or in small groups made up of kin or a mix of kin and community, and for five to thirty minutes they recite prayers at the grave. Women, if they visit at all, do so on weekends, usually with other family members, including men. Only when there are no male relatives to visit the grave do women visit the cemetery regularly. On one or two occasions during our fieldwork, we spoke with women who were visiting alone. In one instance a mother was seeking the burial place of a stillborn infant. The site manager was able to direct her. Male informants and the several imams we interviewed had different versions of the prohibition on women at funerals and in the cemetery generally but were united in believing it undesirable. Most if not all women appeared to accede.

The first forty days after the burial are a significant time of 'quarantine'. For a widow, Muslim tradition requires forty days of seclusion, a ritual seldom possible in London.[40] Another woman who is both a relative and a widow herself should remove the new widow's wedding gold; the widow will then start to wear a sari of plain white cloth. Meanwhile, special prayers are said on the third day after death and burial, when an imam comes to pray. At the end of the forty days, a similar religious event (*milad,* a ritual meal) is held at the deceased's home; both occasions are accompanied by a ritual distribution of rice or meat. Fifty-two days after the interment also mark an important time; prayers are said in the home as well as at the grave. On the anniversary of the death, the *milad* is repeated: this ritual builds up merit for the soul of the deceased as it continues its journey in the afterlife. During the first year, the deceased will also be remembered at important religious occasions, including Eyd, at the end of Ramadan, when we observed family groups – large and small – visiting Woodgrange in great numbers (see chapter 5).

In Islam, the placing of a stone is not prescribed and appears to rest upon economic considerations and family preferences. Thus, there may be no further grave-tending activity, and the grave will remain simple and unadorned. Local Muslims' customs have been changing, however, over the past decade. Stones are increasingly likely to be set, and after shorter intervals after burial than in the past. Moreover, these newer stones may reflect a degree of assimilation toward the styles of indigenous stones and sometimes even toward English styles of inscription. The consequences for the Woodgrange landscape are significant. There is an appearance of irregularity and sometimes unruliness in the central section, where new stones are to be seen against the roughly turned earth. Additionally, as the largest Victorian stones, even those near the entrance, disappear to make way for larger Muslim graves, the scale of the cemetery is changing dramatically, becoming lower lying with much less vegetation.

Insofar as memory of the dead is part of mourning for this community of mainly Bangladeshi and Gujarati Muslims, it has traditionally been activated at the more abstract level of community and society rather than as a material display of individuality. The remarks of older-generation men make it clear that their traditional engagement with the cemetery and their mortality takes place through the nexus of community and collectivity. 'I am here today to pray for myself and for all who are buried here.' Younger people, particularly women, may mention their attachment to a deceased family member as inspiring different and more personal forms of mourning. At Woodgrange, then, the evidence suggests a developing set of practices that include individual and family memorialization. These new customs take the personal and individual into account, along with the traditional and collective. At other cemeteries, groups of Muslims originating in the Middle East and now spanning three generations were reported to have evolved different sets of rituals and practices for burial,[41] sometimes more elaborate and perhaps inspired by emotional affect rather than religious or cultural obligation.

That Islam does not require, and may discourage, the setting of a stone memorial at a prescribed time distinguishes Muslims from other ethnic groups in London. Neither does Woodgrange Park Cemetery routinely embark on more constraining regimes, such as those at the City of London Cemetery, once the first twelve months have passed. At Woodgrange and elsewhere, non-Muslims suggest that attending the grave is never a long-term commitment for Muslims. Although this might be in line with Islamic doctrine – that after death the individual's spirit belongs with Allah, and prolonged attention would be inappropriate, if not blasphemous – the second generation of Muslim mourners is now engaged in activities that suggest a new interpretation.

Conclusion

In the burial and first-year memorial customs observed at these four cemetery sites for four distinctly different groups, we witness those conditions necessary to give mourners the time and place needed to begin to come to terms with loss. This initial mourning period is guided by a combination of forces that include cultural rituals, religious practices, individual beliefs and the ideal practices of both cemetery management and other cemetery mourners. During the first year following death, the character of the relationship between the bereaved and the cemetery managers is negotiated and established invariably around possession of the body and control of the grave. It is also during the first year of bereavement that, among some Christian and Greek Orthodox mourners, the metaphor of garden is developed for the creation of memory and identity. It is the time when the foundations for long-term memorial practices, which consolidate the cemetery as a cultural expression, are established.

In the public space of the cemetery, the first year's rites of mourning are begun and completed. Each of the four cultural groups constructs the end of this year as the point at which survivors have completed the initial, formal processes of mourning. As one Orthodox Jewish woman said, 'I found the stone setting to be hugely significant. . . . It had to do with public things; . . . it marked the end of the year of mourning and acknowledged publicly my mother as good and wise.'

Grief, however – although it may be expressed in different ways – continues far beyond the first year following death and in places other than the cemetery. In the following chapters, we investigate how feelings of loss are dealt with and expressed in the home, in the garden and through long-term rites of mourning. We also explore how, through the continuing creation of memory and the construction and reconstruction of the identity of both the deceased and the mourner, the dead are remembered and the living and dead remain linked.

4

The Grave as Home and Garden

Going to the cemetery is like visiting them at home. I can't go by and not come in; they're here, so I come and see them.

Man visiting the grave of his parents at
City of London Cemetery

As the bereaved begin to confront a recent death, they attempt first to face the loss of the other and then to ease or ameliorate the fractures produced by loss through recourse to everyday domestic activities. Many of the people who participated in this study invoked the metaphors of 'home' and 'garden' in talking about their memorial activities in the cemetery; these metaphors offered familiar territory from which to deal with loss and to try to move toward a level of solace and consolation.[1] The concepts and activities associated with the home and sometimes the garden of the living provided participants with additional resources for rituals dealing with death and loss.

Not all mourning and memorializing take place in the cemetery, of course. The home, full of associations with the deceased and artefacts of shared lives, is an inevitable and complementary site of remembrance.[2] It offers both an escape from the acceptance of reality – 'At home, I do not think of him as dead' – and a familiar, secure base from which to confront loss – 'I have more memories at home; we lived in our home for thirty-five years.' It is from such secular, familiar foundations that survivors face the deaths of others and forge a connection with the place of burial.

In this chapter, we first describe the associations our study participants made between the deceased and the family home – of which the garden was so often a vital part – and then demonstrate how they transferred the concept of home to the gravesite.[3] Just as the home is the material symbol of the self and the family, so the tomb, as home, comes to embody the personhood and meaning of the deceased. First, however – because gardening at the gravesite is such an important part of memorializing at City of London and New Southgate Cemeteries – we briefly discuss the relationship between home and garden in English culture.

The Relationship between Home and Garden

A home with a private garden is an ideal of English life.[4] A fondness for domestic flower gardening developed gradually from the sixteenth until the nineteenth century to become one of the nation's most characteristic attributes.[5] During the industrial revolution, residential densities in urban areas reached slum proportions, and small-scale gardens usually disappeared. The Garden City Movement encouraged the re-emergence of the private garden during the twentieth century,[6] though not all citizens were equal beneficiaries. By the 1930s, two standards of housing had emerged in England: low-density, detached or semi-detached, single-family dwellings with gardens for owner-occupiers, and a growing proportion of terraces and rented flats, with minimal provision for amenity space, in the public and private sectors.[7] Many of our study participants, particularly those at Bushey United Jewish Cemetery and New Southgate, owned their homes and had private gardens. At the City of London, a larger proportion of elderly research participants rented from public-sector or private landlords and had fewer private gardens. Nonetheless, for all the groups studied, gardening was important as the country's most popular outdoor leisure activity,[8] and was associated with the home ownership that now characterizes British society.

Interestingly, many City of London visitors, particularly the elderly and unmarried adult children, although they may not have been home-owners, owned the grave and memorial stone where a partner or parent(s) were interred and where they, themselves, would be buried.

The financial investment entailed in purchasing burial rights and the creative involvement in tending and maintaining the grave and memorial garden gave mourners stakeholder status. As one son who lived at home with his widowed mother explained about his father's grave: 'I feel proprietary about the plot, but it is not the same with our [rented] home. I am more a stakeholder in the grave than I am in my home. The home is something my parents established and which I use. Here, home and grave are the same.' His mother added, 'Our home is through a housing association, and my son will have to move when I die.' Title to a cemetery plot thus appears more permanent and secure than rental tenure, and many visitors may invest the grave property with a commitment of time and resources commensurate with what they believe is a stronger form of ownership. This hypothesis merits further research, particularly for those whose rented flats do not have contiguous space available for a domestic garden and who therefore may subjectively view the cemetery plot as their own home and garden.

To further understand the relationship between the English home and garden, it is useful to consider the writings of Chevalier.[9] To construct a unique domestic decor, Chevalier writes, household members creatively assemble mass-produced objects, collected artefacts and inherited possessions. As they design their gardens, they must transform nature into personalized domestic spaces. The front garden serves as a transition between the public realm and the private, identifying and presenting the household to the outside world. The fenced back garden is a more private place, analogous to the lounge inside the house. Lounge and back garden, according to Chevalier, often display a symmetry in organization and decor: 'The oblong grass carpet of the garden mirrors the woollen carpet of the reception room, each respectively surrounded by the three-piece suite, wallpaper and curtains or by the shed and flower beds.'[10] The lounge and garden are personalized, respectively, with souvenirs and family photographs and with plants and garden ornaments, in either case sometimes inherited from family or collected on holiday – all reminders of life shared. The reception room may contain houseplants, and the garden may have lawn furniture, bridging these interior and exterior spaces. Home and garden are both personalized creations and extensions of the self and family.

Home and garden together are linked with significant life course events and important social relationships – past and current, fulfilling and frustrating. The family home exhibits valued possessions, and the garden displays plants received as cuttings from kin and friends. Therefore, both home and garden provide a way of expressing one's life and family; they make the past accessible and foster identity.[11] Such items, through conscious and unconscious association, have the capacity to create, trigger and evoke memories, feelings and emotions.[12] Family home and garden materially embody the meaning of attachment, mooring and roots.[13] It is from the family home and garden that survivors begin to come to terms with the deaths of parents, spouses and others, and from which a route is established between home and cemetery.

The Connection between Home and Grave

Funeral and mortuary rituals help create a connection between home and cemetery that can be either amplified or neutralized by religious ideology and personal action. In the past, the typical East End burial custom was to keep the body at home before interment. Today, some 'traditional' families with large homes may still follow this practice, which marks a direct link between home and the City of London Cemetery:

> She was in a back room of the house, and the undertaker made it like a chapel of rest with a veil over the casket, candles and flowers. Only the family came. The minister also had a service twice in the house around the coffin. She had died at home, then went to the funeral home and came back home, then to the church for the funeral and to the cemetery for burial.

Many City of London Cemetery families continue to acknowledge this past custom, which connects the family residence and the cemetery plot as the past and present 'home' of the deceased.[14]

Later in the day, following the funeral, kin, friends and neighbours will retrace the route back to the former home of the departed – now conspicuously absent – usually to attend the funeral tea, which celebrates and mourns the deceased. Such practices signify that the dead, whose corpse is now interred in cemetery earth, remains intimately associated with his or her former domicile. In this way, the link between the two sites – home and grave-home – is initiated.

Following an Orthodox Jewish funeral, too, immediate family members return to the home of the deceased, where a ritual meal is served. Prayers, which extend the funeral service from the burial ground into the home, are held evening and morning during the week of *shivah*. People make condolence visits, and it is through conversations held during these visits that the bereaved often learn about deeds of charity the departed might have done privately. They hear stories about the deceased and meet friends and relatives who may have been estranged or previously unknown.[15] Some Jewish mourners visit the cemetery to mark the conclusion of the *shivah* week of home ritual, thus remaking the link between home and cemetery.

For Greek Orthodox mourners at New Southgate Cemetery, the Greek burial ground is the home of the dead, just as the house is the home of the living.[16] Indeed, the Greek Orthodox – like members of the other communities included in this study – refer to the grave by the name of the deceased, just as they would refer to a living person and their dwelling by name. Such practices are effective for the bereaved because they emphasize the parallel and similar activities carried out at the two types of dwelling. The burial ground is always more than a metaphysical place: it is also a social space, an extension of the residence and, like the home, demands ongoing attention. Just as the upkeep of the home reflects the reputation of the family, so the 'critical eye of the neighbourhood' scrutinizes the condition of the grave.[17] Both home and cemetery reflect the moral condition of the living kin, their dead, or both, and an unkempt grave is viewed as analogous to an unkempt house.[18] At both the home of the deceased and at the grave, Greek Orthodox mourners (like those at the City of London who also have their own customary practices of grave tending) clean, wash, plant, weed, water, decorate, furnish, light candles, burn incense, take food and place photographs as well as greeting cards. Because the tomb is only symbolically analogous to the ephemeral home of this life – 'The grave is forever; it's our last and final residence, our eternal home.' – the bereaved attempt to 'domesticate' that reality and, by doing so, to ameliorate and mask the stark truth of death's finality.

The garden at the home of the deceased also extends metaphorical routes and roots to the grave. Many Greek study participants at New Southgate, as well as at CLCC, cultivated their home gardens to grow flowers and plants full of memories, meaning and emotional symbolism. Grave offerings created from these flowers were perceived as more special than those bought from florists: 'The roses and carnations on the grave I have grown especially for her from seedlings.' Growing flowers to take to the grave not only maintained the link between the grave and the deceased's home but also provided an opportunity to display one's feelings publicly.[19]

Adult Children and Family Homes

Adult children closely identify the family home with their parents,[20] and many find it difficult to think about one without the other. This point was underscored by a 68-eight-year-old Jewish man when he discussed the death of his mother, who had died in her late nineties in an old-age home. He pinpointed her death as a person, her 'social death', as the time when she gave up her home and household possessions to enter a residential home. He contrasted this with her 'physical death' years later: 'Really and truly, the turning point was not when she died but when she left her home to go into a retirement home. Going into the home was the upsetting time for us; it was the end of mother's life, she didn't have her own home around her. She only had a photo of father, nothing, no ornaments with her.'

A young Greek Cypriot woman noted that for years after her mother's death she always spoke and thought of the house that her mother shared with her sister as her mother's house: 'That house was my Mum's, never my sister's so much. When I would visit my sister after my mother's death, deep down inside I felt that I was going to see Mum.'

Other adult children, particularly those who never married, may seek to maintain their ties with deceased parents by remaining in the family home. As one unmarried Jewish daughter remarked: 'The whole house is them; it's their home. I can't bring myself to move and start anew.' By keeping up the family house, these adult unmarried children, who often had been caregivers for their parents, sustain their parents' memory. For some adult children it is the garden as much as the home that is reminiscent of the parent – a record of memories and the place where the spirit of the deceased may remain strongest:

> There is something about the garden, I think of him most there; I always see him walking up the path when we come. He worked in the garden, he planted, repaired it. He loved his garden. That is why we do not want my mother to leave the house. His presence is there. We are doing everything we can that she can stay there. We do not want to destroy that link.

For many bereaved families, the family home and garden provide strength and consolation in dealing with death. Flowers, shrubs and trees planted by the deceased are a reservoir of positive memory to be nurtured and sustained. A child still living at home may take over the maintenance of the garden as a way of honouring and continuing the relationship with the parent. One son at the City of London Cemetery remarked, 'I did not have a great interest in gardening until his death, when I assumed that trait of his. Gardening is a continuation of a tradition. I have an obligation to do the garden since he died, to not let it go to ruin.' The home garden, gradually modified by new plantings and design, may also demonstrate how the mature child has appropriated the skills of the parent and now expresses his or her own unfolding identity through the garden. The sequence of the generations is played out in the cycles of the garden.

For other bereaved adult children, the home garden can be a site of painful memories and may be neglected following a parent's death:

> Dad died, I didn't want to come out. My parents used to visit and would come two times a week, and I would take them into my garden and ask their advice. Dad would tell me to move things, and he had lots of gardening books at home and knew all the practicalities of gardening. I couldn't bear to be out there, with him up here [in the cemetery].

In such cases, the home garden may deteriorate as attention is focused on creating a new memorial garden in the cemetery. After a year or more, when the intense pain of immediate loss might have begun to recede, family members may return to the home garden with new design plans. Memories connecting the deceased with the home and garden may be renewed and re-formed by the rescue and revival of moribund plants. At the same time, the altered self, transformed by the experience of loss, may be expressed through modifications of the basic garden layout. These simultaneous processes reveal both a continuation and a redefinition of self following the death of a parent.

Thus, for adult children, the home garden may occupy a range of positions along the connective path between home and cemetery. The family garden, for example, may remain a source of positive memory of the deceased. For this adult Jewish daughter, home garden and cemetery as garden were distinct, and it was in the home garden that her father's spirit remained vital and vivid: 'His home garden is not a memorial garden. It is a living place where I think of him alive. It is not a dying place. I can't think of cemeteries and gravestones there.' For others, caring for the home garden may be a continuation of the parent's role as gardener, and this skill might be extended to maintenance of the cemetery plot. For other bereaved adult children, the home garden may initially be superseded by the cemetery grave garden as the focus of family attention: 'I couldn't go out to the garden. I put my garden at home to bed,' reported one adult daughter at the City of London Cemetery.

Like gardens, family homes are filled with belongings that are integral to memory and identity. In clearing out the deceased parent's home, replete with possessions that represent a lifetime, adult offspring may have to confront directly the identity of that parent, their own identity and often, too, the quality of their relationship with their parent(s). House clearance can be a source of increased understanding and may lead to an enlargement or reformulation of the parent's image, as well as adult children's views of themselves. Papers, diaries and boxes of stored cards, for example, may make known previously unrevealed sentiments the parent had for a child: 'When she died, I found a huge box of paper. She had cut out and stored everything from the newspapers about me . . . every single item that related to my career she had cut out and kept.' A Jewish woman found a trail of notes her mother had left expressing her feelings about various events:

> My mother died in March and I cleaned her flat in May. I sorted through all the papers and read the notes she had left. She wrote down her feelings and when she was angry about things. Some of these thoughts were in booklets, others on notes, and she left notes among her books. I had a lot to read and it was painful. My sense of self was affected and my values shaken. The process of cleaning the flat was also about myself. It was a journey. I feel my mother guided it, by what she left, kept and said with particular things. It was not random. It was like messages from the grave. It was about what she valued, her thoughts about me and my sister. . . . For example, all the birthday cards I sent her she kept, and anniversary cards from my father. . . . Doing this task gave me a different sense of my mother.

The inheritance of treasured items such as family photographs, pieces of furniture, plants, jewellery, china, linens and antiques often signifies family traditions and memories from the child's or the parents' youth. When objects are transferred from the parental home to the adult children's homes, the multiple meanings of parents and of the home and garden – and their intimate attachments and associations to the deceased – are extended to the descendant generations in both material and symbolic form. 'When I look at my father's plants in my garden, I think of my dad and the home where I grew up in.' 'When we moved my father from the family flat to a one-bedroom, I got a hydrangea and a peony from my mother's garden. . . . These are a part of my mother and I look after them like gold dust.' 'We gave our daughter Mum's tea service, which I can remember as a small boy. I look at it and remember my mother.' Such statements suggest that the acknowledgement of the absence of the deceased is related to and also a necessary part of the creation of memory and remembering.[21]

It is often the acts of using and caring for these objects, rather than keeping them in safe storage, that revivify memories – positive, negative, or ambivalent – from the adult child's own life. Moreover, by incorporating inherited possessions into existing assortments of household objects and daily routines or by using them on special occasions, the adult child assumes a dimension of the parent into his or her self and so acknowledges a new status and role. 'It marked a major change in my life, it was the ending of an era. Here I am now, at the top of the tree, the family tree.' This quotation further suggests that death may also involve the remaking of the self and social relationships. Of course the passing down of charged family objects, such as scrapbooks, videotapes, photograph albums and diaries, may not be accompanied by an examination of these items. They may be put aside – perhaps locked away – a potent and acknowledged presence, not forgotten but not interrogated.

The psychological importance of having and caring for ancestral possessions was made especially clear by one Jewish woman whose flat had been broken into:

> I was so devastated when we had the burglary. I was so deeply shocked. I just didn't know who I was without my things. I was the custodian of their [her parents' and parents-in-law's] things and they had gone. I went to the cemetery and I explained to them that it was not my fault. I did not go to them for help, but I went to apologize. Yes, there is a direct link between the home, the things in the home and the cemetery. These things are the benchmarks of life. What you have is part of you. They help to supply a sense of self-identity and how you value yourself. I see myself as the custodian. When we got our things back, I thanked everyone for helping. They are my link with the departed. It consolidates them into a sense of continuity to my home and into the cemetery. The cemetery, too, should have no weeds, be nice and tidy and shining, just like at home, both inside and outside. It is public. The grave is an extension of life. To have it neat is the way for me to handle it. I have to have a sense of continuity in my life.

This woman drew an important analogy between the custodial obligation to maintain, safeguard and transmit family heirlooms intact and the responsibility for making certain that family cemetery memorials were cared for and preserved in good repair. Significantly, both types of inalienable property have a trans-generational life span and represent tangible continuity and preservation of the family through time. Through the ascribed attributes of heritage and multigenerational family ties, they provide a sense of selfhood, self-esteem and rootedness, as well as obligatory caretaking and custodial roles that entail a concern with what will happen after one's own death. Such objects make demands on their heirs: they involve an obligation to remember and thereby continue the 'power' of the dead.

Not only are inherited household belongings conduits of memory, but in the Jewish rites of lighting the sabbath and memorial candles, the spirits of deceased parents are explicitly invited and welcomed into the home. In this ritual act, both the continuing power of the deceased and an assertion of independence and separation from them in order to remember (the dynamically interlinked processes of forgetting and memorializing)[22] may be expressed:

> On lighting the Friday night candles, I welcome the light and all the people I knew who have passed on – I expect them to be there. I enjoy beautifying my surrounding to my taste, and I think I am successful. When I have done something very nicely, I say: 'What do you think of that Claire, do you like that?' My mother would dismiss it, and then tell others, never me, how lovely it was. I need their approval. The fact that they're dead is not important to me.

Many of the adult children from each cemetery site said they continued to talk to their deceased parents at home as well as in the cemetery, seeking their approval and reassurance, soliciting their consent, asking their assistance, or thinking through problems with them. These conversations were often sparked by the presence of inherited possessions such as sabbath candlesticks, photographs and items the parent had treasured. Such objects are the stuff of memory; they help one recall the past and bring the parent into the present. Some City of London Cemetery daughters, for example, said they kept a vase of fresh flowers next to a picture of their departed parent(s) perhaps on the bedside table and might speak to the photograph, asking for help with a family concern. When the situation had been resolved successfully, the parent was thanked: 'Yes, Mum, you sorted the problem out.' In another example, a Jewish woman related how she received her mother's often unsolicited advice, signalled through the stopping and starting of an inherited Swiss clock:

> I carry on talking to my mother. . . . I have her clock in my bedroom and I talk to the clock. . . . If the clock stops, I use this as a sign that I have to re-evaluate the situation. . . . For example, there was a stone setting and a wedding scheduled for the same day. I decided to go to the wedding. But then I worked to get the

date altered for the stone setting, and I was then able to attend both. And the clock started to run again. . . . The clock is the symbol of my mother. I have no idea why. . . it is the first thing I see in the morning and often the last thing at night as I look to see what time it is. It connects to my way of thinking about somebody – I don't know which triggers what – if I am reminded of her and look at the clock, or if I look at the clock and remember her. I am very careful to always wind the clock so that it will not stop. . . . I like my mother's agreement on what I do.

A somewhat similar process of communication was articulated by one City of London son who explained why he now wears the ring his mother gave him as a teenager: 'It's so hard to come to terms with death. When Mum died, something was taken away inside. My wife suggested that I fix the ring Mum gave me; now I wear the ring all the time. I feel she is with me having it on, part of her is with me all the time now.' This man had once given his mother a decorative key rack, inscribed with a poem praising mothers, as a memento from a holiday trip. After her death, he moved this gift from her flat to the cemetery, where he laid it against her gravestone. 'I bought this for her from holiday, it holds keys. I brought it from her flat to here. This is her home now, I felt it belonged here.' Thus the transfer of possessions from the parent's home to the child's residence is paralleled by a relocation of objects from the parent's home to the cemetery, as well as by use of the same flowers for both home garden and cemetery garden.

The numerous material and symbolic associations that adult children forge among the departed, the home and the possessions of the deceased lead to the question, Why, if the home is already a place of remembrance and memory, do some mourners also visit the cemetery? If survivors from all research sites are able to speak to the departed at home, as well as in the cemetery – 'I can speak to her anytime or any place' – and if unsolicited memories and thoughts of the deceased come to the bereaved as they perform routine household tasks or dust family heirlooms, then why do people elect to visit the place of burial? Although various answers are offered to these questions throughout this book, it is useful here to quote those who explained why speaking with a deceased parent in the cemetery was different from conversations at home. Like other study participants, this Jewish woman described a visit to the cemetery as being like a pilgrimage, the making of a special effort:

When there is anything momentous in the family, I come: births, marriage, an upset. It is a mark of respect to go there, it is making an effort on her behalf. It is easy to have a conversation [with the deceased] at home; I do not have to be dressed, I do not have to put on make-up. The cemetery requires special effort; it is not en route to anywhere. It is an offering, an effort to go. . . . It is separate from your domestic space – like making an appointment to make sure that time is set aside to talk about something special.

Many study participants reported that it was possible to keep busy and to store away thoughts of the dead parent while at home, but that a visit to the cemetery was a purposeful act, undertaken specifically to confront the issues of loss, grief, bereavement, abandonment, loneliness and/or absence. For some, the pain of unsolicited memories at home was more difficult to bear than that of anticipated – and possibly more controlled and disciplined – remembering in the cemetery: 'Here in the cemetery you concentrate on the things you want to remember, but at home, things come to you involuntarily and it's more upsetting.' 'At home, thoughts can come unbidden, in a split second. When you're not busy, thoughts come to your mind at home; but here you purposely allow and solicit them.'

The family home and garden were integral to the identity of the parent and remain so in the memories of adult children. In the period of social and psychological transition following death, adult children may revisit this home, both as children mourning parental loss and as adults newly thrust into the senior generation. The clearing out and moving of possessions from the family home to their own homes signify such changes in status. Surviving children may privately endow these inherited objects with multiple and dynamic meanings and memories that allow them to re-create specific qualities of the parent in the present[23] and also permit the initial stages of a shift to a new sense of self.

Bereaved Spouses and Partners

In comparison with bereaved adult children, surviving partners of long-term marriages create a different set of ties between their deceased spouses and the family home, which is replete with shared furnishings, mementoes and plantings. Many mourners, particularly the men who participated in this study, are reluctant to change any details of the home and purposely choose not to redecorate or to modify the garden.

The home itself, with its contents and routines, represents the possibility of an ongoing relationship with the former spouse, as well as with the former self. These homes stand like monuments to the past life shared – and now reflected upon and relived through memory and practice in the present. For widowers, the home remains the domain of the wife's handiwork. Field notes written during a visit directly from the City of London Cemetery to the home of an eighty-year-old man reveal some of the characteristics of the home as memorial:

On entering the home where he has lived since 1936, Tom still called out, 'It's only me!' to his wife, who had died ten years earlier. There were family pictures on the sideboard in the front room – his wife and himself when they were courting, on their wedding day, his wife with a grandchild – all recording significant moments in their shared lives. There were also two Mother's Day cards from the youngest son from after she had died. Things were reportedly the same as they had been when she was alive: the walls were the same colour; the husband's and wife's chairs were still placed near each other. . . . The last two flowers from one of her rose bushes were on the table, 'I never take flowers from home to the cemetery. This is her garden here. That is another garden.' Her *Codiaeum* plant was flourishing in the corner: 'I kept it going.' Other houseplants also survived and looked well. Tom had taken cuttings and all were thriving. The whole house was immaculate. Tom reported that his youngest son won't come to the cemetery, because, he says, 'Mum ain't there, she's at home. He says he can smell Mum's scent.'

The furniture in the adjacent room was shrouded with cloth and plastic – 'Never sat on.' The couple had planned to make it their front room but never completed the task. 'Everything is how she left it.' Tom showed me the wardrobes upstairs, all full of clothes. 'They've never been touched. As she walked out of this house, that's it.' He has never given her clothes away. 'I can't disturb her; I know she's there.' In the front and back gardens, beautiful pink and white hydrangeas were in flower. There were also lupins, dahlias, roses and tea roses that she had planted in the back garden. At the end of the visit, on the way to the tube station, Tom indicated the house a few blocks away where his wife had lived before they were married.

These field notes suggest how the emotional, physical and temporal vacuum created by the loss of a partner becomes attenuated and amplified within the confines of the previously shared home. The home, rich with affective and symbolic meaning, is intensely identified with the departed spouse. It stands in for the presence of the deceased, yet is independent of the departed; it is a place of both association and denial. The home encourages remembrance, yet simultaneously signals loss and separation. It is where the absence of the other is potently present (as Tom remarked: 'I get potty when I come in and there's no answer'), but it is also a world of memory and meaning.[24] Home provides a means of coping with loss – it is the place which allows and encourages intimate rituals of remembrance and where secret, personal rites of mourning are performed.

Home for the surviving spouse also serves as a symbol of domestic and marital continuity, a site of emotional and material investment, a repository of valued objects made more powerful by the event of death. The furnishings and contents of the house – the 'assembled environment, where all the memory-evoking objects of sentimental value remain'[25] – anchor the surviving partner's home as the site of shared marital history and personal meaning. Following a spouse's death, the shared home may provide comfort and continuity of self-identity through the familiarity of daily rituals, through the memories of the other and of shared past events that are evoked by handling everyday household objects or souvenirs from special occasions.

Like Tom, many Greek and Jewish widowers also described how they had left everything in the house intact, in order to preserve the final act of touching by the deceased – 'to make time stand still' and, by doing so, to maintain the presence and continual existence of the departed: 'I would not let anyone touch my wife's things; even her car was left untouched in the garage for two years.' 'Her dress stayed hanging behind the door for such a long time; it comforted me to walk by and see it.' These widowers had constructed a safe and secure barrier – a cocoon – to shelter them against further deleterious change.[26]

Such a home, with its familiar objects and established routines, enables the remaining spouse to continue a similar pattern of living in the present accompanied by the presence of the deceased. Not unlike Tom, another City of London man enjoyed following an accustomed early morning routine from the later years of his marriage: 'I still take tea into her room every morning, share it and watch TV and then have breakfast.' Other widowers in their seventies and eighties at CLCC described the consolation of continuing to live in the family home. They reported with pride, and sometimes sardonic humour, that, alone, they were able to accomplish familiar domestic routines:

We were married forty years. Things at home are the same as always. But I'm not quite so efficient with cleaning, I used to help. I got so good with an iron and doing the shirts that I went to see the doctor – it's not the sort of thing a man does. I always detested cleaning windows, I would get run streaks, so now I don't do it.

I have more memories at home [than in the cemetery]. We lived in our home for thirty-five years, and for twenty-five years before that in another house. I did the gardening myself. Now I have lots of chores: the washing and cleaning and cooking my own meals. I do it just the same as she did, and my gardening too.

In many marriages, a more traditional division of labour between husband and wife[27] often had collapsed in the husband's post-retirement years. Many bereaved older male study participants, for example, reported having helped regularly with heavy housekeeping; they became knowledgeable about and assisted with the household tasks. Bereaved partners from all cemetery research sites often chose to remain in the home the couple had shared for a half-century or more and to adhere closely to the jointly established week's routine of domestic chores. Analysis suggests that it is not only continued residence in the family home but also the assumption of the weekly household schedule, as well as upkeep of the garden, that preserves memory. The acceptance of ongoing responsibility for the care of home and garden is what underpins secular rituals of remembrance.

Cemetery observation further suggests that people who follow a set household routine are better able to cope with the devastating loss of a lifelong partner than those who instead 'take each day as it comes', without an established schedule.[28] The former survivors feel it is their responsibility to 'take care of themselves' rather than become overwhelmed with grief. The regular and routine nature of housework and other home-related chores offers the opportunity to keep busy with distracting tasks: 'When I feel down, I get to work.' One man who redecorated the house – in accordance with his wife's dying instructions – remarked, 'She worked it out so I was busy.'

Taking over domestic tasks associated with women and the routines established by their wives, widowers acknowledge not only their deceased wives and their shared lives but also their own proficiency in accomplishing their wives' gender-specific duties. The purposeful assumption or continuation of domestic routines may also permit a consolidation of the living self and the deceased other. It reveals continued personal growth and pride in the development and achievements of a necessarily expanded self as the transition to the role of widower takes place. In contrast with common negative evaluations of old age and bereavement, late-life mourning can be experienced and interpreted as a time for new roles and responsibilities, for maintenance, if not expansion, of physical abilities and for increased independence.

Whereas older men who were accustomed to helping around the house may find comfort and security in caring for the home, the same tasks can be more challenging for still-working widowers who know little about home maintenance. The learning curve is steep for these men, whose sense of domestic competence may be acquired only after frustrating attempts and perhaps instruction. One such City of London man in his sixties, whose wife had died from a heart attack three years previously, retired to manage the family home where the couple had lived for thirty years. He spoke of the hard times of being alone, of talking to his wife's photograph and of still sleeping in the same bed. His description of his struggles and frustrations with domesticity conveys a deep sense of loss as well as increased admiration for his late spouse:

> I knew the missus when she was fifteen, sixteen. We married when I got out of the army. We go back a long way, forty-one years. . . . It's a bit of an eye-opener with the cleaning, laundry, cooking. We [men] never do it when we're married; we're not prepared for it. You appreciate the different things they used to do: everything was organized. . . . It's hard to pick it all up, a man doesn't understand it. I try to keep it all going, I whip myself up to do it, I could let it slide easy. . . . I tell my son, 'Don't break the routine and then nothing goes wrong.' The old friends of the wife keep an eye on us; the women have keys and take the laundry in if it rains. Yesterday, I left it out all night and it poured. It's not the end of the world. . . . One time I took four hours doing the laundry, trying to iron the double sheets. Then my sister-in-law came over and said, 'No, you don't have to iron socks, pants and towels or sheets. You can hang sheets out.' We don't know this sort of thing.

Here, the widower's attachment to home and commitment to his wife's memory through the maintenance of their family residence were bolstered by the ongoing support of old neighbours and friends. Although we do not discuss such neighbourhood involvement at length in this study, it was important for many study participants and was often replicated in the cemetery at neighbouring gravesites.

For elderly and infirm bereaved widows, who are unable to visit the cemetery the home provides a space where the departed may be remembered in a time and place set aside especially for evocation of their memory. One City of London man in his eighties, with increasing physical limitations, reported that he had an altar in the bedroom:

> It has the Virgin and a nun praying, and Susan is in the centre with her rosary around the picture, and on one side is my Mum and on the other side, her Mum. I pray to it every night and every morning. I never do not do this, no matter how pushed I might be in the morning – something else has to go to save time, rather than this prayer. Susan was a Roman Catholic, and Italian, so I use the Roman Catholic morning prayer and the night prayer they say in church. It helps and keeps Susan happy till I join her. I also have one vase on the altar, which I put flowers in.

In discussing his memorial activities, this man noted that he was similarly proud of the home altar and the cemetery stone monument, both of which entailed significant creative input and enabled him to keep his wife's memory in both spaces in ritual ways.

Many widows who visit the City of London Cemetery also choose to remain in the family home and continue the familiar tasks they have always performed, now also expanding their efforts to the cemetery, which they, too, like the widowers discussed above, view as an extension of the home.[29] In these cases, the continuity of established roles appears to reinforce the self:

> A wife [of my generation] is different from younger wives today. In my age group, to be a wife was to cook, clean, to be domestic. He went to work, decorated the house and gardened[30]. . . . I hate to think [the memorial and small grave garden] is mucky, dirty, not tended to. If you are clean and tidy in your home, you keep the things which belong to you clean and tidy. It is like looking after him at home – like doing the washing, ironing and cooking. There is something here that belongs to him, and I have to take care of it for him. If I didn't come, I would feel that I was neglecting my duty as a wife.

A Jewish woman in her early sixties whose husband had been dead about three years also decided to remain in her home, with its many memories, but to make alterations that helped minimize some of her more painful remembrances:

> My home is a huge resource for me. I have refurbished and decorated my home. I also changed the furniture, so that I would

not see his armchair; it is now out of the house. The house has a lot of memory, it goes back a long way. We lived here nineteen years. I have changed a lot in the house: new lighting, new furniture and carpeting in the TV room. I painted the house and put on a new front. I have now learned to do everything myself. Now I take it on board myself. I am doing two people's work in the house, this time, alone, without my husband. It has made me independent and strong.

In making these changes, this widow extended herself and single-handedly assumed and accomplished tasks that she and her husband might have jointly overseen in the past. Through the material altera-tions to her home, a symbol of the self, she asserted her self-reliance as well as her acceptance of her changed status as a widow. Renewal of her home of twenty years signalled her renewal of self while maintaining a positive definition and continuity of self-identity.

Other bereaved spouses, both men and women, from all cemetery sites had chosen, instead, to move house, not wanting the painful memories, not wishing to handle so much space, or sometimes desiring to be nearer children or other relatives. For many, these decisions marked an acceptance of their widowed status. For others, the clearing out of wardrobes and drawers and the giving away of the deceased's clothing – 'They can't just sit there, you've got to start somewhere' – as well as the decision to stop wearing black, may signal an acknow-ledgement of loss and a following of unspoken social rules about what is expected from the bereaved after the first year of grief. 'I have got rid of all her clothes, giving them to the heart foundation, and her jewellery to the girls, although she gave them some herself; she must have known.'

Some bereaved find keeping the clothes of the deceased hanging in the wardrobe a source of consolation: 'All his clothes were left in the bedroom as if he was coming back home to change.' Occasionally the late spouse's possessions might even yield up new information, as when one City of London widow found a handwritten list of favoured rose bushes in the pocket of an item of her husband's clothing and decided to purchase one of these to place behind his grave. Nonetheless, despite the many protections the home can offer against the impact of loss and grief, it can also be the site of acute loneliness and aloneness. Nights and weekends are reported to be the worst – 'when the door closes behind you'.

Transposing Home to the Cemetery

These post-mortem experiences of home and garden in the lives of surviving adult children and spouses require further analysis to show how a symbolic and material continuum is constructed between the literal home, perhaps with a garden, and the grave, with memorial stone and perhaps a private garden, as figurative home. To demonstrate how the home and garden may be metaphorically transposed to the cemetery home and grave garden, our research findings can be applied to the four-part schema that Rubinstein put forward to show how older people endow their home environments with meaning.[31]

Part 1 of Rubinstein's schema, 'accounting', represents a person's operating knowledge of the totality of the environmental features that surround him or her. Accounting is related to awareness, involves an experiential familiarity with the physical features of a place as a result of repeated use and encompasses a bond between person and place as a consequence of one's having undergone personally meaningful events and experiences there.

Our cemetery research shows the importance to most, if not all, visitors of inspecting the memorial stone and the surroundings of the grave and of becoming familiar with the terrain and the rules and norms that operate at the burial ground. One long-time visitor to the City of London Cemetery, who came weekly to visit the plots of her parents and husband, described her accumulated knowledge this way:

> I like the whole cemetery, I know every bit. I've been here forty-odd years. Every week, I look around generally. I look at all the flowers, both on the graves and on the bushes in the spring. And I look at and read the headstones. I try to see new headstones I have not seen before and to find the oldest, and then I try to beat it the next week.

Part 2, 'personalization', involves the endowment of environmental features with meanings whose referents are the distinctive events, properties, or accomplishments of the deceased's life and identity. These may be unique virtues and qualities in the character of the departed as attributed by the chief mourner. For example, it is the erection of the memorial stone that many survivors say gives them emotional peace by firmly marking the location of the departed. The following comment from a Jewish widow suggests that this process is analogous to that of purchasing and furnishing a home: 'The memorial for your husband is necessary. It's having a home to go to. It's the same difference as having your own home and living in a hotel. You built and organized it; it is a source of pride and sorrow. It's a manifestation of thirty years together.'

As we saw at all of the research sites, the wording of the inscription is crucial for the identification, individuation and personalization of the stone. It includes details of the life lived – name, age, date of death and possibly also place and date of birth – as well as references to kinship relationships, such as 'beloved husband, dad and granddad'. There are also verses on the stone, which may be culled from the stonemason's book, adapted from other memorials, or suggested by a religious text. Some mourners may personalize these elegies further by adding lines of affection such as 'Thank you for being my dad'. Greek epitaphs may include a poem of lament emphasizing the pain of separation and loss and cataloguing the deceased's characteristics.

In part 3 of Rubinstein's schema, 'extension', special elements of the home and garden are used as direct, conscious representations of key aspects of the other. The particular environmental characteristic is chosen because it was close to the deceased person and therefore serves as a heavily charged and significant symbol for identification. CLCC mourners often ornament the written epitaph on the memorial stone with visual symbols of objects or activities that signify the deceased – for example, shamrocks (alluding to country of birth and cultural identification), daffodils (the favourite flower of the departed, an avid gardener), religious symbols (stressing religious devotion and the hope for resurrection) and a rocking chair (representing furniture making, a favourite hobby of the deceased). At Bushey United Jewish Cemetery, one family received special permission to carve a dove on their father's stone, instead of the prescribed Jewish star. The man had been a Holocaust survivor and his faith had been destroyed, but he believed in peace. Additionally, placing symbolic objects on the grave or attaching them to the stone is common for anniversaries and birthdays.

Finally, part 4, 'embodiment', refers to the subjective merging of the survivor, deceased and the environmental object. The meaning of the subjectively constituted environmental feature is so heightened that it becomes closely intertwined with the person who has endowed it with meaning. Through embodiment, the weight of carrying meaning can appear to shift from the individual to the environmental object.

For our study, embodiment is best exemplified by the case of a widow who regularly visited her husband's grave at the City of London Cemetery. His memorial stone was unusual in shape and design: one surface was rough hewn and the other smooth. The woman explained that what her husband had always loved greatly about her was the fact that she had one smooth hand – she had contracted polio as a child and never had the use of her right hand – and one hand that, having to do all the work, was rough. He always held her hands and commented fondly on the contrast, and this, she indicated, was central in their relationship. The woman had not only designed a gravestone like her hands but had also left a space below her husband's name for her own. This kind of embodiment at the gravesite appears to help mourners prepare for and face their own inevitable demise. The same woman continued: 'I call this [the burial plot] my house, and he's down there decorating it for me; this is my second home.' Through the processes of extension and embodiment, mourners similarly use the grave garden to re-create the 'other' in the cemetery. Two unmarried older sisters at the City of London Cemetery told us that the thrift plant on their parents' grave had come from their father's window box, which he gardened during the war years where the family lived. To them, this thrift plant symbolized the 'old haunts': it was reminiscent of their connection to the old neighbourhood and the window boxes there.[32] Another woman explained the provenance of the violas that covered her husband's grave. Originally the plants came from his childhood home; as a newly married couple they had transplanted some to their new home garden. When the husband retired, the couple took the violas to fill the window boxes of their new flat. The life history of the deceased merged with these small purple flowers covering his grave. Through such symbolic reinforcement, the grave not only shelters and embodies the other but *becomes* the other.

A Jewish woman articulated this identification when she described the purpose of her visit to the cemetery as coming to speak with her mother: 'I've come for my mother's stone.' Moreover, tending the grave garden leads the mourner to think about the deceased, and through conversational dialogue at the grave, the self and the other are reconstructed. For many, the nurturing acts of gardening in the cemetery continue the care provided for a spouse at home or in hospital during the illness preceding death. By arranging cut flowers and washing the stone, the bereaved also present the reconstructed public image of the deceased as a unique individual worthy of this special attention. The memorial stone and garden embody both the self (the bereaved) and the other (the deceased).

Boundaries between Home and Grave

Although in the foregoing discussion we have concentrated on the connections between home and cemetery, we must also acknowledge the efforts some people make to keep these spaces separate and distinct.

The boundaries that define and enclose the place of the dead from that of the living may be described as either permeable and fluid or solid and impenetrable. Particularly for Greek Cypriots and Orthodox Jews, issues of contamination rigidly separate the two worlds. Fear arises not from any malevolent intent on the part of the dead but from the polluting essence of the cemetery and the grave itself.

Greeks and Orthodox Jews are forbidden to eat anything that grows in or near the grounds of the cemetery. If a Greek person defiles the *topos*, or geography, of the living with matter that essentially belongs to the 'other side', he or she risks causing an untimely death in the household.[33] One Greek male study participant kept the implements he used for gardening at the cemetery in a box in his car: 'It's not right to bring them into the house, God forbid, this will bring death to the family. Well, that's what we believe and I don't want to take a chance by doing something I shouldn't.' Two Greek women felt similarly fearful:

> I bought so many potted plants for the grave that there were some left over, but I could not take them back home. I placed them on a grave nearby. I know it's stupid, but I didn't feel right to take the flowers for the dead that had been at the grave, to bring death home.

> We all visited our mother's grave, it was a wet Sunday and the ground was muddy. When we got back to my sister-in-law's house, there was shouting and arguing, because some people did not wipe their shoes well enough and brought soil from the cemetery into the house. For us, this is very bad luck. The things for the dead must be kept away, otherwise we are tempting fate. We must always wash our hands when we leave the cemetery.

Relations between the Greek home and grave are ambivalent, however, and as such reflect the sentiments shared by the dead and the mourner during their life together.[34] Although the grave might be feared, it is also treated as the home of the dead. Therefore the deceased and the grave with its genetic and cultural material links will always be, as a study participant commented, 'honoured and respected, but from a certain distance'.

Orthodox Jewish doctrine, too, discourages close involvement with the cemetery. 'You are supposed to limit the amount of death you bring into life' for 'Judaism is a religion of life, not a religion of death.' Jewish mourners ritually wash their hands when leaving the cemetery, symbolically separating the domain of death from the province of life. Many limit their visits to the anniversary of death and to the High Holidays – 'The cemetery is not a place to stay and sit, and it is not what I want to do. It does not pull me back, it does not say "come and see me I'm so lovely."' – and choose to acknowledge loss in the home as well as the burial ground. 'While I express my grief in the cemetery, it is shown even more in the lonelier places at home. There I feel a stronger affinity, I feel much closer.'

Unlike Greek Cypriots, Orthodox Jews do not customarily bring flowers from home to the cemetery, again restricting the continuity between the two domains. As a Jewish doctor in his sixties who had lost both his wife and daughter remarked: 'I am a keen gardener; both my son and I have fruit trees in our home gardens, plantings as a memorial, new apple trees; they grow and are living.' However, for many older Jewish people, like their Greek counterparts, need and sentiment may dictate behaviour and bring them closer to their City of London Cemetery peers. As one Jewish man in his early eighties remarked: 'I come every three to four weeks to my wife's grave; she died thirteen years ago. I feel I get satisfaction from coming.'

Conclusion

Many variables characteristic of survivors – age, marital and health status, socio-economic class, religion and even housing patterns – affect the processes whereby the identity of the deceased is partially transferred from the familiar domestic home to the new cemetery home. Our data suggest that the material and symbolic repositioning of home and garden to the stone and burial plot is realized most fully at the City of London Cemetery, to a lesser degree at New Southgate and only slightly at Bushey United Jewish Cemetery. At the City of London, long-standing religious traditions and newly created customs work together to sustain a 'cult of the dead'. For many bereaved persons, the enduring presence of the body buried in soil allows the creation of an ongoing relationship with the physically located and grounded identity of the departed. Through the processes of extension and embodiment, the memorial stone and the grave garden become synonymous with the deceased in the same ways in which the family home and garden were identified with that person when alive.

The separation between the domains of the cemetery and home is most clearly defined for the Orthodox Jewish individual. The bereaved are encouraged to keep the memory of the departed most fully at home rather than at the burial grounds, although individuals vary. For the Cypriot Greek Orthodox, this boundary between home and cemetery appears more porous; mourners are ambivalent in their attitudes toward the place of burial, and the grave is treated as the home of the departed and the cemetery an extension of the domestic domain. Like the home, the Greek grave is a site of creative investment; mourners bring material objects associated with the departed as gifts to enhance and decorate the grave, thereby regenerating the identity of the occupant and underscoring its identification as the present home of the deceased.

Clearly, home and garden carry multiple meanings and evoke a range of sentiments,[35] as well as providing a template for thinking about other domains of experience.[36] By entering the contemporary cemetery and viewing that world from the perspectives of mourners, we have learned about the many associations made between the ideas of home and grave-as-home. It is through boundaries, physical and social, around the structure – whether the home or the grave – that both connectedness to the deceased and a new sense of individuality are established or claimed. So, too, rituals and practices establish the tomb as the final dwelling place of the once-living body.

People often extend the socio-spatial concept of 'home' to encompass a wider area – whether bounded or not – in which residents experience familiarity and freedom to act with a shared sense of intimacy, predictability and control. Cemetery users often act as though they experience feelings of identification, ownership and involvement with the burial grounds where family members are interred that parallel the feelings they experience towards their own homes. They frequently articulate the same needs for security, safety and control at the cemetery that they feel at home. As the concept of home provides a focus, a grounding, a sense of place and of the past, so, too, can the burial places of kin establish and reinforce claims to rootedness and identity, permanence and stability of self and collectivity.[37]

5

Negotiating Memory: Remembering the Dead for the Long Term

There is an air of permanence about the cemetery which forces you to accept that the person is gone in that form; it is now a stable situation. However, this is the tip of the iceberg, and the other nine-tenths is the way you see the thing within yourself. . . . It is an ever-changing scene, it changes as our own circumstances change.

Jewish widow speaking about the grave of her late husband

Grief often continues after the first anniversary of death as people struggle to come to terms with loss and absence. Memory works in the dynamic space between the figure of the one who died and the life disfigured by the death.[1] Cemetery and home may give physical presence to this psychological space as funerary and domestic landscapes generate complementary resources for emotional processes. The cemetery, like the home, is a place where the social existence of the deceased can be maintained beyond the grave. There is no time limit on grief in either cemetery or home. In the burial ground, the performance of remembrance is encouraged, even imposed. There, the emotions associated with grief are evoked and given expression, yet the cemetery is also a social context in which cultural norms about how mourners should behave and feel are made apparent. Permission and prohibition coexist. Congruent expectations among cemetery visitors may reinforce rules of self-monitoring.

In the years following interment, the involvement of cemetery management is likely to increase as well, as the cultural code of appropriate cemetery behaviour is promoted and enforced. In defining what are acceptable conditions, practices and time frames for long-term remembrance, grave visitors, family members and cemetery owners and administrators may disagree and sometimes conflict. Conversely, the individual, the cultural community, religious authorities and cemetery management may develop relations of trust and confidence even as each brings certain requirements and expectations to the process. These expectations – contested or not – lead to the emergence of a particular cemetery culture and landscape. The character of this landscape, through its visual and practical organization (and the ways in which it is experientially perceived by users[2]), will facilitate or thwart long-term mourners' abilities to construct memory and manage the shifting identities of the deceased and the self.

The character, even the 'mood', of a cemetery arises from this mix of agreements and contests. Consequently, every cemetery has a unique landscape regulated by a particular balance of power and influences. Such landscape outcomes are dynamic: they change and evolve over time as individual gravesite issues are consolidated to become the whole cemetery aggregate. The first year after burial is a period when the bereaved, especially if they have no previous experience of the cemetery, make tentative moves to establish the grave and when authorities and other mourners guide rather than control their efforts. The second and subsequent years of commemorative practice may be different. Ground rules, frequently relaxed at the start, are often more clearly defined. Relationships between grave owners and cemetery managers may become trusting and confident or more suspicious and defiant.

In this chapter we consider the cemetery landscape, the conditions for attending a grave that are set up through managerial practice and the levels of confidence this generates for conduct at the grave and a more or less satisfactory mourning experience. We analyse the ways in which material objects – stones, inscriptions, plants and flowers – along with the dispositions – bodily, emotional and theological – of mourners are entailed at each site, both in the appearance of the grave and in the attributes of accessibility, safety and a trustworthy management for the cemetery as a whole. The different sets of relationships between users and managers that we observed at our four main study sites – Bushey United Jewish Cemetery, the City of London Cemetery, New Southgate Cemetery and Woodgrange Park Cemetery – suggest a continuum.

Three of the four cemeteries are each distinguished by a landscape dominated by one of three commemorative elements: the memorial stone, the grave garden and the practice of visiting to attend both stone and garden. It is around these elements that long-term commemorative practices coalesce and interactions among mourners and between mourners and management take place. To examine the ways in which mourners and managers deal with each of these features, we offer as case studies the cemetery in which each feature appears in its most amplified form. At Bushey, for example, the memorial stone is all important, whereas the tending of the garden as a conduit for emotional expression is most fully developed at the City of London Cemetery. Although garden and stone are integral to each other at New Southgate, the social, familial and religious imperative to remember, through the act of attending both gravestone and garden, brings the importance of visits to the fore. Woodgrange Park, at the time of fieldwork an overgrown wilderness where the safety of both graves and persons appeared compromised, presents a different situation altogether. There, changing practices of long-term remembrance involve a three-party relationship among the private owners, one declining group of visitors and another user population that is expanding.

Cemeteries are arenas where memories, intimate and social, are crafted and where individual and group identities are constructed and given material statement. In the public-yet-private world of the cemetery, communication between the living and the deceased, and between grieving family members and other mourners takes place verbally and through the non-discursive language of stones and flowers. Mourners may use this non-verbal code to compose eloquent, expressive statements about the identities of the surviving self and the deceased other and about their continuing connection. Stones and flowers are conduits through which feelings and significance are communicated at intimate and public levels.

Cemetery visitors, especially the bereaved, appear skilled at decoding the many aesthetic expressions and acts that foster private and public remembering. The authorities, too – both theological and administrative – are in positions to interpret the codified meanings of stones and flowers, though each cultural group and burial ground has its own rules about what is appropriate and correct. Thus, the communities at each of our four sites – and, we speculate, at cemeteries elsewhere – adopt and adapt the basic elements of stone, garden and visit to construct a language through which cemetery norms are communicated. This code is taught, learned, understood and validated by the community of the bereaved. It may evolve over time, and it may be elaborated upon or restricted by managers, religious leaders and new communities of mourners.[3] It is within this context of both community and managerial practice that we examine the long-term commemorative activities of mourners, the construction of memory and the crafting of individual and collective identities and remember-ings – all integral to the appearance of the cemetery landscape. We begin by exploring the relationship between the stone monument and the creation of memory, first at Bushey United Jewish Cemetery.

The Inscribed Stone: Bushey United Jewish Cemetery

The purpose of the tombstone is to name and honour the deceased and to designate a particular grave where family members may visit their dead. For Orthodox Jews using Bushey United Jewish Cemetery, the consecration of the memorial stone eleven months after burial signals the end of formal mourning and symbolizes the fact that the loss in now located in a permanent and irreversible domain. The effect of this ritual is rarely to still the survivors' complex feelings of grief, but the erection of the memorial gives a measure of emotional peace by fixing the site of the bodily remains of the deceased.

At Bushey Cemetery, each grave, fully kerbed and protected by a cover slab, is marked by a standing memorial of marble or granite. Just as the United Synagogue oversees the ritual preparation and interment of the body, so, too, does it regulate the size and text of the memorial stone. Monuments today are smaller and less ornate than many were in the past, when, according to a United Synagogue official, 'wealth and social standing were demonstrated by the quality of the tombstone'. Most families now select a memorial from the designs offered by the United Synagogue-approved stonemasons; very few commission a unique memorial to convey visually and aesthetically their feelings about the deceased.

The wording inscribed on the stone must be approved by the office of the Chief Rabbi. All United Synagogue inscriptions begin with an abbreviation of the Hebrew words 'here is interred'. The Hebrew name of the deceased must appear together with his or her father's name. The official English name of the departed is also used; nicknames are allowed in parentheses: 'Kenneth (Kenny) Goldstein'. With the addi-tion of the deceased's name, the generic stone is transformed into a personalized monument. 'The grave is the marker that you've been here.' The date of death is given in English and optionally in Hebrew. All inscriptions must conclude with the Hebrew words 'may his/her/ their soul(s) be bound up in the bonds of eternal life', repeating in script the words of the memorial prayer recited annually at the cemetery and in the synagogue.

In addition to these standard requirements, the next of kin and the names of all children who were alive at the time of burial may be included: 'Deeply mourned by sons Harvey and Saul and daughters Miriam and Sophie'. Such naming of both the father and the living children and grandchildren of the deceased links the generations in time and space to demonstrate a collective family identity in which the deceased is the central pivot. A short quotation from an appropriate biblical or rabbinic source and a Star of David are also permitted. Individual variations on this model are allowed, but in all cases, religious, familial and individual identity are expressed according to guidance from the United Synagogue on selection of the stone, wording of the inscription and application of religious symbols.

Although some cemetery historians fault today's monuments as dull and unattractive ('the younger the stone, the more uninteresting'), careful thought and consultation go into each decision. The comments of one family who visited Bushey to inspect their memorial a week before the scheduled consecration illustrate this point: 'We liked the look of the stone and what we had chosen for the words – "Loving kindness and truth meet; righteousness and harmony embrace." It is appropriate. We chose an open book and my father loved books; he would have approved. It was correct as we chose it.'

In this case, the stone expressed and also helped to create, through both written text and iconographic motif, the family's interpretation of the virtues, accomplishments and personal qualities of the departed, as well as the nature of their shared relationship. In such processes of choice and composition, mourners also project their own definitions of themselves into the portrayal of the departed. In two telling examples, two different Jewish daughters chose to rewrite the epitaphs their mothers had composed for later inscription on their stones. As one daughter explained her decision: 'My mother left what she wanted put on the stone, but I put what I wanted: "A woman of exceptional ability". . . . We did not use the epitaph my mother had written. It was too long. My husband said we would need a PTO [please turn over]. It was not suitable; it did not describe her properly.'

As the memorial stone marks the burial site of the body and gives material substance to the reconstructed image and meaning of the deceased, it also acts as an agent of inscribed memory for many cemetery visitors. But at each cemetery studied, specific cultural practices and managerial policies affect the relationship between memorial and memory. The ordered landscape and silent stillness of Bushey, for example, can be 'a source of comfort and peace'. 'There is a quietness here, it is a time and place of remembering where I come from and who I am.' The restrained, reverential atmosphere and 'immaculately kept' grounds work to 'concentrate the mind'. The sacred space encourages an interiorized disposition and pensive mood that invites the processes of commemoration and memory. One mourner elaborated: 'Cemetery visits evoke emotions, melancholy, which evokes contemplation. The cemetery is a place where you get your emotions together, rather than your thoughts; you just do it, it is non-thinking, it is not intellectual thinking.'

In this sacred atmosphere, decorum, propriety and piety distinguish behaviour at Bushey.[4] 'We treat this visit with respect. It is solemn.' The protocol that directs proper behaviour is embodied in a dress code: men and women are expected to cover their heads, and women wear skirts rather than trousers, which are considered undignified. People will not make impromptu visits if they are dressed inappropriately. A woman who visited the cemetery office on business explained: 'I am dressed in trousers and will not visit their grave; my parents would say this was OK [not to visit].'

Many United Synagogue members view the yearly cemetery pilgrimage, traditionally made in the autumn during the Hebrew month of *Elul*,[5] as a significant part of their annual ritual cycle and an important way to remember the dead. It gives behavioural form to ideology, to the Jewish sense of a social relationship with death and with the remembered dead. It points to an ongoing regard for the corporeal body in its association with the sacred soul and spiritual self of the deceased. When asked about the 'meaning' of this annual visit, most people replied that 'it is traditional at this time of year to visit the graves of your loved ones and to remember them'.[6]

This customary visit is seen as a helpful way to retain memories of parents – 'a mechanism to hang onto them'. 'I feel closer when I am physically closer to what was them. It's remembering them. It's the closest physical contact you can get with them.' 'It keeps the memory fresher.' Another person explained further how this tradition honours the previous generation, focuses rethinking and provides consolation by continuing the activities parents found meaningful:

> The custom encourages you once a year to make an effort, to focus and to take that journey about your parents who are no longer there. . . . It is a trigger . . . it is their feelings of you and your feelings of them which you can re-evaluate. It is also

knowing that you are doing the right thing and what your parents wanted and that you are showing respect to them.

For some, it is a time of release for stored emotions: 'It is interesting how grief is recessed. We put it away somewhere, and when the dates come, we allow ourselves the privilege of opening the door and letting the pain come through.' Others, however, admit that these annual visits fail to provide consolation and are carried out largely from a sense of traditional expectation, family obligation, or duty.[7] 'The cemetery is not really comforting, but we can't really not come.' And as one woman who had lost her only child said: 'I can't bear coming here. It is a very big effort for me to come. I come here just because I have to.'

Despite the pain and ongoing sense of loss, the annual cemetery visit is held as a tradition that must not be abandoned. 'We come because it's always been done; I wouldn't want to be the one to break the chain.' 'I do not have the courage to say, "I won't go"; I just don't want to be the person who stops.' The weight of custom supports the continuing bond between generations, the same bond that is inscribed on each memorial stone and expressed in the recitation of Kaddish by surviving sons for their deceased parents. 'Even with the passage of time, there is comfort in keeping up with the traditions and in keeping memories alive . . . it's a sense of family and continuation.' Some participants imposed a further moral meaning on the yearly cemetery visit by stressing its religious underpinnings as a reconnection to both spiritual and ancestral roots. 'Coming to the cemetery is about the Jewish religion. It means to go back to basics; it's about what we learned from tradition.'

Customarily, Anglo-Jewish cemetery visits are made on the Hebrew anniversary of death,[8] to attend funerals and stone settings, at times when people 'feel the need' and in the autumn around the time of the Jewish New Year,[9] which is a period of spiritual stocktaking and penitence culminating in the fast of Yom Kippur, the Day of Atonement. A visit during the New Year period is meant to encourage self-appraisal. In the presence of the resting places of parents, and through reflection on the values, lifestyles and viewpoints of past generations, some people consider the paths their lives have taken. Although study participants did not mention it directly, underscoring this practice of self-reflection is the religious tenet that the worthy lives of bereaved survivors – inspired and influenced by the teachings and proper deeds of their deceased parents – can confer an enhanced spiritual state upon the souls of the departed.[10] According to this belief, the living can redeem the dead, their activities enabling the passage of the soul to a higher realm.[11] The Jewish New Year and the traditional visit to the cemetery are occasions of solemnity, times of forgiving and asking for forgiveness and inducements to think through and rededicate one's life. 'It is a time of remembrance, a time of prayers for forgiveness and a time of return. *Teshuvah* is the Hebrew word for both repentance and return – to pray to God in a meaningful place, the final resting place of a close relative.'

Given the sacred and transcendent aspect of the yearly cemetery visit, the memorial stone takes on added meaning as the focus of ritual performance and engagement, the symbolic place where the world of the living and the dead may come into contact. During the visit, most people stand in front of the monument and meditatively read the written text. 'I read the inscription and I'm moved.' They recite the appropriate memorial prayers for a parent or child or pray more spontaneously 'from the heart'. This time of worship and prayers for the soul of the departed and for one's own righteous earthly existence may be followed by a few moments of intimate contemplation of the deceased. Alternatively, a more or less vocal conversation recounting family news and perhaps requesting the deceased's benevolent intercession may take place.

While some wish to leave the dead to 'rest in peace', others believe that the disembodied souls of the departed are present in the cemetery during the High Holidays and that connection and communication are possible: 'When I'm in the cemetery, I have a feeling that my sister's there. That I can contact her – she's there.' Many use the occasion to ask the deceased's intercession for the coming year. 'You pray in their honour of what they did on earth. You receive blessings for your children and family. You pray for health for the family. You deal with your hopes for the family for the coming year, and you report on the past year.' This quotation suggests a spiritual understanding of 'death as a transition to another realm of consciousness, to a state of disembodied awareness in which there is a continued relationship with the realm of the living'.[12]

For some Orthodox Jews, the cemetery is a site for less abstract communion with the disembodied dead. One important, concrete memorializing practice is the careful inspection and care of the stone monument, a metaphor for ongoing regard of the deceased and the maintenance of memory. 'My coming is a mark of respect. To see the memorial stone and see that it's OK, not broken or damaged.' In some families, this examination is tackled first, possibly as a way of deflecting the powerful emotions of confronting again the shock and reality of death. Although people visit the cemetery knowingly to remember and mourn, the process can prove emotionally overwhelming, and moments of distraction and retreat are sought. Each family has its own routine, as one son explained:

Our family has a process of the way we look at the stone: My younger brother brings paper towels and cleans the stone. The whole family looks and carefully appraises the condition of the stone. We employ someone to wash the stone, and we do as well, but the elements take their toll. Our caring for the stone is a demonstration that you care still.

Although marble may appear hard and enduring, in fact its permanence depends upon constant human attention.[13] Visitors acknowledge this reality and are vigilant against the attrition of time, nature and possible human desecration. In the secret yet shared code of cemetery culture, the stone should remain whole, clean and white, resisting signs of weathering and decay. The inviolability of the memorial signals the inviolability of the bodily remains and serves as a metaphor for the upkeep of the name and memory of the deceased.[14] Both the stone and the memory require care and diligence. To keep the memorial in good condition, some families hire a stonemason or cemetery staff member: 'We paid to have it cleaned; it is cleaned yearly to make it look good. We are taking care of our parents' grave, we are taking care of our parents' memory.' Others prefer to do the work themselves: 'We wash the stone ourselves when we are here, it is purposeful. It costs twenty pounds to have maintenance done at Bushey, and we prefer to do it ourselves. I get upset, I do not want the dirt on it when I'm still here.'

The significance of the stone as a site of memory is, we suggest, contingent upon sustained engagement with it, from selection to inscription, erection, visitation and continued upkeep. Study informants endorsed this interpretation; they saw grey, weathered, or broken stones as the material enactment of forgetting. Although cemetery visitors excused an old stone's deterioration by surmising that 'no one is left from the family', decay of the stone suggested to them that the person buried there had been forgotten. 'Overgrown graves are forgotten graves. They look sad when they are dirty, overgrown and stained.' Just as the neatness of the burial ground expresses respect for the departed, so is the condition of the memorial stone seen to reflect continued family devotion and respect, as well as perpetuation of the identity and meaning of the deceased. The need to keep the grave looking clean and unweathered was the reason some families gave for coming to the cemetery more often than a few times a year: 'I come weekly to see the stone is OK.' 'We've come once a month for twenty-one years, to make sure the grave is clean, to show respect for my husband. We like to see it spotless and shining. We do not want to come and see it dirty while we're here.' Such committed maintenance of the stone may also serve to stave off or deny the possibility of forgetting. Deteriorating stones are emblematic of the passage of time and the fragility of remembering, and they raise existential questions about the experience of death and memory.

While the overall condition of the stone is a public signal of the family's concern for the deceased's memory, small pebbles left on the grave reveal to others that the grave has been visited. For Jews, it is customary to leave a small stone on the memorial in honour of the deceased, to show that one has visited the grave and 'to leave something behind'. Suggestions about the origin of this custom are legion. One relates to the Jewish past, when people were buried under cairns to protect them against the elements and unearthing by wild animals. In acts of good faith, passers-by would replenish depleted cairns by adding a stone to each one. Another interpretation relates to a prominent rabbi of the Talmudic era who requested that everyone who passed his tomb add a stone as a symbolic atonement for an unrepented sin. A third suggests that all persons are equal in death, as in birth, and that everyone, no matter how rich or poor can always find a stone to show his or her respect. Yet another explanation attributes the custom to family surveillance in the eastern European *shtetls*: through the requirement of placing a stone, it was possible for elder kin to monitor whether their younger siblings had visited the grave of their deceased parent.[15] Today, the custom continues – to some extent. One Bushey Cemetery visitor said, 'By placing a small stone on a tombstone, we are making a gesture of participation, renewing connection and symbolizing our presence. It is a simple yet elegant language for telling the dead and the living that respects are still being paid.' Another, however, remarked, 'My grandparents have lots of grandchildren and great-grandchildren, but there are no stones on their grave. I feel sad; no one else remembers them.'[16]

Some Jewish mourners find that they need additional contact, to do something more. Bringing flowers to the grave seems to provide a closer connection with the departed.[17] The United Synagogue's policy 'does not actively discourage, nor does it encourage, flowers; we are tolerant of people putting flowers and it is tolerated by the majority,' said one United Synagogue official. To bring flowers to the grave, therefore, suggests a response to personal feelings and a resistance to cultural prescriptions. A father who had lost a child of three explained: 'You're not supposed to put flowers on the grave in the Jewish religion, but sometimes I like to see a few flowers. The cemetery knows us, they tolerate me; they do not take the roses off the grave.'

The placing of flowers is particularly accepted at the graves of children and young people. For example, one member of the cemetery staff remarked, 'Look how they keep the grave of that child alive with so many pots of flowers.' A small minority of families (thirty cases) at Bushey have 'grave maintenance',[18] and roses are planted annually at their graves. Two mothers who had lost adult daughters were given permission by the cemetery manager to plant the oddly shaped areas around their grave plots: 'He said that if I designed a garden for that scrubby bit of land, which was an eyesore, I could have the piece of land and he would help maintain it a bit.' This mother chose grasses and shrubs to mark the ground around her daughter's memorial and put up a wooden plaque with the text, 'That bringeth forth its fruit, in its season, whose leaf, also, doth not wither.' The other mother put in a young fruit tree: 'This piece of land is something that belongs to her.' A trend has emerged in which younger and possibly more Anglicized mourners are visiting Bushey Cemetery at the end of the workday, rather than at the more traditional times of the High Holidays, and are choosing to bring flowers. Nevertheless, despite these signs that flowers may be increasing at Bushey, most graves are still without floral tributes.

This account of long-term memorialization at Bushey Cemetery, with its focus on the memorial stone, reveals consensus among users and acceptance of the ritual and administrative activities determined by the cemetery authorities. There appears to be little improvisatory or innovative activity at the grave, and a state of equilibrium has long pertained between mourner-visitors and the cemetery management. This balance of trust and confidence, assuring that the dead will be appropriately protected, appears not to have been achieved through explicit debate. The conservative mode of operations and the congruence of expectations between mourners and management have not required this. At other cemetery sites, much more debate – and even confrontation – can characterize dealings between users and managers or owners. In some instances, as at the City of London Cemetery, changing customs of mourning and remembrance are managed through dialogue, as well as through dictum as a last resort.

The Garden: City of London Cemetery

At the City of London Cemetery, a similarly transparent and accountable system is in place to regulate the engagement of mourner and management around the stone and its plot. But the configuration of components at CLCC is very different from that at Bushey, not least because the grave garden features as a crucial element. Furthermore, Bushey is an ecclesiastical cemetery; the United Synagogue owns and runs it as a private organization, independent of the local authority. The City of London Cemetery, in contrast, is a municipal, secular, non-denominational cemetery under the direction of the Corporation of the City of London. It has a budget from the corporation, and although cemeteries have been termed the 'Cinderella service' of local authorities and are generally poorly financed, CLCC is well resourced. This cemetery provides an example of the type of relationship that can be established between users and a municipal cemetery management when resourcing is better than average.

Significantly, both Bushey and City of London Cemetery have formal grievance procedures for users' complaints. Negotiation between management and clients is a clearly defined and equitable process. Mourners at both sites are free to visit the cemetery offices to express concerns about grounds maintenance or to report problems with their memorial stones. Such articulated complaints evidence a high level of user involvement, a set of clear expectations about the upkeep of the infrastructure and thus a developed sense of ownership of the cemetery as a whole.

While the United Synagogue's funerary landscape encodes traditional Anglo-Jewish customs of cemetery action and prayer, the post-war lawn cemetery at City of London offers a different architectural structure and process around which survivors build their personal type of mourning. The rationality of the lawn section design, along with the development of public hospitals, professional funeral management and abbreviated mourning rituals, has been depicted as an example of the twentieth century's distancing of death.[19] Paradoxically, however, it is the very geometric simplicity of the rationally designed lawn section and the 'reserve and iconographical emptiness'[20] of its uniform monuments that provide the opportunity for new public and secular expressions of bereavement. A student visiting the grave of his father explained: 'The layout and design of the lawn cemetery are abstract. We are allocated a plot and there is also a permitted shape of the stone. There is a sense of austerity in the design, a plainness and sobriety. It is like the Cenotaph, a kind of *tabula rasa* on which we can project our own individual grief.'

In parallel with the shared cultural identification observed at Bushey Cemetery, the customary rules for lawn graves at City of London centre on the familial relationships of the deceased, emphasizing equality with those in surrounding graves and a striving for dignity. This model follows the aesthetic and ideological principles of the Commonwealth War Graves Commission, which justify the cemetery's regulation of acceptable materials and dimensions for the stone and grave. All memorials – marking full-body burials as well as cremated remains –

must be made of marble, granite or natural stone and are 'limited to headstones measuring three feet high by two feet wide and not less than three inches or more than six inches thick'. Although no specifications govern what is carved on the monument (other than grave number), a drawing of the memorial and its proposed inscription must be submitted by the registered grave owner for approval by the Common Council. Today, most stones are inscribed with the modest details of the life lived: name, date of death, kinship status of the deceased ('Beloved Husband, Dad and Granddad') and a short epitaph ('To Meet Again in Heaven') or verse text.[21] Some mourners may particularize the written epitaph by adding a more private inscription or image. It was these personalized words and meaningful symbols to which mourners often pointed when they talked about the stone and their relationship with the departed.

As at other cemetery sites, the memorial stone is significant to City of London visitors because it marks the 'final resting place' of the deceased and provides a focus for grief. Indeed, a number of families who in the past chose cremation and the scattering of ashes are now electing burial instead, or having the ashes interred in a marked grave. In one family in which most of the relatives had been cremated and their ashes scattered, the lone stone memorial marking the burial of one member had become a collective site of remembrance for the entire family. 'It's making a special place which you can come to and keep the memory.' 'It's somewhere to think and to feel like you're near them; it provides something to fix on.'

When the lawn section was first established, most bereaved families selected the more affordable white marble memorial, which discoloured easily because of its porosity. As at Bushey, survivors at City of London see an analogy between the upkeep of the stone and their ongoing devotion to the memory of the deceased.[22] Some make an annual trip specifically to bleach the memorial marker, using brushes with spirits of salts and even toothpaste to return the stone to a pristine state. 'I feel sad when the white marble is stained; we clean it with acid. We don't like it to look neglected, like no one bothers.' Today, as some families have became more affluent, they may select a more expensive black memorial that 'never discolours and keeps nicely'. Here, 'nature' and the loss of the stone's integrity through time appear to be kept at bay, and survivors' relationships with the deceased may be kept correspondingly constant. In winter, a few stones may be wrapped in plastic to protect them from the elements.

The cultural meanings attached to the lawn memorial at the City of London Cemetery can be fully understood, however, only in connection with its small grave garden. The lawn cemetery has become the locus for a new culture of commemoration created, in part, by people whose working-class grandparents and parents had been buried in unmarked common graves and did not share the mourning customs of the more well-to-do.[23] Their attenuated religious affiliations in a now secularized and individualized society have left many such people 'unguided' and open to creating new practices of cemetery mourning. Exploiting the opportunities of the lawns, they have innovatively linked the maintenance of the 'enduring' stone memorial to the seasonal redesign of the transitory grave garden. In doing so, they have used the non-verbal language of flowers to engage with the grave and the deceased and to involve others.

The 'permanent' stone marker, with its written epitaph, communicates a fixed, abbreviated meaning of the deceased composed at a particular moment in time.[24] The garden, created with ephemeral flowers and plants requiring frequent attention and seasonal renewal, allows a more dynamic and expansive meaning of the departed to be shaped and reshaped over time.[25] One cemetery visitor described the relative importance of these two forms for remembrance as follows:

> It is particularly the process of attending the garden that I enjoy. Gardening is a metaphor for life; it's the organic process of life and death. The garden here is a very important thing. The garden is the memorial. . . it requires a close degree of attention and maintenance; it requires a large degree of commitment. The stone is merely a document. . . . With our grave, the stone is the document and the garden the memorial.

The garden historian John Dixon Hunt underscores this idea in suggesting that the transience of the garden makes it a particularly appropriate form of memorialization.[26] Hunt argues that although the garden is ordered by human agency and domestic care, it is ever changing and subject to the mutability of the seasons and the natural cycles of birth, growth, death and regeneration.[27] The garden makes the consoling cycles of seasonal renewal and regeneration available to the mourner. Its very transience contributes to its meaning as a place of memory, as does the sustained commitment, intimate engagement and responsibility over time required of the bereaved to make the small grave plot into a memorial garden.

Because every garden mirrors its creator, Hunt argues, the memorial garden expresses the individuality of the survivor. In designing the plot to commemorate the deceased, the mourner must reinvent the identity and meaning of the departed and, in doing so, projects his or her own self-image, which is often discovered, expressed, realized and reflected in the process. When people die, they no longer provide a mirror in which survivors may view their own reflections and realize themselves as social beings.[28] For mourners to continue to see themselves still living in and related to the deceased, they must re-create the lost person, and in the process they discover and identify the self. The small grave garden makes available the resources of nature for these parallel processes of memory and identity formation; it gives physical expression to the social psychology of grief and remembrance. The transitory garden, created of short-lived flowers and plants requiring frequent renewal, encourages survivors to shape and reshape the meaning of the departed over time. The memorial plot expresses the reconstructed identities of the survivor and the departed, as well as their ongoing relationship. This idea was clearly expressed by one study participant who spoke about the grave garden he had designed for his deceased mother:

> It's a part of me that's with my Mum. When I come every week, I'm doing something good still for her. I give something of myself. I give my time. My thoughts have gone into how it's prepared – it's quite hard to get it right. I want the garden to look nice because she was nice. . . . I feel she's still with me.

Although many cemetery visitors select the same types of flowering plants, each plot is the unique creation of its designer and reveals agency and purposeful forethought.[29] Some, for example, wish to make the memorial garden more personal and special and so grow plants at home from seed, a process that necessitates detailed planning. Others make trips to the markets and select flowering plants for colour and size – a low garden may be favoured in order not to obscure the inscription and 'allow the deceased to look out' – and for hardiness.[30] Symbolic imagery is also important: rosemary for remembrance, red and white roses for passion, yellow roses for everlasting love. Many visitors seek 'good value for money', whereas others regularly spend large sums for cut flowers as a sign of devotion and sacrifice. Some, restricted by income, may economize by first placing a pot of flowers on a spouse's grave and later moving them to a parent's stone. 'They're too expensive to throw away.'

Like the personalized icons inscribed on the marker, the small garden is intended to distinguish the deceased from others in the line of uniformly sized stone monuments. Through processes of planting and tending, the plot allows survivors to re-create, extol and make materially manifest the remembered personhood of the deceased. Grave gardens often display the deceased's favourite flowers. One widow who had planted daffodils, as well as had them carved on the stone, said, 'My husband loved yellow, it was his favorite colour.' Gardening allowed her to perform and acquire some of her husband's attributes and activities as a gardener and so to reconstruct him in the present while sustaining her role as a caring, devoted wife. 'While I'm here, he's still a part of my life. I feel he still belongs to me. By coming here, I still have got something to do in relation to John. You put yourself out.'

In another instance, a middle-aged daughter brought pink flowers to the grave of her mother who died in 1969. She explained that her father had hated pink and refused to allow his wife to wear it; her floral tributes represented a kind of restoration or compensation. In another example, the grave of a teenage boy who had been killed by a car was planted with the marigolds he had helped his science teacher to raise from seed earlier that summer. These flowers were a visual representation of him as schoolboy and son and were part of the mother's reconstruction of his personhood and their continuing, though altered, relationship.

Sections of the grave garden, although small, give each family member a chance to express his or her own evolving memory of the deceased, the garden as a whole demonstrating the family's composite remembrance. For example, one member might plant bulbs, another might select and prune the standard rose bush, a third might put in the bedding plants and a fourth might arrange the cut flowers or bring potted plants. A memorial vase of cut flowers, to which each family member adds something different, might achieve the same aim. Flowers can, however, express a loosening of family ties after a parent's death: 'My mother kept us a tight bud, but now we go our separate ways,' said one of six children who rarely visited together. In other cases, one sibling might assume control of the grave and exclude the others.

Public rituals of planting at the City of London Cemetery may enable the expression of grief but can also be felt as a cultural imposition.[31] As one participant put it: 'I leave the grave clean, well-tended and presentable so the neighbours will not talk about it, so I will not be the piggy-in-the-middle.' Mourners who have never gardened before report that they are learning to do so by watching others. As one mother and daughter remarked about their beginning efforts at grave tending: 'We're not gardeners, this is an experiment. We live in flats; we went to the garden centre and bought a trowel and hand fork, peat and plants and dug up the earth and enjoyed it. This is our first time planting the grave, it's an experiment.' People acknowledge this public performance dimension of cemetery visits and their awareness that the grave garden is a visible statement about the meaning of the other and the quality of the shared relationship. 'It's almost like a public show, that you haven't forgotten them. People walk past the grave and see the flowers there and know someone is still coming. It is essential to see that the grave is cared for and decorated.'[32]

At the City of London Cemetery, there is an accepted calendar of cultural, religious and secular occasions on which users customarily visit. A decorated memorial, like the small stones left on the graves at Bushey Cemetery, publicly affirms the mourners' ongoing commitment and connection to the meaning and memory of the deceased. Christmas is the occasion when those who visit only once a year come to the cemetery to place wreaths, cards and decorations (Fig. 5.1). Placing a wreath on her father's grave, one woman said, 'It's the thing to do; it's this time of year, it's festive. To let them know we have not forgotten them and as decoration for the grave.' Christmas, birthday and Mother's Day cards are chosen with as much care as are plants for the grave garden. Carrying long, handwritten messages (which allow mourners to articulate their current feelings about the meaning of the deceased and thus to 'update' the inscribed epitaph), they are placed in protective plastic sleeves and inserted into the narrow space between the memorial and the base or sometimes taped to the stone or attached to a nearby tree. Such cards are intended for the dead (though they are looked at, but not read, by other family members who wish to see who wrote them), and others are not supposed to open them. In the memorial gardens at Christmas there is a somewhat similar tradition that mourners bring floral bouquets which they place together in the shape of a large cross, creating a sense of community by symbolizing their shared remembrance of the deceased.

On both special and more routine visits when survivors tend the grave and arrange flowers, most of them think about life as it was with the deceased and about events from the past. For some, this life review is selective: only happy occasions and the positive attributes of the dead are recalled. 'When I'm in the cemetery, I talk to myself of what went on years ago; my mind goes back to when I was young and the good times we had.' For others, remembering the past can prompt a more critical re-examination of lives shared, and sometimes conflicts are resolved.[33] As mourners dig, re-dig and fork the soil, they may gain greater understanding, acceptance and healing through these parallel cognitive and material 'excavations'.

Interestingly, the graveside activities of mourners attending the interred ashes of family members replicate the practices of other lawn cemetery users. A number of these bereaved visitors reported that they had purposely chosen a marked plot rather than a plaque and a rose

Figure 5.1.
Christmas decorations reach from home to cemetery to include the dead. City of London Cemetery, 1998.

bush in the memorial gardens because the stone memorial and its small garden offered the opportunity for greater involvement and thus more time to reflect while tending the grave. As one man explained: 'I need to put flowers, it's nicer to look at and means something more than a rose bush. It makes you think of her all the time. It makes you come to do the flowers and to keep it tidy, and you are thinking more when you come over.' For others with kin in both the lawn section and the memorial gardens, grave-tending practices appeared to be carried over to the memorial gardens, where mourners might polish the brass plaque just as they had cleaned and polished the memorial stone. 'It's the only way I can still give to them physically – I already give to them emotionally.' This need for physical involvement seemed to be a significant aspect of the cemetery visit, whether it was to the lawn section or the memorial gardens.

Mourners at CLCC perceive cemetery gardening as a sacred activity, differentiated from everyday, secular planting. As one daughter explained: 'This is not gardening, it's bringing my mother flowers. When we come, we put flowers on our mother to please her.' The cultural practices of tending the plot and watering the plants justify frequent visiting and provide a legitimate reason for being at the grave for some time. 'It's no good putting them in if you don't take care of them.' Mourners reported that these activities helped to focus their attention, relieve stress and give satisfaction in a productive accomplishment. 'I need to do that, I have to do it for me, for my peace of mind. . . . I have to make it look nice. . . . It helps when you are down to come here, but I do not know why.' Even the removal of weeds assures that the mourner, rather than nature, is the keeper of memory:

> Weeds in the cemetery plot are the imposition of disorder;
> they've undone my labours. They render the notion of planting
> a garden meaningless; they do their own work. It's about control.
> What I do here is garden; it is a bond with my family. . . . It's a
> mediation – it establishes a relationship between me and them.
> I do not know what to do if the weeds are there.

While acknowledging the reality of death, many City of London
users also believe that the 'spirit' of the deceased is present at the
gravesite and that contact and communication are possible. In life, a
person's identity is closely allied with the physical body, and in death,
mourners' behaviour toward the interred body indicates their belief
in an ongoing connection between the 'person' and his or her physical
self. The body and the 'presence' remain a central focus of funerary
rituals. Those who visit graves at the City of London Cemetery hold
a range of views about death and the afterlife, some suggesting that
there are three different 'spirits' of the deceased, or possibly one 'soul'
with different 'spirit' manifestations of 'presence'. Many believe, for
example, that at the time of death the 'spirit' separates from the
physical body and rises immediately to heaven, where it is reunited
with beloved kin and favourite family pets.[34] Others remain uncertain
about an afterlife and ask for signs from the deceased indicating that
they are in 'a better place', sometimes consulting spiritualists for
corroboration. Frequently the same mourners also report that they
feel the 'presence' of the deceased with them 'all the time' or 'at home',
and many say that the 'spirit' of the departed is also 'there' at the
gravesite, his or her new home: 'I see them just as I laid them there.'

Whereas the 'soul' or 'spirit' exists in the eternal time of heaven,
the cemetery-based 'spirit' – the corpse – and the identity and memory
of the deceased are maintained in linear time. Cemetery-based commemorative practices rely on the premise that the identity of the
individual is closely allied with the physical body and that in death
the cemetery-based 'spirit' retains a connection to the interred body –
the physical self – and is sentiently aware of events among the living.[35]
In the early period before the memorial stone is erected, mourners
come to the cemetery to be physically close to the body – to the person
that was. Once the stone marks the location of the body with precision,
it may take on the persona, the 'presence', of the departed. Grief may
be transferred to the monument, at which mourners talk openly:

> When I talk with him, I tell him things that happen (I think they
> already know) about So-and-so is on holiday, people who got
> married, or had a baby – what he would have loved, everyday

things. That's why I come alone, to have a chat. Lots of people I know, friends, say this, too, that they tell them this, that and the other.

For many, the memorial *is* the departed, but the marker gains this attribution only through its proximity to the bodily remains.[36]

The identification of the stone with the deceased is revealed when mourners first arrive. Many visitors greet the stone using the name of the deceased: 'Morning, Henry, how've you been keeping since I was here last?' Many kiss their fingers and then touch their hand to the stone in a more intimate, physical gesture of greeting. On leaving the cemetery, grandchildren are told to 'say good-bye to Nan' and are urged to kiss the stone directly. Through a range of ritual practices, actions and conversations, which we explore further in chapter 6, the dead are embraced and incorporated into the world of the living.

At a deeper level of sacred meaning, to keep the stone and garden is possibly to forestall the effects of time, disorder and forgetting and to deny the inevitable decomposition of the body – to keep the person 'alive'. In cemetery rituals, nature, a metaphor for death and decay of the physical body, is to be kept at bay. At the City of London Cemetery, the ideal is for the memorial stone to be washed and pristine and for the grave flowers to thrive: 'To neglect the stone and flowers would be to forget her.' If plants fail because of the weather, they are quickly replaced. One widow, for example, regularly renews her husband's grave with fresh bedding plants when she visits every six weeks. Control of nature, as displayed through an unweathered stone and vibrant garden, is analogous to 'control' of death insofar as the grave garden is required to belie the putrefaction occurring beneath its surface. The hard stone of the memorial may be a metaphor for the 'enduring' bones of the deceased, whereas the ephemeral flowers may symbolize the more transient flesh. Both are 'renewable' through tending of the memorial stone and the flower garden. The body – bones and flesh – is symbolically reconstructed, and thereby the identity, personhood and memory of the deceased, so closely associated with the physical self, can be sustained.

The attended grave at the cemetery thus mediates between nature and cultural norms concerning death, the afterlife and the continuing bonds between deceased and survivors. But to achieve these connections, the form of the memorial with its garden must be contained. Users at CLCC subscribe to a shared code that guides and, once the first year has passed, constrains how grief is expressed and memory sustained through grave-tending practices. A standard exists, for example, in which the 'appropriate' public display of emotion is 'restrained' and 'not over the top,' a code mirrored through 'proper' planting. One gardener articulated her personal definition of this shared convention: 'Yes, you can go over the top, if the rose bushes are too big, the conifers too large, or the Christmas wreaths too gaudy. I like the garden to be small, neat and pretty.'[37]

If people plant beyond their allotted space or put up fencing or other boundaries, conflict is likely – first with the expressive needs of neighbouring mourners and then with the cemetery's maintenance goals. Although cemetery management claims a 'relaxed' approach to planting restrictions, fences and rocks are said to interfere with mowing and are consistently removed, to the dismay of individual mourners. 'I'm angry, they removed my border. The stones made it look decorative; it was a finishing edge to the grave.' Management is at pains to point out that the regulations attached to a particular type of grave are spelled out at the time of purchase and reiterated when the grave deed is transferred. And indeed, most mourners accept the formal rules and adhere to the informal aesthetic code for acceptable planting.[38] Occasionally, a few will question or try to resist these restrictions in their desire to create a unique memorial worthy of the deceased. The cemetery will, except sometimes with a child's grave, persist in implementing the regulations as a demonstration of fairness to all and as a managerial necessity.

The collective of mourners appreciates this enforcement, allowing that excesses of various kinds – in visiting, elaborating the grave plot and displaying immoderate emotion – are only exceptionally permissible. The first year is a time of dispensation: both mourners and management accept this and, within generous bounds, make allowances. While the cemetery management has tried and tested ways of informing, advising and consulting grave owners, it will nonetheless control excess. If visitors complain, for example, that someone's grave plantings have grown above a certain height, but the owner resists containment, the cemetery's gardeners will remove the overgrown plants. Encroachment on adjacent plots, resented as bad neighbourliness, is similarly curtailed by management.

The City of London Cemetery management is successful in moderating emotional displays and supporting restraint among mourners. It can achieve a consensus because it has legitimacy with grave owners: one consequence of its more than minimal funding for the organization, upkeep and security of all cemetery areas. Although users occasionally complain or express reservations, the mourner community knows what sort of contract it has with the Corporation of London's management. Over time, a relationship of confidence and trust has been established. The norms for conduct have evolved through a dialogue that, though asymmetrical (mourners have generated much of the grave elaboration), is nonetheless comprehended, accepted and expected by everyone concerned. Moderation of the strong emotions associated with death and loss is managed through a culture of tidiness and order, both at the gravesite and across the cemetery landscape.

Such a state of play, in the sense that it is consensus driven, parallels that at Bushey United Jewish Cemetery. It stands in contrast to the arrangements prevailing at New Southgate and Woodgrange Park Cemeteries, at the other end of our continuum of relationships between users and managers.

Visiting Animates Stone and Garden: New Southgate Cemetery

The Cypriot Greek Orthodox sections of New Southgate Cemetery present a complex, activity-filled landscape. Most graves – each with its inscribed stone, its glass case for the *kandele,* which should burn constantly, and often with a photograph of the deceased – are set within their own gardens of potted plants in colourful profusion.[39] The two elements, stone and garden, are spoken of as the inextricably linked ideal, the more extensive and elaborate the better. Some plots, which can be three or four metres square, have seats or benches and resemble a garden or patio in a way to which graves at City of London Cemetery can only allude (Fig. 5.2). Such plots offer great scope for regular activity, and mourners are drawn to the grave often to attend to its upkeep.

Indeed, it is visiting the grave that animates and validates it to perpetuate the memory of the deceased – a doctrine that is explicit in Greek Orthodox theology and in Greek practice. Without visiting, the grave has no purpose, and the unremembered dead become a rebuke to the Greek Orthodox and Cypriot community. In Greek Orthodoxy, regular memorialization of the deceased through cemetery rituals is a religious and moral requirement that benefits both the living and the dead. Forgetting by 'moving on' or 'getting over' the death is anathema and is perceived as a fate worse than death. This dedication to visiting has consequences for the nature of mourners' interactions with the grave plot, the cemetery site and the owner-managers of New Southgate.

The first anniversary of a death and the subsequent annual memorials at church and cemetery are the most heavily attended of all Greek Orthodox mourning events. Held on the Sunday nearest the anniversary, memorials in church are so heavily attended, even by those

Figure 5.2.
Benches, pots of flowers and miniature trees create a grave garden at New Southgate Cemetery, 1998.

who may not ordinarily go to church, that people say, 'We should thank God for the dead, for they bring the living to church.' Large groups of people, often made up of three or four generations, make their way to the cemetery after the church service to attend the grave ritual and prayers. The bereaved family prepares *koliva*, the customary wheat dish, and take a special bread, *prosphoro*, to the church and the cemetery, distributing them to everyone in memory of the deceased. Thus religious obligations to commemorate the dead are discharged, to be repeated at subsequent memorials and on important occasions when the grave will be visited.

In between ritual occasions, much private visiting takes place, to check on the grave and work on the garden. The *kandele* is evidence that the grave has been regularly and frequently visited. The lights flickering in the glass boxes in the Greek Orthodox section of New Southgate distinguish it in a visually striking manner. 'By keeping the flame alight, the deceased's memory does not fade; it's as though the light on the grave shows us the continuity of their existence.'

At least two ritual tasks may be performed even during ordinary visits. One is the burning of incense and olive leaves, which is done at each visit to purify and sanctify the grave. Sometimes the olive leaves are taken to the church to be blessed before they are brought to the cemetery. The other ritual is the watering of the grave, which is not only part of tending the plants but also has symbolic meaning, because dry earth is bereft of life and denotes lack of care. 'Watering the grave refreshes it and the deceased. A watered grave is a grave that is cared for and looked after – it has the potential to sustain life.' These ritual practices, along with the need to keep a complicated grave and vigorous garden tidy and under control, provide many opportunities – or obligations – to visit the cemetery.

Traditionally in rural Cypriot communities, death and cemetery rituals were associated with women, especially the responsibility for looking after the grave. Women prepared the funeral and memorial foods, arranged the ecclesiastical memorials, prepared the body for burial, lamented the deceased and made regular visits to the grave to perform the various rituals. Usually, elderly female relatives assumed a prominent role in these activities. In London's Greek Orthodox community, such activities are no longer so strictly gendered. Men and women visit the cemetery in almost equal numbers, often arriving as family groups and representing all generations. Although it is still the older women of the household who are more likely to prepare the *koliva,* both men and women participate in the cemetery rituals and tend the grave garden. Younger visitors, nonetheless, are more likely to depend on older relatives to carry out some of the religious rituals: 'If my mother and her sisters were not here or they couldn't prepare the *koliva* or come to the cemetery, I would do it, or my brother would do it. I don't know what the rituals mean but I would do them anyway because this is what she [my grandmother] would have wanted.' A typical distribution of tasks was described by this young woman:

> A lot of the things we do at the grave are part of our religious duty. And I am happy to do it. I wouldn't feel guilty if I didn't; no one is forcing me to do this. I want to be here. I bring her cards and flowers, and my gran does the *kabnisma* and lights the *kandele.* My uncle cleans the headstone and comes here more regularly, especially in the summer to water the plants on the grave, because he works close by.

The pattern of visiting for the Greek Orthodox in London has altered from that usually seen in Cyprus. Whereas Saturdays were normally allocated to cemetery visiting in Cyprus, the popular time to visit at New Southgate is on a Sunday after the church service. Name days, falling on the annual festival of the saint for whom the deceased was named, would have drawn visitors to the Cypriot cemetery; birthdays generally substitute for name days in present-day London.

Along with other Londoners, Cypriots in large numbers visit graves at Christmas, Easter, Mother's Day and Father's Day. Second-generation Cypriots often explain that being near the grave provides a stronger sense of consolation in their experience of bereavement than going to church or praying. Loss and love are expressed by bringing special flowers and ensuring that the grave is well looked after. Planting, weeding, watering, cleaning and incense burning all justify one's being near the deceased in active and purposeful modes. Still and silent contemplation or praying by the grave is no longer the norm in the Greek Orthodox section. The cemetery becomes a public arena for active expression of the significance of the loss.

The grave garden, initiated in the first year, matures to become an important conduit for the regular expression of strong emotions of grief. In turn, those emotions are materially transformed into a highly visible, elaborate garden that demands continuing attention through visitation. It might be argued that theological and spiritual concerns with the deceased's soul, which are purportedly in decline, have been transferred to the body, which, in its grave, becomes the object of attention for the bereaved. Whereas death itself and the preparation of the body have largely been turned over to professionals in modern secular society, thereby leaving survivors out of direct involvement with the dead, the cemetery invites a set of activities at the grave and garden that enable survivors to remember and remain connected with the deceased.

The various actors involved in grieving rituals for the Greek Orthodox dead include the Church, the funeral directors, the cemetery managers and staff, and the bereaved themselves. In the immediate and longer term, each of these can act, individually or collectively, to hinder or facilitate the grieving process. Insofar as mourners perceive their grieving to be hindered, their experience of loss can be exacerbated. At New Southgate Cemetery, where people purchase grave plots from the owner-managers and thus consider themselves rightfully entitled to maintain the plots as they wish, the Greek Cypriot cultural emphasis on frequent visiting and creation of elaborate gardens and memorials can occasionally result in tension between users and managers.

One study participant, for example, concluded that the cemetery management would 'like us not to come back once the funeral is over; they don't want us to visit, we get in their way. The less time we spend there, the better for them; the less we do to the grave, the better for them.' Such sentiments were voiced less explicitly at other cemeteries, though we heard hints that, beyond the common rhetoric of caring for the dead and the bereaved, grave owners and cemetery management had goals that could be divergent. At New Southgate, the transformation of the grave into a small garden, already seen in moderated form at CLCC, is a laborious enterprise. As each grave becomes a unique and individually crafted garden, expressing something of the deceased and the bereaved, management is likely to say that mourners 'see the grave as their own personal garden'. This is at odds with the owners' perspective on how the cemetery should be managed as a public place where individual emotion must be contained in order for all mourners' expressions of grief to be facilitated.

Cemetery users' urges to place boundaries around the grave or the garden seem generally to be strong. Where the grave garden is sizeable and houses many accoutrements to mourning, boundary marking and securing assume even greater strength. Many types of enclosures are placed around graves at New Southgate, even soon after burial. These are not simple demarcations of ownership and possession but signify the identity of, and protection for, the grave and the body. Although management at New Southgate does not raise the same objection to fencing as at the City of London Cemetery – that it interferes with maintenance – they are keenly alert to the appropriation of territory, not least because other grave owners are likely to resent and challenge the encroachment. From a managerial perspective, placing large paving stones around the grave is an expansionist strategy and must be controlled. The bereaved state other rationales: 'We put the paving stones so that we could have somewhere dry to stand, especially in winter when everything is so muddy.' They may also voice concern over the lack of security guards at the cemetery, suggesting that the graves are vulnerable to theft and vandalism and need to be individually secured in the absence of organizational security measures.

Greek Orthodox study participants occasionally articulated what they viewed as restrictive practices. They occasionally spoke with some force. Referring to his wife's grave in the separate section owned by Saint Sophia Cathedral and controlled by its committee, one man said:

> When I buried my wife here I was the first in this section to put iron railings. It makes the grave more secure; it looks much better. I grew plants up the railings and as you can see it's like a walled beautiful garden. It's for her, she loved her flowers and her garden, and it's what she would have liked. I am a scientist, I don't really believe in the existence of souls – it's for love. . . . The bishop told me to take the railings down or he would instruct others to pull them down . . . . Why don't they leave us alone to deal with our loss and pain in our own way?

The cemetery manager suggested that the different, more lenient standards permitted in the Saint Sophia Cathedral section of New Southgate set problematic examples for mourners with graves in other parts of the cemetery. The grave owners disputed this, but it indicates that management may not always be seen as consistent or predictable. This is quite different from the situations at Bushey and City of London Cemeteries, where notions of consensus among mourners and between management and mourners determine conduct – and the landscape that emerges from such activity.

The strong sense of individual or family responsibility for Greek Orthodox graves at New Southgate, though it undoubtedly arises from long-established Greek Cypriot custom, may also receive a boost from management's rather 'arm's length' approach to service delivery – an approach that is increasingly associated with greater deregulation in the United Kingdom. That is, the 'end user', client, or customer ostensibly has control, in this case over the grave plot, but within limits set by service owners, often private-sector entrepreneurs. The entrepreneurs' ultimate goal is maximizing profits from their asset – the cemetery site. Commercial operations sometimes require rapid changes in strategy, in order to keep costs in line with revenues, but such shifts can appear to cemetery users simply as inconsistency and unpredictability in policy. Moreover, reinvestment of part of New Southgate's profits in infrastructure and support services, though appreciated by users, may seem erratic. Some people suggest that these improvements 'arise more from commercial requirements. . . .' This may be the case in a privately owned business where turnover and profit are of concern. This view differs from users' perceptions at Bushey and CLCC, where there is across-the-board agreement that an acceptable proportion of revenue will be ploughed back into the grounds to maintain infrastructure.

At New Southgate, the religious, familial and social injunction to remember the dead is expressed through long-term commemorative practices of attending both memorial and garden. The Greek Cypriot patterns of frequent cemetery visiting and highly individualized elaboration of stone and plot, as well as mourners' concerns over the security of the grave, are often perceived by users to be at odds with the priorities, policies and practices of management. Dynamic tension, rather than negotiated consensus, appears, from the perspective of mourners, to characterize relations between users and owner-managers. This interpretation helps to explain the uniquely exuberant appearance of the Anglo-Greek memorial landscape at New Southgate Cemetery.

Old Stones, New Stones and Changing Visitors

At the time of our fieldwork, the cemetery at Woodgrange Park was being transformed by an increasing volume of burials of Bangladeshi and Gujarati Muslim immigrants and the cessation of burials representing the original East End English population, even though the latter continues to hold grave space and burial rights. The Muslims who now live in the area are making financial and emotional investments in Woodgrange Park Cemetery at an accelerating rate. Consequently, Woodgrange is a somewhat 'contested' territory. The private owners and the site manager, who is present daily and has a detailed knowledge of the cemetery, mediate an implicit and subdued contest between the incoming and the outgoing groups. A number of strategies are open to the cemetery owners as they find unused space and sell it to the Muslim community for single-depth graves. Space in the earlier, nineteenth-century graves, which were dug deep enough to accommodate large families, remains available because many of these graves were never fully used. The disruptions of two world wars and repeated economic upheavals meant that local families dispersed and burials took place elsewhere. The upper spaces can now legitimately be used, because human remains are unlikely to be disturbed.

Many of our mostly male Muslim informants denied that long-term memorialization of the dead through a focus on material symbols such as gravestones and gardens was important to them at all. Instead, they focused on visiting the cemetery to pray for the deceased's soul. Many of the Muslim families who use Woodgrange live near the cemetery, and following a burial, visiting is frequent. Some male family members may visit more than once a day, and certainly several times a week. This intensity of visiting is likely to be maintained for several months and sometimes longer. For example, a father visiting the grave of his thirty-day-old child, dead three months, said: 'I come three or four times a week now. Less than before, but I cannot forget him and have to come.'

Some Muslim participants said that Islamic custom was to resist extravagance at the grave. 'Once one dies, the body does not last long. It is the spirit that does. Why pay too much attention to protecting the body and then go on to forget the soul?' They also described an unworldly approach to maintaining the grave:

> There is no requirement in the system of Islam to clean the grave. After death the body and all physical things have ended. All that matters are the spiritual things. We are not thinking of these things growing all over here [pointing to a six-foot-high bank

of brambles]; this does not matter to us because what we do here is all for the spirit and for the glory of Allah, peace be upon him.

Another Muslim mourner, however, made the following remark about habitual treatment of the grave when family members visit: 'First we cleared away the leaves and the small weeds. We changed the flowers; then we prayed the prayers from the Qur'an. It is our duty.' And many indicated that they were uncomfortable with the disorder that had prevailed in the cemetery until quite recently:

It must smell nice – it should be like home – that's the most important thing. There shouldn't be all this rubbish like this, it might make people not want to come and visit if it just looks like a junkyard. Some people are frightened and they think, 'I don't want to go there, with all the dead bodies,' so it should be clean so that it's like home. I say my prayers from the Qur'an, then I say a prayer for everyone in the graveyard.

Whether disorder around the grave indeed represents an Islamic preoccupation with the spiritual and the afterlife, to the neglect of the mundane, is questionable for those who now bury their dead at Woodgrange. We found evidence, as illustrated in the preceding quotation, that certain aspects of the disorder are as disturbing to Muslims as to English Christian users of the cemetery. Muslims expressed just as much distress over broken gravestones as did members of the older English population. Broken stones hint at vandalism and sometimes racism and generate intense anxiety as well as anger. The cemetery terrain went equally unprotected for both groups until management fenced and secured the perimeter in 2001. Apparently the newer clients, engendering a vital cash flow for the cemetery owners, command more attention when they complain. The older users have exerted some influence by forming a group called Friends of Woodgrange, but they have waning expectations that their traditions will continue to be upheld, not least because they do not generate income to the same extent as the Asian Muslims.

The Muslim graves at Woodgrange Park Cemetery show that such burials have taken place from the 1960s onwards. The memorials that mark the earliest clusters of Muslim graves, representing the first – generally male – immigrants from Bangladesh and Gujarat, are modest and plain. They are in white stone, sometimes rectangular, sometimes with the horseshoe-shaped Muslim arch. Inscribed with black lettering in English, they give the deceased's name and place of birth, along with the date of death. A more recently established cluster of graves also records the exact time of death. An Arabic inscription invoking the Prophet as Allah's messenger is always on the stone, generally below the personal details. There is little evidence of plantings at the early graves, and it is unlikely that anything more than the strewing of cut flowers was done at the time of the burial. Islam does not encourage elaboration at the grave or extravagant embellishment or decoration.

Nearly half a century later, Muslim burials at Woodgrange continue to be those of immigrants – first and second generation – from the same regions. Up until the mid-1990s, when our fieldwork started, graves tended to be as simple as the ones just described. Since then, two parallel trends have led to greater elaboration of graves. First, numbers of burials have increased markedly. This represents an Islamicization of cemetery space and an accompanying intensity in the 'consecration' of the land. The increase in burials is a demographic inevitability as Muslims increasingly choose burial in the United Kingdom instead of repatriation, often because family formation has reached three generations and there are now grandchildren to visit grandparents' graves.

The generational changes that help anchor the family in London are accompanied by economic changes within families and across the Muslim community that uses Woodgrange. Greater wealth – though still modest – is displayed in the extensive improvements that can be seen in nearby housing occupied by this group. It may not be unreasonable to attribute the appearance of larger, more elaborate gravestones in the cemetery to this upturn in economic fortunes. There is some supporting evidence in that quite substantial stones are now being placed on some of the earlier, 1980s burials. Increasingly, the temporary brass and wooden plaques that mark new burials are being replaced by memorial stones more closely resembling those chosen by users of, for example, the City of London Cemetery. Islamic injunctions against spending appear to have been somewhat relaxed with the more recent Muslim burials and their grave gardens at Woodgrange Park (Fig. 5.3).

At the same time, Muslim features persist. The grave continues to be oriented towards the east, and the headstone reflects this. Arabic inscriptions continue to appear, though the personal details of the deceased are more extensive and the epitaphs, resembling those on indigenous memorials, are more likely to be inscribed in English. For example, the epitaphs 'Beloved mother/father' and 'In loving memory', as well as references to kinship relationships, are common on newer Muslim gravestones. Shrubs and flowers now appear inside the concrete kerb surrounding the grave.

Figure 5.3.
A recent Muslim grave with stone and garden, Woodgrange Park Cemetery, 2002.

The contract between Muslim mourners and Woodgrange manage-ment is for the digging of a suitable grave; management generally makes no wider commitment to maintain the plot or the cemetery for either Muslims or Christians. One consequence of this style of opera-tion – which offers certain freedoms – is great discontent on the part of the original English users, who see a cemetery landscape with which they have had long family connections changing in radical ways. Many of the original monuments have been broken up for removal, though the Friends of Woodgrange have 'rescued' a number of the older stones and continue to try to protect what is left of its heritage.

A different strategy has been adopted by the Patel Trust, a group of Muslims who have purchased a piece of land from the cemetery owners. This fenced compound, once marked by the graves of English East Enders, has been cleared of monuments and top-filled so that new graves can be dug. Surrounding this enclave, within the fencing, is a boundary of Leyland cypress trees that provides a dense, high screen. This section is markedly different from the open and wilder Muslim areas. The gate is always closed – though not always locked – and has a notice prohibiting entrance to anyone 'unauthorized'. Alongside is another plot, leased rather than owned, yet to be fenced, but displaying a sign of the East End Muslim Welfare Trust.

Whereas order, achieved through generous funding and enforced regulations, is the hallmark of the City of London Cemetery, disorder is said to characterize Woodgrange. While CLCC has embarked upon an experimental programme to establish user advisory groups as a focus for negotiation between management and clients, Woodgrange continues to organize negotiation at the individual level: face-to-face between the client and the site manager or via his mobile telephone when emergencies arise. The Friends of Woodgrange group has managed to exert some influence over some management decisions. The group's capacity to 'negotiate' has been backed by the Woodgrange Park Cemetery Act, but is still minimal.

The long-term commemoration practices of the Muslim communities that bury at Woodgrange take the form of annual visits to the cemetery on the holy day of Eyd, at the end of Ramadan. Such visits to the cemetery site itself, as well as to specific, individual graves, are acts of remembrance at the level of community and collectivity for all the Muslim dead. Men, dressed in prayer clothes, visit in large groups and recite traditional prayers near the area of Muslim graves. There is evidence, however, that with the second generation, some of these practices are changing. Just as the style of memorials is evolving, there are suggestions that new forms of commemoration are being developed. How these practices will affect relations between users and owners and how they will be reflected in the cemetery landscape will be seen with the third generation, who were born in Britain and often knew and lived near their grandparents.

Conclusion

As the anthropologist W. Lloyd Warner wrote, 'The cemetery is an enduring physical emblem, a substantial and visible symbol of the agreement among individuals that they will not let each other die.'[40] Once the first year of mourning has ended and grief moves on to an extended trajectory of years and even decades, how do constellations of activity around the stone and garden and the contractual or informal agreements between mourners and cemetery managers support or interrupt the establishment of preferred patterns of memorialization? To what extent do people at each of our four study sites, and by extension at other cemeteries, manage to re-craft a sense of self and identity by making links with the deceased at the grave and through the garden? How is the cemetery a place where ongoing grief is managed?

At the City of London Cemetery, agreement, accommodation and trust obtain between users and management. The tidiness and upkeep of the grounds tacitly signify safety, confidence and support – the landscape demonstrates that both management and mourners are prepared to take care of the dead in respectful ways. This balance of trust, sustained by the safe, orderly and accessible grounds, has encouraged a shared cemetery culture built on the English interest in gardens. This and associated rites of memory have now become omnipresent at the City of London Cemetery, where many mourners reported that they had never gardened before but were learning through the examples of others.

At Woodgrange, too, there is also a lot of learning going on. Here it is the newcomers, the Bangladeshi and Gujarati Muslims, who are transposing and adapting patterns of grave attendance to a new cultural setting. The data suggest a degree of accommodation with local custom – for instance, in adopting a more Western style of memorial stone and practices of gardening – but this may be as much for convenience as a reflection of assimilation. The laissez-faire approach of management, with few restrictions, provides an open atmosphere that allows for these processes of cultural adaptation and assimilation as well as statements of group identification. At the same time, it creates an atmosphere of insecurity because of the lack of overall cemetery maintenance. This feeling pertains to the newer Muslim users but is particularly acute for the increasingly displaced original English population. What is certain, however, is that the purchasing power of the Muslim group is such that the cemetery management has recently found it worthwhile to make accessibility and security greater priorities than previously, when the original grave owners – no longer a source of income – were numerically dominant.

The memorial stones of mourners at Bushey United Jewish Cemetery and the stones and gardens at CLCC appear relatively uniform, and users are reminded when they persist in breaching communal conventions and managerial rules. This climate of supervision at both sites (in contrast to that at Woodgrange) is accompanied by a sense of security that can encourage regular and even frequent visiting. New

Southgate mourners, as well as those at CLCC, may attempt to resist or circumvent managers' regulations; and such acts may result in management's reappraisal of what is appropriate for the stones and the plantings. As the former superintendent of CLCC said: 'They're the customers, you have to cater for their needs.' Accommodating, as it does, several denominational groups, New Southgate has to manage in such a way that flexibility sometimes outweighs consistency.

Other interesting comparisons can be made among the four study sites as well. For instance, burials at Bushey and Woodgrange are managed according to religious precepts that everyone concerned accepts, yet the landscapes of the two cemeteries appear very different – one highly ordered, the other less so – and must be interpreted differently. Burial in the Greek Orthodox sections of New Southgate, too, is framed by theological and ritual customs with which all concerned are well acquainted, but this site is again different from either Woodgrange or Bushey. A great deal of individualistic interpretation intervenes between Greek Orthodox theology and practices observed at the grave, and this introduces levels of improvisation similar to those at City of London Cemetery. City of London may lie at a distance from these three religiously formed cemeteries in that mourners there are much freer to move among secular, spiritual, ecological and religious idioms as they create grave gardens that allow the kind of long-term memorialization they consider appropriate.

What we see in these four cemeteries – and we suggest that to some extent our observations may be generalized to other cemetery sites – are patterns of visiting and styles of tending stones and plants, along with sets of rules and regulatory practices, that combine to produce very different landscapes. The characteristics of the resulting landscapes are not limited to the aesthetic. We argue not only that the character and mood of a cemetery arise from habitual activity and disposition on the part of users and managers but that this atmosphere in turn generates the material and emotional conditions for future mourning. This is essential for mourners because grief is ongoing. At the same time, mourners who visit cemeteries come to acknowledge the secret and coded idiom that shapes what is acceptable as the expression of private grief in a public place – the grave in the cemetery. Just as the urge to bound the grave with fences and ornamental stones is thwarted by management, so any impulse to emotional excess is restrained and contained by pressures exerted through the coded cemetery idiom, expressed in stones, plants, visiting patterns and the wider cemetery landscape.

We argue, then, that an optimum level of regulatory activity on the part of managers is required for the emergence of the coded cemetery idiom. Where regulation is too heavy handed and restrictive, the code cannot be developed, learnt and practised, so that mourning is felt as unsatisfactory and may be displaced to another arena, possibly to the domestic setting. Where managerial activity is absent, partial, or unpredictable, mourners may be reluctant to invest effort and other resources in establishing a grave for the longer term. Again, the coded language, built upon a 'syntax' of tidiness and order of stone and plants, more or less elaborated, will be stunted where nature, particularly the overgrowth of vegetation and the erosion and decay of inscribed stones, chokes development and expression. 'It's a cemetery I can't settle in; it seems a shame you pay for a stone and grave and it's not kept tidy.' Insofar as they experience frustration in attempts to impose order on nature, to build elaborate structures of significance for grieving, or even to visit in safety with the desired regularity, mourners will be compelled to turn away from the grave to find other ways to contextualize their loss. Sometimes this will mean displacement of memorialization to places that express affiliations other than that of the cemetery community, which so many of our informants had found to be enriching and supportive.

6

Keeping Kin and Kinship Alive

The continuity of the relationship between the living and the dead is a result of their mutual dependence as well as their mutual identity, what remains of the dead in us and what the dead have taken away that is ours.

Maria Catedra, *This World, Other Worlds: Sickness, Suicide, Death, and the Afterlife among the Vaqueiros de Alzada of Spain*

In his classic 1970 study of kinship in London, Raymond Firth briefly discussed the social significance of the dead by noting how people continually referred to their deceased kin with affection and cited them as links in family genealogies.[1] In this chapter we expand Firth's study into uncharted terrain in order to examine ongoing ties between the living and the deceased. We ask about the content, meaning and duration of the relationships that surviving family members renegotiate and reconstruct with their deceased kin (particularly their parents, siblings, spouses and children) and about how the cemetery-centred practices linking the living with the dead and the living with the living constitute an arena for the creation of culture and the making and performance of memory.

By talking with mourners at the City of London Cemetery and Bushey United Jewish Cemetery – where the visitor populations have been resident in London long enough to have buried three or more generations of family members – and by discovering whose graves they visited and why, we learned that at least this self-selected group wishes keenly to maintain ties of kinship and connection with the dead.[2] Its members do so by tending the graves, talking with the deceased and spending contemplative time in the presence of the deceased's memory. And through this behaviour, they enact an ethos of kinship that values reciprocity between generations and certain cultural definitions of a devoted parent, grandparent and child. Parents and grandparents bring children to the cemetery with the aim of inculcating these principles and practices of memory (Figs. 6.1 and 6.2).

Whereas most studies of kinship in Western industrial society do not include the actual (as opposed to the ideal) practices of mourners toward deceased family members, in this chapter we explore this area and ask how mourners determine how they wish to behave toward

Figure 6.1.
A woman at the City of London Cemetery contributed this photograph of herself visiting the cemetery as a little girl.

Figure 6.2.

As an adult years later, the woman shown as a child in Figure 6.1 tends a family grave at the City of London Cemetery.

their dead kin. Individual judgement[3] is shown to influence bereavement activities, and personal choice moderates learned ideas of moral obligation and responsibility.[4] As one study participant explained: 'Visiting the cemetery is a degree of choice, not obligation – I still only visit relatives I particularly knew and am fond of.'[5]

Although scholars have explored cemeteries as public sites for the cultural performance of rites of mourning and commemoration, cemeteries also offer intimate, private spaces for the ongoing construction of personal memory and meaning. It is the quiet of the cemetery that many mourners say provides the atmosphere, the private time and space needed to address grief. 'Here . . . you're in a different frame of mind, and the pace of life is different.' By talking with mourners about their private conversations with the deceased and by examining cemetery visiting patterns, we have been able to chart the meaning of the dead across the survivor's life course. We begin by examining visits made to the graves of parents by mourners of different ages. Throughout the chapter we concentrate on both maintenance of kinship and the private, emotional interaction in which each mourner engages in the public ritual space of the cemetery.

Visits to Parents' Graves

The religious injunction to 'honour thy father and mother' and the Orthodox Jewish prescription to mourn parents for one year and to visit their graves annually underscore an internalized sense of moral responsibility that some children at both Bushey and City of London Cemeteries felt toward their deceased parents. 'To come to the cemetery is a duty, but not a tiresome duty.' 'I would get this odd twinge if I did not come and make this little pilgrimage.' Some cemetery visitors, however, rejected religious precepts in favour of more private feelings of respect and affection: 'This is a sentimental journey, to relive memories, show respect; it is a personal, not a religious journey.' The deceased were sometimes seen to reinforce the moral obligation and sentiments of parental honour. They expected to be visited and made their wishes known: 'She talked to me when I was washing up at the sink: "Are you coming out to see me?"' 'I feel she might be sitting above in eternity and looking down and not see a stone on the grave.' 'She'll look down and say, "My Ann's making that garden for me."'[6]

Implicit in every decision to visit the graves of parents was a code of intergenerational reciprocity. This ethos included the cultural ideals of a 'proper' mum and a 'good' dad. 'I had a good mother; a good mother cares for her children and brings them up the right way.' 'We had good parents, they always put us first, before themselves.' Mourners held expectations concerning the appropriate duties of parents toward children, and it was the parents' having fulfilled this role that some gave as the reason supporting their visit. That is, at a much later stage and in a different way, cemetery visitors repaid the services their parents had performed in raising them in their early years. 'I like to come, my parents were devoted to me. I can repay them in some way.'

Most City of London study participants who were born in the East End described their mothers in traditional, idealized terms as women who had raised many children, often took in additional work 'to put food on the table', and were there as a source of comfort and emotional support. 'She was always a shoulder to cry on. . . . If you were poorly, she was there to take care of you.' Before the mother's death, adult children would meet regularly at her home, and her pivotal presence kept siblings close. The 'typical' East End father, in contrast, worked long hours and went to the pub on Saturday and Sunday afternoons, but his companionship, advice and supportive counsel, particularly concerning matters of work, were valued. When queried, mourners from other cultural groups also articulated the attributes of a good parent. In more well-to-do Orthodox Jewish families, for example, the emphasis was on moral training, whereas in less well-off Jewish homes, a 'good mother' was described differently:

> She shouts at the family occasionally, always puts food on the table and is worried and concerned about you – about all her family and the extended family. [She is] someone who gets money to help others, takes the husband's [son-in-law's] side over the daughter, is a font of all knowledge and will do without to give to her children first.

For many adult children, it was the fact that the parent had never abandoned them that underpinned their commitment to visit. One City of London woman broke into tears as she explained why she and her husband still tended the grave of her mother, who had died thirty years before: 'It's my duty. She was a proper mother: a proper mum looks after you, she thinks the world of you, she never leaves you. She never left us.' Importantly, many mourners described their relationship with each parent differently, often depicting a closer connection with one over the other. Although many people visited the graves of both parents, they did so with subtle differences in behaviour that revealed how public memorial conventions were privately manipulated to convey contrasting feelings. As one City of London daughter explained: 'She was not very close; I was closer to his [her husband's] dad than my Mum. I have no feeling when I read her stone, but I do with my father-in-law. . . . I read both his name and the verse each time, but I do not always read the bottom part of Mum's [inscription].'

City of London study participants interpreted the choice of earth burial over other forms of disposal as entailing an implicit commitment to visit and maintain the grave of a parent. 'If you decide to have a grave, the family should look after it. If not, it is best to choose cremation.' 'If you're not going to come, why go through the motions of a stone?' Frequently, however, it was only one person within the family who accepted and fulfilled this unwritten contract, usually someone who had already selected himself or herself as the 'designated mourner'. One City of London mourner explained this kinship principle: 'It's in you to come or not; it's related to the kind of relationship you had before they died. I was over there every week to see my Mum. I visit my sisters and know the family news.' In many traditional East End families, it was either the oldest or the youngest daughter who assumed the customary responsibility for living close by and caring for the mother in her old age. As the 'closest' child, she inherited her mother's jewellery and visited her grave. 'You have a responsibility as the youngest child. I was there for her and helped her.

I got her ring, sovereign, watch and bracelet, and I will pass these on to my own daughter.'

We found it difficult to learn more about family members who chose not to visit the cemetery; study participants had accepted their absence and did not question their reasons. One Bushey woman was typical in her explanation: 'I feel the need to come, but my sister does not feel this need, nor does my younger brother, and they do not come.' In a few cases, we heard explanations such as the following for not visiting: 'It upsets her too much, she can't handle it.' 'He believes that once you go, you're gone, your spirit is gone.' 'He feels their memory lives in your heart and your head, and you don't need to come to the cemetery to express your grief.' Many families had no tradition of going to the burial ground. As one son at Bushey Cemetery explained: 'My parents had no expectation of my visiting their grave, and I was not brought up to go.' In still other cases, the non-visitor lived too far away or was too elderly or unwell to visit, or had chosen other places to remember.[7]

Sometimes the parent's perceived lack of support through desertion or divorce was the expressed reason for not visiting the grave, for choosing to forget. One United Synagogue daughter, for example, was sent away to boarding school while her sister was kept at home with their mother after their father's death. This woman no longer remembered where her mother was buried and did not visit. In some such cases, the kinship connection had long been gone: 'I lost track of my mother, they broke up when I was six and some relatives raised me.' 'I lost contact with my mother many, many years ago.' 'I do not visit my mother's grave. She left the family, I was fourteen at the time.' And in a notable case reported at the City of London Cemetery, the epitaph 'Sadly Missed by Wife and Family' was scratched out on one gravestone and 'Child Abuser' written instead.[8]

Visits to the graves of parents were thus based on an internalized sense of duty that was mediated by an underlying code of reciprocity between generations. In most cases, the decision to visit the cemetery was an individual one, often acknowledged and accepted before the parent's death. Because analysis of the data suggested that differences in the meaning of cemetery visits were age related, in the following sections we examine the nature of visits at different times in the life course.

Visits by Elderly Children to Parents' Graves

For people seventy-five and older who still visited the graves of their parents, memories ('of both the good and the bad times, the trouble and the headaches'), respect and affection were what endured over time.[9] A City of London couple in their late seventies articulated the continuing feelings of grief shared by many older persons when they remarked, 'It don't matter how many years it is, it never goes away' (Fig. 6.3). Many older persons reported that when they stood in front of the stone they were able to 'visualize' the deceased, and through this process of 'seeing' they were able to recall life shared in the past, 'like mementoes of reflection'. A Jewish couple in their late eighties who had been visiting Bushey Cemetery since the wife's father had died forty-five years earlier explained: 'We still come to the cemetery and still think of our parents and see them as they were. You think in your mind, we do not talk, but stand and visualize and say the prayers.' An elderly City of London woman explained further how the cemetery visit was a purposeful time of memory of the years when her parents were still living: 'In my mind I talk to them about the earlier years and what we used to do . . . when we were younger and how everything used to be.'

Figure 6.3.
Many older couples continue to visit the graves of parents. City of London Cemetery.

For these people, cemetery visits encouraged reflection on past experiences when parents were still alive and thereby provided continuity between older and younger selves by linking past activities with present lives. Grief and a sense of loss continued but were coloured by positive recollections: 'When they are gone, you put things into focus and forget about the bad. It sifts out the bad, and now it is only the nice things I remember.'

For the very old, frail, or chronically ill, trips to the cemetery were often accompanied by an awareness of their own impending mortality. 'This is my last visit to see my mother's grave. I am very ill and will not come again.' In the senior generation, the wish to put both worldly and otherworldly affairs in order was often the meaning attributed to the cemetery visit.[10] One 99-year-old Jewish woman, for example, requested that her niece bring her to Bushey so that she could see her own reserved grave plot: 'Now I will have a long talk with my nephew and ask him to say Kaddish for me; I want to leave everything in order.' A 73-year-old man who had had four heart attacks in the previous eighteen months came to the City of London Cemetery specifically to plant the family grave. In his conversations, he subtly explained that he had chosen to expend his limited energy on activities that signified a tying up of loose ends, an acknowledgement of his ongoing duty as caretaker of the dead and a preparation for his own demise. 'It will not be long before I get in here,' he said. Such cemetery visits suggest that some older people come to place themselves between the domains of this world and the next.

Often, older persons who traveled to the cemetery by public transport were forced to postpone visits because of illness or inclement weather.[11] Each day they assessed the state of their health and the cold and wet, and when all conditions were passable, they seized the opportunity. 'I came today because I might not be able to come next week. I do what I can, when I can.' These people often made it 'easier' on themselves by coming less frequently, by not visiting during the winter months and by cutting back on plot maintenance. 'I made it easy on myself and plant geraniums, which get on without water.' For some older City of London visitors, even the small plot had become demanding: 'Sometimes it's nice to have just the stone, to express feelings without a garden. When it's new, you come regularly. Time goes on, you get older, and the gardens get neglected.' Thus, for many older persons the cemetery visit signalled an acknowledgement, acceptance and expectation of their own mortality and also stood as a significant accomplishment that demonstrated their ongoing participation in meaningful activities.

Elderly people who were no longer able to visit the cemetery devised strategies to maintain involvement with the graves of parents and thus to ensure that they were properly tended. One City of London woman still accompanied her children to the cemetery, even though she was unable to leave the car. She participated by paying for the Christmas wreaths used to decorate the family graves, handmaking the small bouquets of flowers for the cremation plaques and, upon leaving the cemetery, providing the pound coin 'to thank the guards for taking care of the dead'.[12] When they could no longer visit, some pensioners hired cemetery staff to maintain the plot or left arrangements of plastic flowers so that the grave had some colour. Others received a full report from children, nieces or nephews who visited in their stead. Such ongoing interest revealed the significance of the cemetery as a place of connection and people's continuing sense of responsibility that the graves be tended.

Visits by Middle-aged Children to Parents' Graves

The cemetery visit made at Christmas or the Jewish New Year, on the death or birth date and on Mothering Sunday or Father's Day was often a time of emotional catharsis for persons who had lost parents in mid-life. As one middle-aged daughter explained about her visit before the Jewish New Year: "You store up grief all through the year and it is appropriate to unload, to off-load at the graveside. I do not know how I will feel until I'm here. . . . It is a question of the interaction of the weather and my feelings. It is in public, but here I can quietly cry.' Another Jewish woman described the ongoing pain of loss through a metaphor of the cemetery landscape: 'We always come home exhausted; it is a bleak, cold, sterile place. Yet it always rekindles the richness of the life we had and the learning to live without the people you loved. It's a hard road, leaving empty spaces which you can never fill up.'

For others, the contemplative atmosphere may prove too emotionally demanding: 'It is not an easy thing to come to the cemetery; your emotions are recalled, you think of your own mortality. I should go, but when you go to your father's grave, it is much more than your father's grave.'

The remembered experience of coming to the grounds with an elderly parent who was now interred in the same grave was a significant component of cemetery emotions for many middle-aged visitors.[13] For some, part of the experience was the acknowledgement of a pledge to maintain the grave: 'My dad kept it as it is now and I told him I would keep it.'

Many adult children in their fifties and sixties brought family concerns with them to the graves of their parents. During cemetery visits, the wisdom, moral authority, advocacy, approval and support of the deceased might be sought. In these cases, the cemetery visit was not just delayed compensation for services rendered in childhood but also a request for the continuation of support and guidance. The deaths of the senior generation had left many people with increased family responsibilities, and some middle-aged persons used the occasion of the commemorative visit to reflect on family issues from the perspective of their parents. 'I'm the patriarch of the family now, I have no older brother; it's all up to me to make decisions, there is no one past me.' Despite sometimes ambivalent feelings toward a parent – 'My relationship with my mother was not good, she was a difficult woman.' – cemetery visits were a strategy for gaining guidance on family matters. 'You come to the cemetery when something is wrong; you come to discuss things with someone, someone who can't talk back. Maybe you come to discuss it with yourself.' Here the role of the deceased parent was to act as sounding board, wise counsellor and silent discussant in thinking through a difficult family problem. One 57-year-old Jewish woman explained this process and emphasized how the burial ground provided a unique, meditative space:

> I've come to work out family problems. . . . I ask: 'How would they [her ancestors] have dealt with it?' . . . You stand and think and talk in your head about what's going on. . . . In the cemetery you can think through something with these people. When I am here, I see that solutions are not locked into time and place. People and family relationships are the same no matter when or where the people lived, so ancestors from the past can give help by giving their perspective from their thinking and their time. History can illuminate our lives – how they would have dealt with the situation, how I deal with it and the adjustment between the two to get an alternative way of thinking about and looking at it.

Other middle-aged children perceived deceased parents as having power and agency in the affairs of the living and sought their intercession and advocacy for health, work or family crises. 'I used to pray: "Please, God, let so-and-so happen"; now I say, "Please, Mum, let so-and-so happen."' A daughter further explained how going to the cemetery to ask for assistance gave her a feeling of confidence and empowerment:

In speaking with my mother, I feel I'm connecting with her in some way . . . and it's reassuring. I tend to ask her for assistance . . . with problems, for myself or others. It's satisfying for me to have done something constructive in my head, I've taken action, I've spoken to someone about it, the way you go to any agency for assistance.

This process of asking for intercession was observed directly on a cold, rainy morning in April, when a woman in her early fifties came to Bushey United Jewish Cemetery. 'I have things on my mind and I want to talk to my mother and to ask her help.' As the woman crouched down and touched the base of the memorial, she spoke in low tones about a family member who was not being appreciated at work. When she had finished speaking, she rose, placed stones for herself and other family members at the base of the memorial, kissed her fingers and then gently smoothed them over the inscription: 'Most near, most dear, most loved, most far'. She explained: 'I come for her guidance, to get outside help . . . and I ask her to sort it out.' Later the woman remarked, 'I'll ask her to give me a sign – like breaking a good plate. Even if it's not related, I make it so that it is. I feel better when I talk to her; she's the only one I might talk to about this.' In this typical example, the image of mother as supportive confidante and trusted ally was reconfirmed, and the daughter, in alliance with the deceased, assumed this same representation as wise, protective parent within her own immediate family.

In other families, the deceased mother retained her status as moral arbiter and family matriarch. This ongoing role was demonstrated when two widowed cousins came together to Bushey Cemetery with the purpose of telling their mothers that each had found a new partner and would remarry. 'We were both married many years, and we both are thinking of remarriage,' one said. The women visited the graves of their dead spouses, who had been told earlier about these new relationships, but it was at the gravestones of their mothers that the women hoped to gain acceptance: 'My mother was my mentor; I used to ask her for advice. When I come to her grave, I wish she could speak – I want her approval.'

As adult children grew older, experienced more of life and gained new insights, the cemetery offered a place and process whereby the image of the parent might be gradually modified. For many, mid-life was a time to think through and confront complex and often contradictory emotions that had not been fully addressed when the parent was still living. As adult children became more aware of their own mortality, middle life was a time of coming to terms with 'self' through a greater understanding of the deceased parent as 'other'. Death gave distance while the cemetery provided immediate, though often painful, intimacy. Visits to the grave brought the parental relationship to the fore. One middle-aged Jewish woman explained the unique possibilities of the cemetery visit: 'There is no more contact – that's why you go to the cemetery. To say things you did not say or couldn't say, because they were too difficult or too painful. . . . Death is so final you need to continue the relationship, the unfinished conversation, to keep it ongoing.'

Whereas some cemetery visits were occasions for resolution, others were about a striving for understanding, and still others were made with ambivalence and a sense of grievance. For some people, the cemetery visit was a time of re-evaluation and acceptance: 'I love him more for what he stood for – things being right and high standards. I can accept that more since I'm now much older and have more understanding.' Others brought an unresolved sense of guilt to the graves of parents: 'I feel I could have done more and said more before, when they were alive; it's partly self-punishment and partly self-flagellation.' Resentment, regrets and ambivalence coloured still other generational connections: 'I only had a fair childhood; little things were not right.' 'I regret what we never did together. It was hard for me to communicate with them and he with me; I feel I missed out.' In some cases of forgiveness, visitors reported that they had already come to a point of reconciliation and then brought peace-making to the cemetery. 'I had a word with her today [in the cemetery]. I whispered about the years when we were estranged and that it was for a reason. She knows now why it happened and that I am glad I was able to love her again before the end, in her later years. And I said I am glad she's at peace and happy now.' Or as another daughter explained: 'As I am getting older, I have a great appreciation of her abilities. She had many fine qualities and plenty of flaws. Now I accept both, but in the early days, I saw only the flaws.'

Even in cases where the parent-child relationship was impaired and where the same behaviours were being passed on to the next generation, the ideal of the parent as nurturer was often upheld during the cemetery visit. Some middle-aged adults, for example, who had not been to the City of London Cemetery since the funeral many years before, returned to visit the grave of a parent in the hope of reconstructing the parent-child bond and thus, perhaps, ameliorating a lifetime of failed relationships. 'I miss her so much. There is no one to talk to. I had a bad life and no one to turn to – there's no one to take my mother's place.'[14]

While visits were sometimes about the expression of a continuing sense of loss,[15] a request for intercession, or the articulation of emotional issues, they were also occasions for the linkage of generations and the transmission, enactment and reinforcement of kinship ideology. At Christmas, Easter, Eyd and the Jewish New Year, many middle-aged mourners brought family members together to visit the cemetery. These visits endorsed the pivotal position of the senior generation as those who now linked past and future generations and were the repositories and transmitters of family history. At the Jewish New Year, for example, cemetery visiting groups were customarily composed of individuals related by blood, not marriage, and were usually limited to two generations, because it is traditional for children not to visit the burial grounds if their parents are still alive. (Thus, the cemetery is first experienced with the death of a parent or grandparent and is not a place most Jews come to as children.)

One typical Jewish family group was composed of a widowed mother, her brother and sister and her two sons; their itinerary included three different cemeteries. Among London Jews, it is customary at the New Year to visit the graves of ancestral kin, which often necessitates trips to older burial grounds: 'You have to go from place to place to find them.'[16] In speaking about the New Year visit, the widow emphasized her intention to use these cemetery occasions to impart family history, traditional cultural ideals and the responsibilities of kinship to her adult sons:

> We do the rounds. We have always come as a family from when my father died, and we went with my mother. This is a family day to share thoughts, feelings, to reminisce, to make contact with our past. We talk of old times and my children learn the history of the family, about who they were and who was what. We remember our childhood and our parents, the happy and the sad things, the ups and downs. . . . This morning we looked at old photographs and talked about old times. We pay our respects all the way around. And by doing so, it becomes a tradition in a family network. Soon my sons will come to visit their grandparents and take the whole day. The cemetery is very important for coming together.

At the City of London Cemetery, in contrast, Christmas was the occasion when three-generation family groups made their annual pilgrimages to memorials in both the newer lawn and the older Victorian sections. Whereas the recent graves of immediate family were visited more frequently during the year ('love over duty'), at Christmas a wider kinship network of the deceased was customarily included, replicating traditional practices of making contact with a larger circle of relatives and friends during the holiday season.[17] 'Christmas is the time you think about them. We have a big family; we are all together at Christmas and now they're missing. On Christmas Day, we toast to absent friends.' Most visitors ornamented the graves of family members with Christmas wreaths, though a few chose to express their feelings with more elaborate displays – baskets of flowers, traditional holiday decorations, oversized cards – thereby temporarily disregarding the customary boundaries of restraint. At CLCC, Christmas was a time of remembrance, memory and thinking about the past, often recalled in nostalgic terms despite the difficult reality of the post-war years:

> When I come to the cemetery at Christmas, I think of the good times gone by, I think of my childhood. They were good times, we didn't have any money, we were working people. The people all down the street, we were all the same, we shared more then. After the war, we all helped each other. Life was better then. . . . If someone were ill, the neighbours would get their shopping. Now the Old England is gone.

One representative three-generational group that came to the City of London Cemetery to visit the graves of kin at Christmas was composed of a mother, age seventy-three, her two daughters, forty-nine and forty-six and a granddaughter, thirteen. (Unlike people who followed Jewish customs, some adults at CLCC had visited the cemetery since childhood.) The daughters explained the significance of this Christmas visit as a way of honouring their deceased parent: 'Our father had three close family graves which he attended, and we did this with him at Christmas as soon as we could walk. We have kept on with this duty, which we do now once a year at Christmas. This walk shows our respect and love.' As the family continued through the older parts of the cemetery, the mother commented: 'This walk is full of memories, of years of bringing others up here, and now of coming to see them. Now I'm taking my granddaughter so that she will learn to do the same as we do.'

These yearly family 'pilgrimages', for both the City of London and Bushey Cemetery communities, set the order of the grave visits (the most important – 'the hardest' – to be visited first or last), established which few relatives were still cherished and passed on family lore. Individual biographies and family histories were thus written and traced on these landscapes of memory. As mourners walked through the burial ground, their travel back in time was marked by the dates of death of the deceased and the many decades they had been visiting. There in the cemetery, past, present and future were brought together and experienced simultaneously. Over the years, such annual visits helped preserve and revitalize the memories of grandparents and great-grandparents who might not have been known personally by their descendants ('They have now become a part of me'). When the parent who kept these graves died, the established route – now also including the grave of the recently deceased parent – was sometimes continued as a tribute to him or her. For example, two middle-aged Jewish sisters continued to visit annually the graves of their great-grandmothers, for whom they were each named. 'We always brought our parents, and when they died we carried on; otherwise people get forgotten.' However, if the graves of grandparents had never been visited, their location was frequently lost. One City of London visitor explained: 'I never came with my father to the cemetery to visit his parents' grave. My father's parents may be here, but I cannot locate the grave.'[18]

Knowing the place of the burial plot, as well as personal likes or dislikes founded on childhood experiences often determined whether a grandchild visited the grave of a grandparent. As one young visitor made clear: 'I was very close with my mother's father. . . . He was my best friend. We shared all our interests in sport, boxing, football. He took me when I was a kid, and I took him when he was old. I never had a father-son relationship like that I had with my grandfather.'

Particularly for City of London visitors, a close relationship shared with a grandparent often included time spent together in the cemetery (Fig. 6.4). Some grandparents used such occasions to talk about their own parents and, by the example of the visit, to inculcate a kinship code of reciprocity between generations and the cultural definitions of a devoted parent, grandparent and child. One thirteen-year-old granddaughter supported this observation: 'Through our conversations, I have got to know more about my great-granddad.' Interestingly, the girl's mother, too, had been brought to the cemetery by her grandmother. There thus appears to be a skipping of generations as grandparents, the teachers of cemetery traditions, instruct the young. One City of London couple explained:

> We bring our grandchildren here to teach them not to forget. We tell them as much as we can about our father and mother, and about death. We tell them all we can about the grandparents, the work they did as dockers, and that the father was head of the family and we all respected him. We pass this on, so that they respect us, too, in the same way.

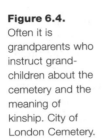

Figure 6.4.
Often it is
grandparents who
instruct grand-
children about the
cemetery and the
meaning of
kinship. City of
London Cemetery.

There were the many people in the middle-aged group, too, who
knew the locations of grandparents' and great-grandparents' graves
but who gave reasons for not visiting them. These data reconfirm our
argument that cemetery behaviour is directed by personal choice, and
they give insight into the ways people make decisions about which
graves to visit. For many, the grandparental grave was in an older
cemetery with difficult access. 'It got overgrown; there were brambles,
you slipped in the wet – it was awful and there were funny people
there.' For a few, the decision not to visit was based on the assumption
that the grandparents had not treated their own child, the study
participant's parent, well and thus did not merit the extra effort
required to visit their grave. For others, 'Just knowing where they are
is enough for me.'

Some middle-aged people, occupied with work or child-rearing,
started to visit grandparents' graves only later in life, after their own
parent had died. 'I now visit my grandparent because I still feel it's
part of my mother; it was her mother.' For most, 'It's something I intend
to do, but never did.' And for all, it was an existential question of how
far to extend connections backward or forward in time. As one middle-
aged man at Bushey Cemetery eloquently phrased the debate:

> My parents died, but who were their grandparents? I know my
> grandparents but not my father's grandparents. How far back
> can you go? How far back are you expected to go? The family
> bond? I love my children and my grandchildren, but should I
> love my great-grandchildren and my great great-grandchildren?

If I am alive, or if I look down, how far does the obligation of love to family go? How far back? How far down?

In contrast to the older adults who brought their children and grandchildren to the cemetery in order to encourage kin relationships, a second group of middle-aged persons – many of whom had not married or had children – tended to make visits that were less about the future and more about the past. An unmarried 87-year-old man explained about the bimonthly visits he had made for the past thirty years: 'I lived with my parents and they lived with me. They're the only ones I've got to remember; I don't want to give up my memories of them.' In such cases, keeping the grave was also preparation for the visitor's own future 'home', because unmarried or divorced children were often buried with or near the parent. Memorial landscapes such as the City of London Cemetery thereby exemplify the basic kinship structure of English society: couples were buried together while unmarried or divorced children shared a grave with a parent.

Visits by Younger Children to Parents' Graves

For mourners who had lost one or both parents before the age of fifty, the quiet and unhurried space of the burial ground furnished a private place of remembrance and conversation. Like older adult children, many younger mourners explained that they continued to talk with a deceased parent, often in the cemetery. But the focus of most of these conversations was guidance for one's self rather than requests for intercession or counsel on family matters. For many, this 'dialogue', spoken in a 'low conversational tone', was a significant component of keeping the dead parent 'alive'. 'I know he's here, I speak to him; he really hasn't left us. We keep him informed of all the news, we do not just come and put flowers on the grave and move away. He's listening.' For some, an initial phase of talking had ceased: 'I talked to him when I first came, but not now. . . . I feel like he's not here any more . . . now he's up with God.' For others, talking could continue for a lifetime.

The shared notion that the dead parent was able to listen and could be kept 'alive' by talking was described by a 28-year-old woman at City of London Cemetery who had lost her mother when she was eight: 'It's just as if I were talking to her. It's like you phone your mother and give her an update since the last time you saw her. I still talk as if she's still alive.' Such updating of the deceased constructed a concerned and involved parent. It also allowed the surviving daughter to self-reflexively describe her activities and thereby define and re-create herself to her 'living' parent. Both strands of this intertwined process went on for years.

For those who lost a parent when they were adolescents or older, cemetery conversations kept the deceased as a life guide and were modelled after earlier, shared talks held when the parent was living. One woman detailed this process:

> When we have a problem, we come here and sit. When Dad was alive, you would tell him your problem and he would say, 'Oh, go on, you don't want to worry about that,' and he would be supportive and let you vent all your feelings. He would say, 'If you want to do it, do it,' or, 'Don't do it because I wouldn't like it.'

Cemetery conversations provided reassurance, courage and empowerment of the self, though one Jewish son was more analytical: 'It is really asking questions to yourself and knowing the answers your father would give. It is a legitimization of what you want to do. You ask permission, seek guidance. It's an opportunity to stand on your own.'

For many young adults, it was the freedom to talk frankly in the presence of the parent – to hold nothing back – that was beneficial about the cemetery visit. One 42-year-old City of London man explained: 'If no one is about, I let my emotions go. . . . I'm a different person when I'm here, more relaxed, more open.' In other examples, a daughter used family visits to her father's grave at Bushey Cemetery to speak candidly about personal issues with her mother and brother, 'as though talking in front of [her] father'. A Greek Orthodox son described 'thinking myself at one with my father', and another Jewish woman explained:

> When my mother was alive, I shielded her from upsetting things, but now I feel she knows and sees all. . . . Over the year, I have been storing things up to say to her about what's happened to people in the family. . . . Since my mother's death, my conversations are more confidential . . . now I can tell her intimate things which I never shared before. . . . I can do this because she is not alive anymore; there is just her spirit, she can't be hurt or worried anymore. Now she is like a force, a positive force; what is left of my mother is love. This knowledge and her force are strengthening and very supportive and protective.

It was the same sort of intimacy, support and guidance that other surviving children, particularly sons, said was lacking from their lives. Sometimes they blamed the aloof and distant parent for their troubles. Sometimes the cemetery visit was a search for self-understanding and insight: 'I go to the cemetery when I feel depressed. . . . I want to understand him. . . . I credit my father with my depression, it caused a certain atmosphere at home. . . . When I go it helps me to get less angry.' For other young adults, cemetery visits offered a way to change the past and construct a different future: 'When you grow up, you need a father figure to take the lead from and to set an example. Without it, you have to work it out for yourself. . . . If I had more time, it would have been better. Coming here, I am spending time – sort of making up.' These typical cases, like those discussed earlier, suggest that even in death, an improved relationship, one closer to an imagined ideal, could be built and a more positive self-image might emerge.

In the presence of the benign deceased, who could not talk back, some young adults now felt it was safe to confront parents and reveal long-kept secrets. As one CLCC male confided: 'I have come to the cemetery to deal with problems from the past. . . . I was abused sexually by my brother. I want to say what I couldn't say, to express it, to get it off my chest; it saves you.' For many sons in their twenties and thirties who had unfinished business with their fathers, each visit offered temporary closure; the same or slightly different questions were examined repeatedly at each visit: 'It's like closing a chapter in the same book, which you keep rereading.' Thus, for some individuals, cemetery visits seemed to share some of the processes and tasks of psychotherapy and to offer the possibility of self-healing over time. One son explained this process of change as follows:

> He was not a man you could be close to. I brought a wreath the last two years, but this Christmas it's not the same as all the others and maybe the flowers show it; they're all fresh, colourful flowers. I do now talk to him about my problems, I do try and communicate. All I know, if I come over here and communicate, I feel a lot better when I go.

Commemorative visits to the graves of parents, then, had different meanings over the life course, and the nature of such visits appeared to be related to a number of factors: the age of the mourner at the time of the parent's death, his or her stage in the life course, the survivor's perceptions of the relationship shared with the parent (which could still evolve and change over time) and whether or not the mourner believed that connection between the world of the living and the world of the dead was possible. Of course, whereas individual cemetery visits offered a time for private remembrance, traditional occasions such as Mothering Sunday, Father's Day and the Sunday before Yom Kippur saw thousands of people making the pilgrimage to the graves of parents (see Appendix 5). At such times, many mourners expressed solidarity, a feeling of community and a shared bond of grief with fellow visitors:[19] 'They're all together in heaven – here we join with others, all the people who come here feel as we do, a loss for their loved ones; we feel community with others.' 'All the people were here today to pay tribute to their Mums; everyone is the same here, the same as you, they're all visiting their relations.' Others, however, found the cemetery on these crowded occasions 'impersonal': 'It's like a football match – I get far more satisfaction on a weekday like this when it's quiet.' Paradoxically, on the major holidays of commemoration, the separation between the sacred, bounded space of the cemetery and that of the secular world outside the walls is broken down. On Christmas Day, indeed, the usual direction of influence between the sacred and profane appears to be reversed: instead of the secular world's encroaching on the quiet of the cemetery, the sacred peace of the cemetery is now mirrored across all of London, which is still and peaceful, without traffic, congestion and noise.

Visits by Sisters and Brothers to Parents' and Siblings' Graves

Siblings may share bonds of intimacy, understanding and support, and these ties were often evidenced in cemetery behaviour. Close relationships and shared visits to the burial ground were seen by mourners as acknowledging the moral force of a parent's wishes ('He liked to see us together.') and provided emotional comfort: 'It's a nice thing, you're brought together; we phone and make a time to meet and come together – you all feel the same pain and same sorrow, you all share the same loss.' One Jewish woman described the absence of her recently deceased sister, with whom she had formerly visited the graves of their parents and grandparents:

> We used to go to the cemetery together. . . . It now feels lonely when I go alone. When we went together, we talked about memories, we shared saying the prayers, and we walked together to see the other stones and remembered together people we knew. . . . It was a shared experience, with warmth and memories.

Unlike the graves of married persons, which were traditionally attended by their spouses or children, the graves of unmarried people usually became the responsibility of their remaining siblings. One Irish Catholic woman affirmed this obligation as she looked after her older sister's plot: 'I haven't neglected her, and I'm still here with her.' This assumption of care for unmarried siblings was also seen as a way of acknowledging a devoted parent, as one City of London woman explained: 'This is my brother's grave; I looked after him after our mother died. I had a very good mother; it's a way of showing what she did for us.'

Reports of avoidance or contention among siblings during cemetery visits suggested, however, that the sibling bond was also fragile – open to jealousy and competition as well as affection and sharing. One self-selected sibling, for example, may assume sole responsibility for the upkeep of the parent's grave (and memory) and reject the flowers brought by other grieving kin: 'We went to the cemetery, but we found we were not welcome; our plants had been tossed out and were just left lying there, near the edge of the plot.' Earlier disagreements over the treatment of a terminally ill parent or disputes over the distribution of money or jewellery also sparked tensions. Long-standing sibling rivalries for the parent's affection became focused on inherited property: 'She said I took control of Mummy's things and Mummy.' In families where divisiveness was already present, such antagonistic situations frequently caused a rupture in family ties that was expressed in cemetery behaviour, as in the case of this City of London daughter:

> I usually come with my younger sister and the children; our other sister comes on her own, we don't talk. Things were not good beforehand, things happened and it finalized it – how Mummy left things, she had a little jewellery to be shared equally. Our older sister wanted her engagement ring. But when we were clearing Mummy's flat, we found a will she wrote, and it said that 'the engagement ring should be sold and the money divided among the grandchildren'. My sister and I, we were the closest, and we got some nice pieces. All the family, they do not talk to my sister and me; they disowned us.

Later disputes among these same siblings focused on issues of memorialization. The sisters disagreed over what to put on their mother's stone: her surname from her first marriage, her surname from her last marriage, her maiden name, or all three. Three years after her death, the mother's grave remained unmarked.

Visits by Husbands and Wives to Spouses' Graves

The death of a spouse is likely to be a painful rupture. For some widowed study participants, the cemetery provided a place for continued contact with a lifelong partner (Fig. 6.5). For many spouses, the trip to the cemetery may also have been a search for a part of the self that had been lost with the death of the other: 'You grow alike; after fifty-five years, what I like she likes. You have lost a part of your life.' For still others, however, the experience proved too painful, and they limited their visits. 'It's a bit miserable coming here, it brings back all the memories. . . . It's hard to come, but I do.' One Jewish man found that visiting the graves of his wife of over sixty years and his favourite daughter, who had died at twenty-eight, was 'too emotionally upsetting'. Even though it is customary for Jewish people to visit the graves of close family members when they are at the cemetery for a funeral or stone setting, this man – with the advice and permission of his surviving children – now visits his wife's and daughter's graves only twice a year. Thus, an inability to visit the cemetery may reflect an ongoing grief as intense as that experienced by some who visit the cemetery more regularly.

Importantly, research at the City of London Cemetery (see Appendix 5) showed that 38 per cent of cemetery visitors were over the age of sixty-five – the group most likely to be widowed – and in that age group, 46 per cent were men. Nonetheless, the assumption that it is primarily women who visit the cemetery was maintained by some male mourners themselves and even by the guards at the City of London Cemetery entrance, who stated that it was mainly women who tended graves.[20]

For the older widows and widowers, visiting the grave could frame strategies for coping with the years to be spent alone. The first of these strategies was to maintain an ongoing connection with the deceased through intimate conversation: 'You feel as though you're with them. We stand and talk, like they are right beside us talking.' The cemetery appeared to offer a different type of solace from that of the memory-filled home, with its photographs and objects acquired over a lifetime together. As many bereaved men in their seventies and eighties explained: 'There is someone here to come to.' 'It's a comfort to come up here to talk; we were married fifty-three years.' 'I look forward to coming on a Thursday; it's visiting the wife, visiting her memory.' 'We were happy for fifty-four years. I feel at ease, I feel better for coming down.' Such comments suggest that the cemetery is a place where a continuing relationship with the deceased can be maintained, despite death, through conversation and by being 'near' the other. Couples still grow old together – 'She would have been eighty-two this year' – and birthdays and anniversaries are acknowledged by a visit to the grave.

For many surviving spouses, it was the deceased partner with whom they talked about the pain of loss. One telling comment by a 72-year-

Figure 6.5.
Visiting the grave of a lifelong partner, City of London Cemetery, 1998.

old widow – her husband had died nine years before, and she now visited the City of London Cemetery every two weeks – revealed a set of ideas and practices that were typical of many cemetery users and seemed to underlie their cemetery behaviour:

> If I'm depressed, I come, I sit and talk, like to a friend, and I feel better, like my old self. . . . When I'm here, I'm near him, I laid him there, his body's still there. . . . I see him as I knew him, not as a skeleton down there. . . . I feel there is something after death. . . . I'll be with him. . . . I love to come to the cemetery, it's a day out. . . . When you're on your own, it's nice to talk to people. . . . It takes you a long time to come to terms.

Grave-tending activities were not generally seen as an aid to the soul's passage to heaven ('He was a good man in life and does not need my help for his soul') but as a way of keeping alive the memory of the deceased and maintaining contact. For many, cemetery conversations with the deceased spouse involved the exchange of everyday news, the recounting of family and neighbourhood events and the reporting of one's schedule of activities – all in the manner of chatting to an old friend. 'I ask her how she's going, [tell her] that I've been to see the daughter and had my holiday with her. There is an engagement party and I've come to let her know where I'll be.' Importantly, as mourners spoke about coming to the cemetery to visit with their departed spouse, they simultaneously acknowledged that the person was dead and that only the bones now remained. As one widower noted, 'I know she's not there, really, the body deteriorates – but it's nice to have somewhere to come to appreciate the life we had together.' Thus acceptance of the reality of death and the maintenance of an ongoing relationship with the departed could coexist and helped with coping.

The second coping strategy shared by many elderly mourners was to embrace the Church's idea of an afterlife and the belief that the deceased was already in heaven, so that a reunion of some unspecified kind was possible. 'I've always believed there's a life thereafter and we will meet, but I don't know where,' remarked one widow. Connected to the idea of a heavenly reunion was an ongoing sense of the presence of the spouse. 'His presence is wherever I am, really, that's how you learn to cope; you mustn't think they're not here with you.'

Maintaining a regular pattern of visiting the cemetery constituted a third coping strategy. During the week, bereaved spouses generally visited alone, but on weekends many would be accompanied by a son or daughter. Men who visited alone on weekends saw Sunday as a special, perhaps sacred time, appropriate for the cemetery visit: 'It's the best day, it's the proper day, being more religious. I do my worship here, instead of going to church. . . . I come on Sunday and make it a holy day.' Many women described daily visits after the spouse had first died, then gradually reducing their visits to a few times a week ('I won't go so often') and later to weekly or once a fortnight. Men, however, tended to follow a regular schedule from the beginning and usually visited on the same one or two days every week. As a man in his late seventies who visited every Monday and Thursday noted, 'It's a normal week.' At both City of London and Bushey Cemeteries, long-term widowers visited every month or so.

Some participants described their weekly cemetery visits in the context of their previous caregiving efforts and as a continuation of those activities: 'It would be no good doing this if I never looked after her in life.' Yet some felt a lingering guilt that they could have done more: 'I wish she could come back and say, "Teddy, you done what you could, you've nothing to repent."' On first meeting, some spoke about what the caregiving experience had been like toward the end of the deceased's life: 'I looked after her for two and a half years; she couldn't hardly breathe. . . . I did everything – washed her, cooked, nursed her.' Caregivers often had a need to review this experience and found others in the cemetery with whom they could talk. In cases where the deceased had been very old or would have been left physically impaired by illness, death was accepted: 'If she survived, the doctor said she would not have been able to get out of bed, so it was a comfort and best that she went. We were married sixty-four years and knew each other sixty-six, so I consider myself lucky. I am consoled with my wife; it would not have been the life she would have wanted.'

Visits to the cemetery and the simple exchange of information with other mourners at the water tap ('I've been to my husband in the memorial garden, and now I'll do my sister,') also seemed to provide affirmation, support and social contact with 'the other regulars' who tended graves, an activity often disparaged outside the cemetery gates: 'I've met people who say, "What do you go over there for? You can't do anything."' As another widow explained:

> Here is the right place to express feelings; you have time at home, but not in public; this [the cemetery] is more. Everyone comes, you're in the same situation . . . it makes you realize you're not the only one; there are so many others like you. People say, 'Oh, how can you go over [to the cemetery]? They forget, they do not want to know . . . . How can you shut it out? They're just as important after as before, how can they shut them out of their life when they were so important?

For widowers, the long rows of memorial stones provided a baseline – an abundance of mortality statistics, a fund of comparative information – to contextualize their current experiences. 'I look around the cemetery and compare my situation with theirs; we all seem to do this.' Some widowers used the dates of death on the other markers to corroborate as normal their own painful grief and feelings of despondency. At double graves, they looked to see at what age the first spouse had died and then calculated how long the widowed partner had survived alone. 'I notice people die two years later [after the death of first spouse]. They pine and neglect themselves – it all adds up, and they get depressed. I do, I get more so now than I used to, even when it first happened.' There were men and women at all of the research sites who similarly reported that the pain of loss did not subside with time. For many it 'stayed the same' – 'I miss him as much' – but for others it increased: 'It's worse than ever.'

Many bereaved widowers had internalized a view of the life course common to their generation, a view in which widowhood, age barriers and devotion to the memory of the deceased were seen as determining their later years. 'I gave my life to her. I took the vows, to always love her, ashes to ashes, dust to dust.' 'I'm very sentimental and old-fashioned. I could not become interested in a girlfriend. It would be impossible, I just couldn't do it.' The stage of life when the two were a couple was over, and a few men voluntarily commented that they were now too old to find a new partner: 'What's the point now, I'm eighty-odd, I have to try and look after myself.' For men, this later phase of life was dedicated to the memory of the other and to taking care of themselves. Most adopted wellness as a goal and made their physical and psychological health a priority. For women, too, the emphasis was on health and attitude, but with a different slant: 'Be cheerful, look after yourself and eat the same; after all, you've got to carry on. If you're miserable, no one wants to know you, do they?' Both men and women carefully dosed the amount of emotional pain they were able to bear. However, for a few men, mourning had become a full-time commitment: 'I can't get over it, I don't want to.' 'This visit is not a one-off for me. I come every day or twice a day. I did not want counselling; I felt I could not confide in a stranger, it's just a job for them; I do not feel I would benefit. For the first eighteen months, I just watched the box and read.'

Writers on grief have suggested that female and male survivors cope differently with the death of a spouse. Stroebe and Schut,[21] for example, posit that coping involves times when people confront loss and focus on bereavement experiences and times when grief is avoided and new roles are learned. Women were found to be more likely to talk about their feelings with friends and to confront loss more directly, whereas men typically used more problem-focused strategies and retreated from acknowledgement of their feelings. Close examination of our research findings on both men and women who visited the cemetery, however, suggests that most study participants employed both strategies and that they called upon the skills they had developed throughout life to deal with the stress of grief: 'I can get through it on my own; I did most things in life myself.' Male and female mourners fell on both ends of the continuum between confronting and seeking diversion from feelings, between expressing grief and containing it. Some widowers, for example, seemed willing to face and talk about their feelings openly, and they articulated deep sorrow and sadness while talking about the illness and death of their spouses. The following quote from a widower who went every Friday to tend his wife's grave is representative of those who speak openly about their feelings with others:

> I've not had a dry day since she died, there are so many memories. Different people have different ways of mourning and I have this way. They know me in the shop where I buy roses. She saw most of the grandchildren grow up, and nine great-grandchildren. I've been lucky, we met at school together and I went to her fourteenth birthday party. . . . As we got older, we got more devoted. . . . We had ups and downs, our rows; she would look at me with pride and we would make up. When she was dying she said, 'Teddy, let me sit on your lap and cuddle.'

Other men, however, found talking about their wives to be difficult – 'It brings it all back' – and quickly sought escape in the tasks of grave tending: 'I was peaceful until we started talking. It hurts more, talking about it and trying to verbalize how you feel. . . . If I start thinking, I get something to do.' One woman described her experience of this oscillating process: 'There is one point when you really want to think the thought, and simultaneously it is too much and you don't want it and you rattle around and do something else . . . when you can't face it.'

The cemetery is a resource for spouses coping with loss. It is a place where private emotions can be freely expressed, but it also offers ready distraction in the tasks of polishing the stone and tending the grave garden. Our research suggests that men and women who use the cemetery demonstrate strategies that confront loss directly and retreat from that loss – the process of talking to the deceased as if present while simultaneously acknowledging the disintegration of the body lying beneath the stone and garden. Our findings suggest not just an oscillation between these two strategies but their simultaneity. 'It seems though I accept they're dead, they're still with me.' It is this ability to acknowledge death while maintaining an ongoing relationship with the deceased – to accept that the dead are truly dead while continuing to converse with them – that gives many mourners the resources to deal with the powerful, often contradictory and conflicting emotions that accompany the death of a lifelong partner. For some, the cemetery, the deceased's new 'home', provides a second, private space, complementary to the couple's formerly shared residence, in which to visit and talk with the departed: 'Because I can't see my husband at home, I come here to see him.'

Significantly, for many bereaved spouses the tending of parents' graves is resumed with the death of the partner. The leisure of retirement and the death of a significant other during a later phase of life combine to structure cemetery visiting patterns, providing both the time and place needed to grieve. During the educational, work, child-rearing and caregiving phases of life, regular visits to the graves of parents and grandparents may be suspended or decreased in the face of more pressing work and family responsibilities. Thus, visits to the graves of kin, as well as the emotional dialogue that takes place during such visits, seem to be strongly related to age and marital status. It is a significant death, such as that of a spouse, that may (re-)initiate and intensify the cemetery visiting patterns of the surviving partner, but also those of other family members. For example, an adult son who may not have visited the cemetery since childhood may now start to accompany a parent on weekends to visit the grave of the recently deceased spouse, the adult child's mother or father, and grandchildren might be brought along as well. Many CLCC men and women recalled visiting the grave of a grandparent when they were very young but not coming again, or visiting only intermittently, until their own parent or spouse died.

Such examples suggest a variation of visiting patterns among family members and across generations; one grave might receive a range of visits of different frequencies and intensities over time. Visits to the grave of a spouse may take a linear form, beginning intensively and gradually declining, but visits to that same grave by children and grandchildren might be more staggered as these generations pick up and leave off visiting. An analysis of our data reveals that cemetery visiting patterns can fluctuate widely over the life courses of men and women and across generations. The following quotation illustrates this finding and suggests that when either the speaker or her spouse dies, the cycle will be renewed:

I used to come regularly when my father first died. I was twenty-four then. I came every Sunday with my mother. And I still came when she was too old to come; I came weekly when I could. Then when she died in 1981, that's when we moved away for my husband's work. I had the stone cleaned and refurbished when my mother died. . . . I used to come yearly on their birthdays and at Christmas. . . . And now, over the last years, I've not been well. My daughter and her husband used to come occasionally in my place – she knew her Nan – but they've not come for the last few years because they have a couple of children. It takes me two and a half hours to come. My husband is seventy-eight and I'm sixty-eight.

Remarriage

Observation of and discussions with study participants who had found new partners revealed another manifestation of the process by which people oscillate between maintaining a connection with the deceased while also being committed to a new relationship. The comments of widowed people who have made new partnerships later in life suggest that the meaning of the first marriage remains special. 'I won't forget my first wife; we set up our home together. I have good memories of our times together.'

Many widowed study participants preferred that their second partner be another widowed person, rather than someone who had been divorced. They recognized both the positive similarity of experience and the negative possibility of rivalry. One widow, for example, who was visiting the grave of her deceased husband at Bushey confided that she had met 'someone new' who was also widowed and that their shared empathy was helpful. 'You know what the other person is dealing with,' she commented. While acknowledging the continuing ties of her first marriage – 'It was a happy marriage that will not disappear. I will always have that feeling' – she recognized that her new partner held fond memories of his former marriage, too, and that these could be a source of envy and competition. Another widow explained:

> With a new relationship, you have to take on board the other person's life and their partner. You can't push it away because of jealousy. In a way, I have to share him with her, and to listen when he talks of her. That's the difference between being a divorcee and a widow – she was the best part of his life, she walks with him every day, she was the mother of his children.

Many decisions concerning second marriages and the often simultaneous shifts between ongoing ties to the first partner and attachment to the second relationship are registered on the cemetery landscapes. One arena in which potential conflicts over ties to both a deceased spouse and a current partner play out is decision-making about the surviving two partners' future place(s) of burial. An important consideration for a second relationship is the selection of the memorial stone. Within the Orthodox Jewish community, for example, decisions must be made within the first six months following the funeral about whether to reserve a burial space next to the grave of one's former spouse and whether to purchase a single or a double stone. One woman in her late fifties recounted how the stonemason had dissuaded her from buying a double stone and advised her to purchase a single memorial in case she married again. Although the possibility of remarriage seemed 'incredible' at the time, she followed the advice. Soon afterwards, she met her current husband. Together, and 'for the sake of the children', they have decided that each will be buried in the plot reserved for him or her next to their respective first spouses. In many cases of second partnerships, however, the issue of where to be buried is never discussed. Cemeteries are filled with reserved plots and never-used grave spaces.

The surviving spouse often brings the news of a new partner to the grave of his or her deceased spouse. One widow shared her conversation and reflections at Bushey as she stood in front of the grave of Larry, her former husband: 'I hope Larry is pleased that I'm friendly with Sam [the new partner]. . . . Sam makes me laugh. It's lovely. Sam cries, his eyes fill with tears when he speaks of his wife. Even if I remarry, I will never forget Larry. I will always come to the grounds. Sam says, "I know Sarah and Larry would be happy we're good friends."'

Sometimes, the surviving spouse brought the new partner along to the grave of the deceased. Such occasions revealed the survivor's ongoing deep regard for the former spouse, acknowledgement of the new relationship and possibly a sense of guilt. 'I felt very strange, standing there with another man in front of my husband's grave. I am still having a problem of coming to terms that Harry was there, laid into the ground.' In a number of cases, this transitional phase was eased: 'permission' had been given for the bereaved to remarry, 'not to be alone'. 'We agreed that if either of us died, the other should get married as soon as possible to the right sort of person; we gave each other permission.' In another example, an ill wife had indicated a specific woman she thought would be appropriate as her successor, and the husband was now seeing this woman. Without such 'permission', some felt uncomfortable in a new relationship. In discussing his second marriage, one widower confessed, 'I felt guilty when I was first married, as if I had gone off with another woman.'

Courtship and remarriage are simultaneously a time of remembering the former spouse and forging a relationship with the new partner. One City of London couple, for example, met in 1966 while tending the graves of their mutual spouses and married three years later. They have maintained their ties with the deceased for the following twenty-eight years: 'We always tended the graves together once we started seeing each other. People think it's strange we go to the cemetery, [but] it's the most important era of your life when you first marry . . . and start a family. Even though there are so many years in between, we still uphold it.' In another case, a man brought his new partner to his wife's grave at Bushey and introduced them, assuming his wife's permission: 'Barbara, not that you don't know already, this is Sarah. I'm sure it's OK with you.' A widow who had been courted by a widower said:

> When we were still going out before remarrying, I would see him in the drive selecting one of three pot plants, a begonia, to give to me. The others were for his wife's grave and his father's. I was not offended, I understood. At that time I was still visiting Abe's grave two or three times a week and would take flowers, leave tokens, write notes. I was not offended that he chose pot plants for the dead and for the living. It was comforting.

When this couple married, the cemetery landscape registered the change in her status from widow to new wife:

> I even improved Abe's stone. At the foot of the grave, I did not want to plant anymore . . . so I had chippings put there, where I could lay flowers. . . . It was an alteration, I improved it. I did it when I got married and was going to live in the country and would not be coming to attend to it. It symbolized the end of one chapter and the start of another.

It appears that for widowed spouses, one of the keys to a successful remarriage is the inclusion of both past partners. It honours oneself, the deceased and the past shared life:

> When people remarry, both sides have to accept their previous lives. . . . You must bring your former spouse with you; they're a part of you. . . . You can't cut off the previous from the present. . . . You are an amalgam of your own personality and what came from living with another person for a long time. There are four of us welded together; remarriage is a four-way relationship, a quadratic equation.

Or as a widower at Bushey summed up remarriage:

> My wife died seven years ago, she was fifty-five. I go to the cemetery two or three times a year and this is when the tears flow. The cemetery is very emotional for me. . . . In the early days of the new partner, I used to excuse and justify it, and say life goes on and I hope you understand. Now we two are four – we're like a load of old friends; you have a relationship with the old

and new spouse, we're all in the same club. In fact, I feel like her [the new partner's] husband is like a friend. . . . A new relationship, however, is not the same. With the original partner you brought your children into the world and sacrificed together. With a new relationship, it is mutual respect and love.

Visits to Children's Graves

The tendency of bereaved parents to articulate, both verbally and through grave elaboration, the intensity of the loss of a child can provide a deeper understanding of the dynamics of grief. Greater diversity in permitted styles and materials for children's memorials, as well as wider choices of cemetery landscape settings, might support a broader range of strategies for coping with loss.

At all research sites, parents who had lost children described feelings of overwhelming anguish. 'When you lose a child, you think about it every day.' It was common for many grieving parents, either together or singly, to visit the cemetery daily, or even twice a day for long periods. An Afro-Caribbean man described coming to the City of London Cemetery every day for five years: 'I had the feeling to come, the need to look for Mark.' Other parents said they 'couldn't get past' the loss: 'It takes five years to think straight.' Some found that the cemetery offered no comfort, yet they still visited: 'I could not bear to come here every day; it's not comforting, it's upsetting, but we still do it.' Others visited regularly on certain days; most came 'whenever they felt the need'. One mother whose seventeen-year-old son had died ten months earlier depicted her grief not as a constant, intense state but as more erratic and variable. It was the difficult times that propelled her to visit: 'Some weeks are much worse than others, I feel more down, tearful, lonely.' Her husband, a practising Buddhist, rarely visited the cemetery but instead sought out the spot where their son had died. Some found their faith shaken; others rejected formal religion altogether.

Many parents of deceased children wish 'to maintain the continuity of a relationship' and to keep their son or daughter as part of their life. One grieving father explained this by contrasting the death of a young child to that of an elderly parent: 'There is a difference between young people and old people dying. With a young person you need to keep in touch, you need to spend time, you tend to cling onto them; if you lose a parent, you don't.' Or as the mother of twins stated when talking about the death of one of these babies: 'I always knew it was something I didn't want to forget or get over.'

In the case of another deceased twin whose body was cremated, the parents took a less direct route to remembrance, thereby illustrating the wide variety of responses to the death of a child. Initially they were unsettled about what to do with their daughter Mary's ashes, but they 'felt they needed a focal point, not just a plaque'. Their friends, study participants at the City of London Cemetery who had lost their own young child, offered to have Mary's ashes interred in their daughter Ann's plot and to keep an extra vase with flowers for the little girl. As Ann's mother explained: 'I was an alternative parent already when Mary died . . . and was devastated. It brought up all the feelings of my daughter Ann; Mary died on the thirteenth anniversary of Ann's death.' Although Mary's parents seldom visit the cemetery, Ann's family has come regularly since 1978, and as parents and 'alternative parents' they tend the plot for both daughters and put roses in each vase. 'They know that her ashes are there and that we put flowers on the grave and they are happy for us to remember Mary.' In this case, like those of family members discussed earlier who did not visit the grave themselves, just knowing that the plot was carefully tended was a possible source of comfort and continuity. The two mothers share a special bond: 'We both know what it's been like and is like – there's something there.'

Some bereft parents saw the cemetery as offering an opportunity to establish a special space of remembrance, separate from the all-too-present memories at home. As Ann's father remarked: 'I've adopted protection by doing other things at home, in the garden, work, ordinary things. It's really disastrous in your life – you push out the disaster and replace it with the everyday. In the cemetery, it's making a special place which you can come to and keep the memory.' For the family of a twin who died a few days after birth, his grave was the 'special place' where his surviving twin brother could bring gifts identical to those he received at home or on holiday: 'a live rabbit for Jim, a stone rabbit for John'.[22] In the cemetery, this East London family had devised a set of practices to maintain the living presence of both boys.

For the parents of a stillborn baby, the significant decision to conduct their own funeral service with poems and songs, their self-described 'obsessive behaviour' in designing and crafting a unique memorial stone and the drawing up of a special planting plan were all vehicles the parents employed to construct and maintain an identity for their child and a role for themselves as loving parents. As the mother explained:

A person who has been around is a person. But for Arthur, he was not anything much; if we did not make something of him, we would have been left with nothing. . . . When a baby is stillborn, it does not have a proper existence. We wanted to say he was our son . . . take pride . . . make sure everyone knew about him. Otherwise, he would just disappear. . . . I feel I need to come to the cemetery for our son to be part of my life, still. . . . We planned a garden on the grave. The scheme is white and small . . . everything is low growing. Originally the plan was to plant it permanently, but with such a small space, it is impossible to choose. We keep changing it all the time.

This example reveals how grieving parents act and use the materials and the processes of memorialization – sketching out the gravestone and the planting of the grave garden – to construct their deceased child as a person with special qualities and, by doing so, to claim an identity for themselves as caring, protective parents. By selecting small, cream and white living plants, they created an image of their child as a small, fragile, pure baby with an ongoing existence. Their repeated selection of new and different plants and their seasonal revision of the grave garden metaphorically suggest that the death of a child may remain emotionally unresolved. The parents' pressing need to be active at the grave, to bring or do something, to redo and rearrange may express an ongoing sense of loss, both conscious and unconscious, that characterizes parental grief. At each cemetery site, the boundaries of activities considered appropriate were expanded to accommodate the parents' expressions of mourning of deceased children.

Because of the cultural meaning of a child's predeceasing his or her parents,[23] it is useful to examine which criteria parents used in selecting a cemetery for their child and the needs so articulated. Information about this process of choice comes from research data collected at East Sheen and Richmond Cemetery, where, for the same cost, families can choose an upright memorial in the lawn section or a fully kerbed grave in one of several landscape settings. These data also allow comparison of the needs of parents who have suffered the loss of a young child with the needs of those whose daughter or son died as a young adult.

In selecting East Sheen and Richmond Cemetery, the parents of Arthur, the stillborn baby just discussed, 'were protective of their son and needed to find the right place,' which felt 'familiar' to them. They first considered the burial ground where the mother had walked as a young girl on her way to school but found it 'too wide a community: there were too few babies and too many people who had lived a full life'. East Sheen and Richmond Cemetery proved 'perfect' because the graves were smaller, it offered a community of other grieving parents and the couple lived nearby. As the father explained:

> We chose an area where the children's graves are together – a community. Here we do not have to speak. It is a shared experience. The other parents know our story and we know theirs. . . . It is a beautiful open space; there are trees, and it is peaceful and quiet. . . . It is the cemetery of Jack and Mark and Arthur. I have the notion that the children are playing and that they are together. You make a connection with their families; it's supportive. . . . We came here once, six months after Arthur died, and Jack had just died and was buried and his parents were there sitting down, around and over the grave. And Mark's parents were here and it was his first anniversary and his mother was pregnant. It was like we could see our past in Jack's parents and our future in Mark's parents. It was a hopeful experience.

For the parents of children who died in their teens and twenties, the important selection criterion was that the grave be a full-size plot in an informal, natural setting. 'I chose a proper grave for my daughter who died in 1993. I wanted something to do, somewhere to come where I could have some activity. In the other [lawn] section, there are just headstones and grass, and I did not want to just look at the stone.' One mother who had lost her son at seventeen and who also chose a full-size grave remarked: 'I like the natural part, it's softened. It makes things seem natural – it's a natural thing that happened. It makes it more acceptable in a way. . . . It makes, if possible, it makes the pain a bit easier.'

Two important points emerge from these quotations. First, the bereaved, even those traumatized by the loss of a child, often recognized their special needs and made informed choices about a suitable cemetery site and an appropriate type and size of grave. Second, 'nature' and a more 'natural' setting were seen as desirable and palliative. This nature was not, however, the 'wildness' of some London cemeteries, where nature had reasserted itself in a succession of vegetation, or the older, more overgrown parts of the cemetery, which were described as 'creepy'. The 'open' sections, protected by a backdrop of informally planted trees, where these parents tended their children's grave gardens were viewed as less 'institutional' than the tidy and 'a bit bleak' lawn section. For some parents, the informal style of the landscape paralleled their informal style of planting, which mirrored their emotional need to express grief fully and freely. As one father noted:

I do not need the cemetery to be neat and tidy; I prefer it to be less tidy. I prefer this side's more natural feel, less tended. To be manicured is to be institutional. If I had known they existed, I might have preferred a woodland burial. . . . There is no pre-planning, no planning goes into this grave – unless it's subconscious. . . . This garden comes and goes; there is no set pattern. This is why I keep it this way – it has varied a lot in these three years.

These ideas of nature as less controlled, as more a partner, parallel the redesign of old churchyards, now covered with wild flowers, as well as the concept of the woodland burial, discussed in chapter 8.

Whereas for some bereaved parents, nature was a desired palliative, for others whose religious preferences or geographical location dictated a specific cemetery site with a carefully maintained and tidy landscape, the need to keep busy at the grave and to make it a more personal memorial for their child remained significant and was possibly intensified. At Bushey – in examples also mentioned in chapter 5 – two grieving mothers each chose trees, ornamental grasses and shrubs to memorialize their daughters in a manner that other visitors seemed to understand and accept. Meanwhile, a bereft father tended the large garden he had planted on the grave of his deceased daughter and the two adjoining plots reserved for his wife and himself. At New Southgate, the graves of deceased children were laden with plants and colourful flowers. As a mother talking at the grave of her 24-year-old daughter explained, 'The grave is beautiful and is a reminder of how lovely she was and a reminder that my child is gone and that's all that's left.' At the City of London Cemetery, the lawn grave of a Maltese son overflowed with plastic flowers, potted plants and cut flowers, while in the newly created special section for babies, soft toys were in abundance. Another father at Richmond and Sheen Cemetery 'did not want the formality of a headstone' and 'put in the fir tree instead, to give it scale'. He also noted, 'Graves are a personal thing; it's how you feel about people.'

Although many bereaved parents learn to grieve within the traditional strictures of their cemetery, others seem to want more freedom for individual expression and personal involvement with the grave – in memorial designs, in planting styles, in landscape settings. Such findings suggest that cemetery owners and managers would do well to offer parents (and possibly all bereaved survivors) not only a range of burial options and permitted memorial styles but also a choice of settings, from the tidy, manicured garden to areas where nature is less formally managed and more readily available as a comforting support and healing partner.

Conclusion

Our research suggests that the cemetery must be appreciated as an important site for the creation of culture and memory. In it, the notions and practices of kinship – of ongoing ties between the living and the dead – are articulated, reinforced, contested, renegotiated and reconstructed through memorial behaviour and personal conversation. Today, transformations in society affect how people think about and deal with their kin, both during their lifetimes and afterward. Increased life expectancy; divorce, separation, widowhood and remarriage leading to reconstituted families; changing gender roles; more open gay partnerships;[24] and mobility, migration and growing economic distinctions among family members combine to leave gaps and uncertainties in the ways people choose to behave toward their kin. Cemetery ritual practices, we believe, are arenas where such shifts are evidenced and accommodated. Decisions concerning the gravestone and epitaph, because they deal with the finality of death, are often opportunities for productive dissonance that bring unresolved issues and structural ambiguities to the fore. In cemetery-centred rituals, family members negotiate and struggle to reconcile the traditional expectations of kinship with present-day social realities. Through such practices, they keep, embody and transform tradition and prepare the ground for future memory.

Age, for example, has been shown to have a dynamic effect on cemetery activities. Family members are living longer today (often with terminal but chronic conditions), and death in old age, rather than in childhood, is the norm. Our survey findings clearly reveal that the majority of cemetery visitors are adult children in their fifties and sixties who visit the graves of their parent(s) and older widows and widowers who come to tend the graves of lifelong partners.[25] As longevity extends parent-child dynamics, sibling bonds (or rivalries) and marital partnerships, the cemetery offers a physical site for the continuation and extension of long-established social roles and family attachments as well as for their possible renegotiation through resolution and reconciliation. Age – of deceased and survivor at time of death – and years since death influence who visits, what they do during a visit, when and how often they visit over the life course, their reasons for visiting and the meanings ascribed to these visits. The behaviour of men and women from various cultural groups further reveals how gender, class and culture may combine with age to mediate ideas about obligation, sentiment, religious prescription and custom in relations between the living and the dead and between the living and the living. (For a further discussion of this point, see chapter 7.) Such cemetery activities form the micro-practices of memory ('We are a very close family and affectionate, we are here to make sure we remember.'); they inform our understanding of how memory operates and how it may change and evolve with societal transformations.

Moreover, as mourners visit their deceased kin, many find that the cemetery is a place where they can express private emotions within the performance of public rites of commemoration. In the world outside the cemetery, people are discouraged from articulating feelings of loss: 'In the circles I mix in, real grief is an embarrassment; people give you a hug and collect money for flowers, but this is all people want to deal with in a public context.' The cemetery is a locale where personal memories are gathered into a collective space to the benefit of individual and group identity. For many, the loss of the other is also a time of mourning for the self, and the cemetery prompts visitors to contemplate and prepare for their own future deaths, to 'take stock', to think about where they will be buried and about who, among their kin and friends, will visit and remember. Cemetery visits thus express and exact a relationship with the self as well as with the deceased, a relationship that evolves and expands from the individual to the group to society.[26] Kinship and memory here work together as a benefit for the group and society. In the cemetery, private, personal feelings of grief inspire a more public conversation, and thus a new language emerges through which today's debates on kinship may be articulated and the meaning of death and memory in late modernity become manifest.

7

Cemeteries as Ethnic Homelands

Home is where your loved ones are, dead or alive.

Greek Cypriot woman visiting at New Southgate Cemetery

In the foregoing chapters we explored the capacity of the cemetery to transform the emotions, dispositions and perspectives of individuals and families as they look out onto a world changed by the death of someone significant. In this chapter and the next we examine the ways in which larger cultural groups use both the hidden and the explicit meanings of the cemetery to transform their self-perceptions and the views of others. The legitimacy of claims of belonging is strengthened by the marking of places where kin – both immediate and those more distant – lie buried. We argue that the cemetery enables those separated through migratory dislocation to forge new connections with their places of origin – in effect, to bridge time and place.

In the absence of the more complex nexus of family, community and territory which characterizes places of origin, kinship, with its blood ties and affinal bonds, may feature more prominently in the network of relationships that bind people to their new place of settlement. The network may be further extended and given deeper significance if the dead are encompassed. This may be effected through memory, ritual activity and emplacement nearby in burial grounds, which, over time, come to mirror the generational realities of settlement and the new nexus of relationships that increasingly, with the passing of time, become territorialized, involving and rooting the living as well as the already settled dead. Cemeteries, as liminal places where geography and chronology are reshaped and history is spatially spread out, are diverse and relatively unexplored sites for examining the processes involved in the contemporary reconstitution of memory of self, family and group, in place and trans-spatially. Rituals associated with death may bring the younger generations of both indigenous and ethnic groups into places – notably churches, mosques and cemeteries – where they otherwise might not go. Such rituals are dynamic: they renew social and family ties and create and re-create the bonds of relationship and interaction.[1] Burial grounds are thus places in which to explore whether rituals – and cemetery behaviour generally – have acquired a new quality in diaspora.[2]

In describing the ritual activities of mourners in these cemeteries, we have been been alert to the literature on syncretism across cultures.[3] At the same time, we place our observations of emergent practices – particularly at New Southgate and Woodgrange Park Cemeteries – alongside our analysis of the way people share codes of mourning and memorialization that are founded on loss and change, as well as upon cultural appropriateness. Although we found talking with the dead to be almost universal in our research sites, the modes in which such 'conversations' were depicted fell within cultural parameters. Muslim men, for instance, tended to account for their meditations and 'conversations' in terms of a universal brotherhood; the fewer Muslim women we met tended towards more personal accounts underpinned by sentiment and kinship. For Greek Cypriots, the mode was emphatically one of kinship.

Structural frames for the reconfigurations of space and time for which we argue in this chapter include notions of symbolic – if not sacred – capital.[4] That symbolic capital is to be accrued through virtuous cemetery visiting is clear from the remarks and claims made by study participants whose voices are heard throughout this chapter. It is perhaps debatable that symbolic and sacred capital arise from social capital – and indeed from capital at all (in other words, from material, financial and property resources that give rise to a sense of empowerment) – as a consequence of the increasing lengths of time in which immigrants have been settled in London, but such a progression can be construed from the remarks offered by the informants quoted here.

More tentatively, we speculate about the ways in which sacred and material capital sometimes offset or compensate for each other. In chapter 4, we argued for an alignment between home and the grave and their attendant practices. For incoming groups, with reduced material reserves, expenditure on burial and the grave may often be disproportionately high. But the symbolic and sacred capital accruing from the 'investment' sometimes appears to compensate; where the family may have to occupy poor and sub-standard housing, often under a rental tenure, the grave represents a form of owner occupation or property ownership. Elaboration at the grave may also represent a freedom to demonstrate cultural preferences and power denied at the family home, where the landlord's preferences prevail. Professionals frequently commented that elaboration and expense at the funeral and in its aftermath were most likely to be associated with lower and middle socio-economic status. In a society where owner occupation is now the norm, it is not easy to make the case that grave ownership compensates for lack of ownership of land or a house. Yet historically and currently, those least likely to own land and property seem most likely to relish owning a grave plot, thereby gaining sacred and social capital within their group and a sense of identification and belonging within the larger host society.

Cemeteries as Ethnic Homelands

Immigrants to other countries, living far from their homelands, work to establish and then to maintain community in their new places of settlement by selectively preserving and recovering traditions, often in hybrid forms.[5] Burial in the diaspora – in the new place of settlement – may be seen as an attempt at 'creating communal spaces of belonging'.[6] Here we explore how cemeteries and rituals of mourning help to foster a sense of ethnic community among the most recent immigrant groups in our study. We concentrate on the Bangladeshi and Gujarati Muslims who started to arrive in the United Kingdom in the 1950s and also on the longer-established Greek Cypriots who began migrating in the 1920s. Although nineteenth- and twentieth-century Irish immigrants were not among our primary study groups, we did collect data from Irish Catholics who visited graves at many of our study sites, particularly at St Patrick's Cemetery, located in the East End of London and close to the City of London Cemetery.

Just as ethnic identity is significant to a person's sense of self during life, it is likely to be an important part of identity in death. In London, for example, Greek Orthodox cemeteries are sites that stand as surrogates for the homeland, their memorial landscapes carrying constructions of self and communal identity at once de-territorialized and re-territorialized.[7] Ethnic cemeteries record, in their totality and through individual stones, communal change through accommodation and assimilation to the host society. They also reveal cross-cultural exchanges between groups. For example, some who maintain Irish, Italian and other Catholic graves near the Greek Orthodox section at New Southgate Cemetery have adopted the Greek aesthetic and now elaborate their graves with icons, votive lamps and potted plants, transforming the plots into small, colourful gardens. The newer Muslim memorial stones at Woodgrange Park Cemetery include local stylistic features, and the shapes and styles of some older memorials at the United Synagogue's Willesden Cemetery resemble Nonconformist Christian grave markers that were established contemporaneously at Abney Park Cemetery.

The transformation of a burial ground to replicate an original homeland cemetery may be an intentional and financially calculated decision taken at the managerial or institutional level. For example, in addition to using sand-coloured gravel reminiscent of the Cypriot landscape, the management of New Southgate Cemetery also publishes brochures and other advertising material that include photographs of Greek Orthodox clergy at the cemetery's Orthodox site. 'If they cannot be in Cyprus, then re-create it,' is the slogan. Alternatively, correspondences between homeland and new cemetery landscapes may arise from individual decisions taken simply as personal preferences. Whether the process is institutional or individual, the outcome is revealed in a remark made by one Greek Orthodox informant: 'This is now a small part of Cyprus in London. Look all around – on a bright sunny day you could forget that you're in a foreign place.'

Burial or Repatriation

The most fundamental decision an immigrant must make regarding his or her own burial – or that must be made by survivors – is whether to be buried in the new place of settlement or be repatriated for burial in the land of birth. When immigrants begin to choose to be buried locally, they launch the establishment of a new, ethnically affiliated burial ground that can become a focus for their ethnic community and its maintenance (or re-creation) of a sense of homeland.[8]

Often, the stated objective of the first generation of settlers is to return home when their economic situation has improved. In the case of Greek Cypriot immigrants to London, the first generation's identity was rooted in the homeland, and this generation was most likely to choose repatriation. With the second generation, whose members may return annually to visit Cyprus, the choice of place of burial is often less clear-cut. Their children and relatives may decide to bury them in the Cypriot section of the nearby cemetery, where these descendants can fulfil their traditional obligations to visit the grave regularly to perform Greek Orthodox rituals. 'Although he was born in Cyprus, this is where he lived. . . . This is where I live, why take him back?'

Until the 1980s, the ideal and the norm for Catholics of Irish origin or direct descent was repatriation for burial in the home parish. Repatriation in many such instances could be an act of defiance towards a colonizing power that had exploited the labour of generations of Irish immigrants.[9] But some who had set down roots, at least tentatively, remained to be buried in London. Economics was only a small part of their decision. Becoming part of a community, albeit an almost exclusively Irish-born one, and particularly having children born in London set the scene for burial in an English plot. One study participant explained how his old-age intention to be buried in London came about. Along with his first wife, who had died young more than thirty years earlier, he, too, would be buried in London, although he really preferred the idea of burial in Ireland: 'When I go there, everyone knows who I am.' He said that there were now grandchildren who, as Irish Londoners, would need to visit their grandparents' grave. For him to insist on repatriation would, he imagined, mean a split in the family, something he was not prepared to set in train. For some members of immigrant groups – perhaps key members who have established a 'family tree' – such decisions may be inevitable. As in this instance, the decision may well make itself as feelings of personal identification lie with spouse, children and grandchildren, rather than in the past with parents and grandparents.[10]

For many of the first generation of immigrant Bangladeshi and Gujarati Muslims, now in their seventies, retired from work, speaking little English and having as many connections in the subcontinent as in London, repatriation is both a possibility and an actuality. Those whose children are now in London, often with children of their own, may, however, feel greater tension as the two sets of networks and the two countries pull against each other. Pragmatics and concern for the future deceased self undoubtedly enter into the decision on where to be buried as people ask, 'Who knows me well enough to visit my grave for a while, if not forever?'

In deciding, however pragmatically, to be buried in the place of settlement following migration, members of ethnic groups make personal statements about the place they see as home for themselves and their descendants. Our study participants did not explain decisions to be buried in London in ethnic terms, however. Rather, they spoke in family terms – of the need for grandchildren to know something of a grandparent. They generally were anticipating the time when grand-children might wish to visit a grandparent's grave. The ethnic status of the informant – the grandparent – was rarely mentioned in these accounts, even though it was one of the facets of identity that resonated with descendants. Individual decisions about the place of burial appear to be guided, then, more by emotion and by religious and kinship sentiment than by ethnic or economic considerations. The requirement to fulfil ritual obligations by attending to the graves of the deceased, particularly for the Greek Cypriots, further reinforces this personal decision. The costs of repatriation and local interment were approxi-mately the same, at least for the Greek Cypriot, Muslim and Irish groups we studied.

The establishment of places marked by the bodies of forebears – cemeteries where succeeding generations of locally born ethnic groups might learn about and perhaps identify with their heritage – may not have been conscious acts on the part of the earlier generations who chose local burial rather than repatriation. Nevertheless, the choice to bury the dead and carry out traditional memorial customs in London further committed the group to its new home, making its members more settled and rooted. This was dramatically illustrated in the case of two study participants who had returned to Cyprus and attempted to resettle there but found it very difficult. 'Our daughter is buried here [in London]; we could not be away from her. We tried, but this is our home now, where her grave is. So we sold up again and came back to London to be near her.' Or as a widower poignantly remarked:

> There are five relatives here, five that I have to do *kabnisma*. They're all up there waiting for me . . . may God have mercy and forgive them. That's what we Greeks say when we talk of the dead, the *Makarides*. I am glad they are buried here in London so that the rest of the family can look after them. That's what family is for, to look after the dead. I visit once or twice a week. . . . She died ten years ago. I'm retired now and should go back to Cyprus for the last few years left to me. But she keeps me here, I can't leave her.

Such loosening of ties with the homeland and generational distance from the immigrant experience were widely shown by people's reluc-tance to repatriate the deceased when close family and kin were settled in London. 'I will not go back. My wife is here; this is where I belong.'

'They're all buried here because it's where we live now; like it or not, it's our home. Cyprus is too far. How can you trust others to care for the graves in the same way as us – as me – who feels for them?' The grave seems to root the individual further and deeper within the 'diasporic space',[11] and 'the homeland' becomes fixed in the mind as forever distant. The earlier generation, opting to remain in the new settlement for burial rather than be repatriated, sets up a symbolic store for its descendants. Its interment close to hand offers multiple possibilities for the imaginings of generations yet to come, in a way that repatriation might restrict.

Safety in Ownership

Because the cemetery plays a role in fostering and sustaining identity for immigrant groups, ownership and control of the grave plot and the cemetery terrain become a concern, if not a preoccupation, for both newly arrived and settled social communities. The possibility that the dead – often the older generation, who are closer to 'home' – might become a surrogate community for the living is likely to intensify the need to control the land where graves are established.

The nature of urban cemetery ownership and grave tenure in England reflects patterns of urban settlement by incoming groups, first from rural areas in the British Isles and later from abroad. Acquisition of cemetery land accompanies settlement as members of a particular class or ethnic group reach a critical mass. At first this land may be earmarked for the elite members of the group who, for political reasons, might not be able to choose repatriation. One of the earliest Greek Orthodox burial sites, for example, was established in the nineteenth century at West Norwood Cemetery.[12] Around the same time, higher-status Muslims established an area for burials at Brookwood Cemetery near Woking. Land for burial of the immigrant majority is likely to become crucial as the group expands. For example, seventeenth-century Ashkenazi Jewish settlers purchased land for the Alderney Road Cemetery next to, but separate from, that of their Sephardic brethren, upon whom they had originally relied for burial space.[13] Also nineteenth-century Irish immigrants, who, as Catholics, had been barred from owning public property until the restoration of the Catholic hierarchy, established two burial grounds in London in the mid-nineteenth century, as soon as this was legally and economically possible.

The pattern of land acquisition through private purchase or transaction continues for settling immigrant communities to the present time, as witnessed by the expanding Greek Orthodox sections at privately owned New Southgate Cemetery. In contrast, indigenous groups who choose burial tend to use the municipal cemeteries, which may sometimes be more responsive to their requirements. The practice of providing special denominational sections in municipal cemeteries, where the ground is consecrated according to the rites of the group, is now unusual in London cemeteries, where space is extremely restricted.[14] Although several local authorities have tried to provide at least minimal space for Muslim groups,[15] opting for interment in a municipal cemetery means that full Muslim burial rituals – particularly the imperative to inter within twenty-four hours of the death – may not be guaranteed. Some groups, notably Catholics, appear to have accepted compromise more readily than others we studied, who continue to prefer specially consecrated and/or demarcated grounds for burial.

Interestingly, at both Woodgrange Park and New Southgate, distinct subgroups have set up bounded burial areas within the cemetery. Access to these is more selective, and gatekeeping is controlled by members of the ethnic group rather than by the cemetery owners – at Woodgrange through the Patel Trust and at New Southgate through the Saint Sophia Cathedral Committee and the Baha'i Burial Committee. The ideal of owning and controlling the burial ground is achieved only in part for each of these denominational groups. For Catholic groups, the land may be owned by the Church. This is also true for the Saint Sophia Greek Orthodox section in New Southgate and the earlier Greek Orthodox section at the Hendon municipal cemetery. The private cemetery owners, however, control the burial territory of the majority of the Muslim group we studied, as well as the majority of graves at New Southgate. In both instances, these owners have initiated or agreed to changes that transfer a degree of control and ownership or have otherwise accommodated ethnic preferences.

The degree of control that can be exercised over individual plots or the whole site promotes greater or lesser confidence within the minority group that ancestral remains will be undisturbed. But even outright ownership of burial land cannot always guarantee security. St Patrick's Catholic Cemetery elected to overfill a four-acre section in 1966 with six feet of earth to make new ground for future burials. Earlier graves and their markers were covered by this layer. Some small Jewish cemetery plots in inner London boroughs have also disappeared under new developments despite vehement local protest, and old burial grounds in the square mile of the City of London have made way for commercial development over the past three centuries or more.

The notion that burial is 'in perpetuity' is fast unravelling in the London metropolitan area and in other, similarly congested parts of the United Kingdom.[16] The Jewish community may be an exception, because there is a strong rabbinic tradition of respect for burial places. Jews are buried in perpetuity and Orthodox Jews oppose the disinterment of any Jewish burials. The Board of Deputies of British Jews takes responsibility for many 'orphaned' cemeteries throughout England, for which there is no longer an organized Jewish community, and also maintains nine burial grounds in London.[17] All of the London Jewish sites (fourteen pre-1900, seven of them pre-1850) are protected by high brick walls and locked gates, and many are kept vegetation free to deter vandalism and desecration.

For the newer Greek Orthodox and Muslim communities, some comfort appears to be drawn from the dedication of ground to individuals from the same family or from users sharing the same ethnic and cultural origins. Some groups customarily consecrate burial land that remains in private rather than municipal ownership, a practice that may be seen as a form of 'possession' alternative to purchase or financial transaction. The Muslim group does not formally consecrate its burial areas, arguing that the burial of human remains serves to consecrate the particular plot and the terrain more generally.[18] A sense of control may also be secured by accumulating the resources needed to select and buy a particular grave or to choose a preferred location and reserve adjacent places for other family members. This comment from a Greek Orthodox informant was echoed by others: 'We bought a double plot, and each grave can take two people, so that when we go they can bury us with our daughter, and when my son's turn comes there will be enough room for him also.'

The same study participant spoke directly of the immigrant's special desire for the security of the gravesite that arises when burial grounds in the homeland have attracted religious, national or ethnic aggression. As was the case for this man, the territorial violation that had precipitated his group's particular wave of migration had extended to desecration of the burial site where family members had traditionally been interred: 'I bought the grave so that she [his mother] can have something more secure. She died wanting to visit her parents' graves, but they're in her village which now the Turks own. We hear horror stories of what they did to the little village cemetery down there.'

The distinctiveness of cemetery ritual, which may be a source of security and comfort as people settle in a new place, is nonetheless grounded and visible. The cemetery terrain may be marked in the same ways that the homes of immigrants can be identified and so may also become a target for violence. Such burial sites across the United

Kingdom have, from time to time, been vandalized and desecrated. Although other graves are also defaced and damaged, there is little doubt that some of the aggression towards Muslim graves is racially and ethnically inspired. Financial hardship or uncertainty for the first generation of immigrants is likely to preclude expenditure on reliable security measures. Because of their sense of vulnerability, it was important at least for the most recently settled of the groups we studied to have burial spaces close to their residential areas. One informant made this clear, along with the proviso that the plot be owned: 'The dead must be near the living. To buy the plot gives you security.'

A certain self-consciousness, if not defensiveness, may enter into the wish to have the dead of one's immigrant group close by: 'This may sound silly, but there is safety in numbers. When we are grouped together in one place it not only creates a bond between us but they have to listen to us, and our wishes as a group can't be ignored.' The need to feel comfortable while carrying out special rituals was another aspect of security, as highlighted by this Greek Cypriot informant: 'They are all together here. It's good for our dead to be together, and when we carry out our traditions you don't have people thinking that we do strange things.'

Ethnic Markers in the Cemetery

As members of immigrant groups come increasingly to be buried in denominational burial grounds or special sections of larger cemeteries, customs of burial and memorialization physically mark their graves as belonging to a certain ethnic group. For many, the earth itself in which burial takes place is significant. Some Cypriots, for example, symbolically place their dead in Cyprus by throwing Cypriot soil into the grave.[19] For Muslims, contact with a generalized and elemental 'earth' and with the *desh* of homeland is an ideal, sometimes realized if the burial is uncoffined but more often represented by the bare earth that remains exposed over the central part of the grave and by the cut flowers and branches strewn on this topsoil until they wither. But it is the memorial stone or other monument that most visibly and directly identifies the deceased as a member of an ethnic community. We found, for example, that for the Irish, Muslim and early Anglo-Jewish groups, reference to the place of origin on the gravestone was fairly common, so that the village, town or region where the deceased was born or came from would be named. This practice was less common among second-generation Greek Orthodox.[20]

When place of origin was not mentioned on the stone, ethnic or cultural context was invariably referenced through symbols incorporated into the design. A particular lettering such as Gaelic or Arabic script was often used, sometimes exclusively but often together with English words. Other symbols of origin or nationality included shamrocks, harps, Orthodox and Roman crosses and the Star of David. There was some evidence that particular religious symbols – and undoubtedly other, more secular images – clustered in particular spans of time.[21] At New Southgate, generational differences among the Greek Orthodox were evident in the balance of secular and religious symbols used for memorialization. Graves of younger people displayed not only traditional icons, crosses, votive lamps and incense burners but also plastic flower arrangements (for example, in the shape of a car), wind chimes, medals, garden ornaments and photos of the deceased, sometimes in secular situations such as on a motorbike or with a toy animal. In other words, the graves appeared with all the accoutrements now found in secular settings such as the City of London Cemetery.

Sensitivity to or anxiety about others' interpretations of nationalistic or political symbols may influence the choice of displays. The changes in style over time that we observed in the gravestones of Irish-born people, for instance, suggested a wish or need for a low profile in the 1950s and 1960s but a shift from the mid-1990s onwards towards an increasingly assertive and declarative style. Expressions might be limited to ephemera or attachments to the stone, such as an Irish flag or rosary beads, but occasionally an expression of national identity was explicitly inscribed on the stone, as on one that read:

> If they ask you what your name is tell them it's McEvoy
> For there is no blame and there is no shame in an Irish name my
>   boy
> And if they ask you where you came from tell them friend or
>   foes
> That it's near Killarney & its lakes and fells 'tis the land where
>   the shamrock grows.
> Rest in peace Dad

One possible interpretation of this change is that Irish first and subsequent generations began to feel safer physically and increasingly self-confident with their ethnic or national identity in late twentieth-century London.

Just as grave memorials carry symbols of ethnic affiliation, so do they display features of syncretism and assimilation to the dominant culture. At Woodgrange Park, for instance, Muslim stones increasingly incorporate features of Western memorialization. The prayer may be written in Arabic script, and the positioning of the stone may often reflect the traditional orientation – facing outwards rather than towards the deceased and the grave – but heart-shaped stones and open book forms have appeared, along with inscriptions predominantly in English and incorporating local expressions such as 'in loving memory'. For these, the inscription, following the pattern for indigenous Britons, is likely to be dominated by the kinship place occupied by the deceased, such as parent, grandparent or sibling. The same is true for some of the more recent immigrant families, but some evidence suggests that the more personal form of memorialization takes precedence only with generational depth and concomitant distance from the homeland. As cultural-religious connections change over time and may be replaced by the more secular and individual values of Western society, terms expressing family relationships come to supersede those of cultural-geographical origin.

Cemetery rituals teach and disclose signs of assimilation and acculturation, yet at times cemeteries become places where ethnic dilution and assimilation are also resisted. National, ethnic, religious and personal symbols become fused at many cemetery sites. The example given earlier of the Irish placing the national flag on the grave shows that political statements are no longer anathema to this group. The other groups we studied appear to be more circumspect; to date, we have seen no nationalistic emblems for the Muslim group at Woodgrange. At New Southgate, a proposed memorial for Greek Cypriot dead and 'missing' since 1974 and memorial services held for the dead of Northern Cyprus are similar examples of ethno-religious features or events with political overtones.[22] It is now customary to include a memorial service at New Southgate on the anniversary of the Turkish invasion of Cyprus, conducted by local Orthodox priests, bishops and the Archbishop.

Many burial grounds have sections of war graves and memorials to servicemen with no known graves. Such national war memorials may link ethnic group sacrifice to British and Commonwealth history. In two United Synagogue cemeteries, for example, Remembrance Service prayers and psalms are juxtaposed with the Israeli national anthem and with the British traditions of lowering flags, placing the memorial poppy wreath and singing 'God Save the Queen'. Such occasions, as well as the plaque at Willesden Cemetery remembering by name those who died fighting in the Boer War, articulate an Anglo-Jewish identity and commemorate Jewish military participation and contribution to national war efforts.

Perpetuating Community

Members of immigrant or longer-established ethnic groups who visit cemeteries are both creators of and audiences for the types of material symbols just described. Indeed, it is the very act of visiting the cemetery amid such symbols that fosters people's identification with the ethnic community and teaches younger people to value their connection with that community and with their ancestors.

On special ritual days such as Eyd, at the end of Ramadan, the very large numbers of Muslim visitors to Woodgrange Park Cemetery include many young children and babies in family groups. The goal is to expose younger generations to their cultural tradition: 'It is important to remember our past, and if we come here it will remind us to lead good lives. This is a very strong feeling and I feel it when I come here.' The middle-aged male spokesman for a three-generation family gave an account of its visit that, although characterized by family sentiment, also made links to wider collective contexts: 'We've come to see their grandfather [the speaker's father]. We don't bring flowers, we praise Allah. We come with the children to visit their grandfather; they must know their family is here as well as at home.'

Young Muslim men, often those in their late teens, tend to visit Woodgrange in small groups after attending the mosque, particularly on Fridays. The cemetery is only one of the places where these young men will become socialized in the ways of Islam, but it might be argued that unlike clubs, schools and shops, the cemetery, through the collective presence of many hundreds of Muslim graves, is particularly powerful, perhaps even more so than the mosque, in permitting acculturation to a collective past through kinship and extended group affiliation.

Many older Asian Muslim men visit Woodgrange Park at least daily, sometimes alone, sometimes with peers or family members. Their accounts suggest that the Islamic religious duty may frequently override more personal motivations for visiting. Their explanations were generally formulaic as they justified their visiting and praying by reference to Qur'anic scripture and Islamic law. Yet an element of community identity ran through these visitors' accounts, too. One man, for example, explained his reasons for coming to the cemetery by saying, 'I am here today to pray for myself and for all those who are buried here.' He did not have a particular grave to visit in the cemetery, since his brother's grave was in the north of England, yet he clearly identified with the Muslim community represented by the dead of Woodgrange. More explicitly, a middle-aged father visiting the grave of his two sons explained how visiting made him 'feel part of the community, the living community, because all Muslims come here to pay their respects.'

Greek and also Jewish participants in our study stressed the primacy of personal links and actions toward deceased kin in explaining why they visited the cemetery. The meaning of 'homeland' and 'roots' for these respective groups was kinship and ancestors, the continuity of generational connections and the links between the family of the present, the family of the past and the family of the future. Like members of the United Synagogue, those in the Greek Orthodox community called upon similar metaphors to characterize their cemetery behaviour as one link in a continuous chain forged by their parents, who acted in similar ways toward their parents: 'I'm just a link in a long, long chain that goes back to my great great-grandparents in Cyprus,' said one. Another remarked, 'It's traditional to come [to the cemetery]; we're doing what our parents, grandparents and great-grandparents did.' The links with the 'old country', in the long chain of belonging, are increasingly relocated to London's burial sites.

After the annual visits to the graves of kin in an older cemetery, Jewish relatives often walk together through the grounds, noting the inscriptions, commenting on the stones and telling stories about the people whom they knew. Such journeys, which encourage social comment on the values of the past in terms of the present, articulate, reinforce and also modify traditional cultural ideals. In Greek community rituals surrounding the memorial stone, sentiment and practicality dictate visits mainly to those relatives known personally. A disposition to curtail grave visits after two or three generations and to follow Orthodox obligations only to deceased parents and other close kin, works to advance the transposition of the concept of Cypriot homeland to the new place of residence.

When communal ethnic identity is viewed as a form of membership in a greatly extended kinship group, then burial at a specific site is ascribed for members of the ethnic group. Horowitz regards ethnicity as a form of extended kin membership established through birth.[23] Correspondingly, this membership encompasses an assured place in a specific burial site. 'After all, that's what it's all about, closeness; we are one blood. There is no separation between the dead and the living; we are all part of the [Greek] Orthodox community.' In both the Jewish and Greek cemeteries, ethnicity, lineage, ancestry and history are united. 'To be buried in a community cemetery makes me feel that we are with our own people; here where my parents are buried, there is a small part of Cyprus.'

This strength of group membership and its identification and affirmation through burial were exemplified in the remarks of a United

Synagogue member whose brother had married outside the religion and was buried in a non-Jewish cemetery: 'We will not say the ritual prayers at his grave, but we will leave a stone to show we've visited.' Thus while the surviving sibling found it inappropriate to recite the traditional prayers of mourning at the grave of his brother who had been buried in unconsecrated soil, he did choose to leave a pebble affirming the continuation of the family bond.

In many of the cemeteries we studied, occasions arose when those who were at the periphery of the local community could move towards the centre through a public display at the cemetery. These sites had annual days of remembrance when the wider ethnic community gathered, as described in chapter 5. At New Southgate, for example, these special days were occasionally accompanied by services arranged by the cemetery management. Even when this was not the case, the participation of the second and third generations was facilitated by the communality set up by the occasion itself. Thus, those who might have lapsed from religious or cultural practice were brought back into the ethnic community through obligations to deceased parents and grandparents. These ritual occasions were the times when the young and men attended religious places in greater numbers and so relearned to be both Greek and Orthodox, Asian and Muslim, or Irish and Catholic, as well as Londoners in Britain. For the individual, ethnicity and an ethnic identity might come to provide a vital sense of continuity of self, a self that rests not only on assumptions about the past but also on aspirations for the future.

The grave and, in some cases, its garden become the encoded material expression of this identity of self and memory of other. It is 'read', observed and endorsed by other members of the cemetery community; the processes of individual identity construction are appropriated by others and become emblematic of communal identity. Evolving customs of memorialization link personal memories with a re-created sense of community consciousness: 'I'm here with my grandmother; she does the *kabnisma* and lights the *kandele*. She has been bringing me here for six years now, visiting my granddad's grave. She talked to me about him, about the things we are meant to do in the cemetery and what not to do. We're always speaking in Greek.'

For communities whose ethnic identities lie at a distance, the cemetery is a memoryscape, a reflection of their 'homeland' and an expression of collective experience. The cemetery is a culturally constructed place used by those living in the diaspora for the transmission of collective memory, both material and cultural. Like memorial monuments which reflect the cultural influences of the host society, the behaviour of cemetery visitors also reveals the assimilation of younger people and sometimes their resistance to community traditions. Young Muslim men visiting Woodgrange Park after attending the mosque, for example, are more likely than the senior generation to wear ordinary dress rather than prayer clothes. Muslim women are discouraged from visiting the cemetery, yet some visit out of emotional need or as an act of resistance. The few Muslim women we met at Woodgrange Park tended to conform in their explanations of visiting with ideas of duty, remembrance of the dead and reminders of mortality, but it was also among the younger women that the strongest divergence from the 'party line' was likely to be encountered, as in the following instance:

> I am a Muslim – sort of. But I don't really believe now, I don't know really. Some people do hold to all the rigorous rules and all that, but I don't. I did go to my father's funeral when all my relatives, mainly the extended family, were trying to tell me not to. But it's really up to the individual. It was my aunties who were telling me that I shouldn't go, but some were saying that it's OK for the closest relatives to go even if they are women. I just said, 'I'm going and that's that.' So they let me go. And I haven't got any brothers either. It's up to individual families. Sometimes I bring my sister's children because she won't come down here, she's a bit scared of graveyards, but she wants her kids to come, so I bring them here for her. And they can see the grave of their grandfather.

Older Greek women, dressed in black, have been widely depicted as dominating the public space of the cemetery, but today the Greek cemetery in London receives almost equal numbers of men and women. Usually, family groups dominate the cemetery grounds. Some Greek Orthodox are breaking with the tradition of visiting on Saturday and come instead on Sunday, which doctrinally is a day associated with life and resurrection rather than with death. Through such practices people use the cemetery as a site for reworking the dialectic between assimilation and resistance.

The processes of globalization are focusing attention on issues having to do with the preservation and re-creation of identity in a world where traditional ideas of people as members of fixed and separate societies and cultures no longer hold.[24] In today's world of economic migration and global interconnectedness, the search for a new sense of 'homeland' within and between spatial and temporal boundaries raises associated questions about the 'remapping of memory'[25] and about the contemporary reconstitution of memory of self, family and collectivity. Drawing on research data from the immigrant Greek Cypriot and the Bangledeshi and Gujarati Muslim communities, we argue that for members of minority and immigrant ethnic groups, cemeteries can play a significant role in creating a sense of community beyond the strictly familial. Such sites act as magnets drawing ethnic groups together, physically and cognitively, thereby re-creating a sense of communal homeland. Cemeteries both evoke the place of origin and reflect the genesis of a new situational identity. In today's world of global economics, the decisions of individual migrant families to bury their dead in the new country of settlement rather than to repatriate their kin initiates the grounding of this new sense of rootedness and homeland. As liminal, betwixt-and-between sites where geography and chronology are reshaped and history is made spatial, cemeteries are places of social, religious and ethnic continuity and belonging. Cemeteries act as bridges between two worlds – the home of the living and the metaphorical home of the dead, the home of origin and the home of settlement.

8

Change and Renewal in Historic Cemeteries

Our roots are around here. The cemetery is like remembering
the old way of life. It's like coming home.

Man in his sixties visiting the grave of his mother at
City of London Cemetery

Throughout this book, we have examined the cemetery from the
perspective of mourners as a centre of emotional attachment and felt
significance.[1] The cemetery is a place were space and nature have been
appropriated and transformed by management and by the remembrance practices of the bereaved into a legally sanctioned physical
setting appropriate for the disposal of the once-living body. Such sites
are not static but are continually reproduced and also altered by
individual and institutional actions that reflect (but also help direct)
changing cultural attitudes linking death and nature. The cemetery is
a place but also a process. In it the thoughts and feelings of the bereaved
are evoked, socialized and constrained in their culturally appropriate
behavioural expression, in the same way that memorial practices also
produce, shape, perpetuate, modify and transform the prevailing
cultural customs and codes. In the previous chapter we discussed how

study participants from ethnic minority groups are using cemeteries to create new landscapes of memory that link death, cultural identity and ideas of homeland. But what of older and disused cemeteries that are no longer being regenerated through new memorials and the remembrance practices of recently arrived ethnic groups?

The landscape of the cemetery, including those of older burial grounds, is always open to reinterpretation. Some current re-readings reflect changing attitudes about society's relationship to nature and the environmental importance of older, disused grounds as valuable sites of ecological biodiversity and urban green space. Other reinterpretations are based on a growing awareness of the need to preserve the heritage value of these unique cultural landscapes. In this concluding chapter we bring into sharper focus the significance of old burial grounds from both of these perspectives. We revisit the complex concept of cemetery as garden to examine how the image of the emblematic Garden of Eden is being reformulated to include a woodland landscape, as well as notions of home as a place where relationships among kin are made material. Do old and historic cemeteries and changing ideas of nature and the cemetery as garden suggest new narratives? If so, are these relevant to the formation of future policies and practices regarding issues such as reuse of grave space, cultural diversity and ecological sustainability? How do past memorial landscapes inform our present understandings of death and the meaning of the afterlife? Do they offer new models for innovative cemetery landscape designs?

In this chapter we examine how East Enders and members of the United Synagogue, as well as members of newer, geographically based communities, are reinterpreting older burial grounds as sites of community history and collective significance. We argue that disused burial grounds have not exhausted sacred purpose and meaning[2] but continue to bind present generations to their forebears and to future descendants in new ways. All urban settings change over time, as do ideas about nature and – as we have argued throughout this study – the landscapes, purposes and meanings attached to cemeteries. It is in old cemeteries that memory ends and history begins.

Old Cemeteries: Repositories of Cultural Significance

The years since the publication of scholarly studies on burial grounds in the 1970s and 1980s have seen growing public appreciation of nineteenth-century English cemeteries as repositories of a unique architectural and landscape design history.[3] Between the 1950s and the early 1980s, however, many of these historic sites had been threatened by a lack of funds for repairs and maintenance, by the demolition of buildings and the wholesale clearance of monuments, and by the shortage of available burial space.[4] By the mid-1990s, the need to conserve and protect historic burial grounds was increasingly being recognized.[5] With this raising of public consciousness about the heritage qualities of English cemeteries, the United Synagogue and the Greek Orthodox Church were similarly encouraged to revisit their older burial grounds as sites of cultural significance. Alderney Road Jewish Cemetery, maintained by the United Synagogue, and the Greek section at West Norwood, in trust to the Hellenic Community, were each re-evaluated and researched to document the group's collective past and to publicize its contributions to English society.[6] During our study, two occasions marked an accelerating recognition of the significance of these older ethnic cemeteries.

In 1997 a tricentenary service was held at Alderney Road Cemetery, marking this site – established following the readmission of Jews to England in 1656 – as the oldest Ashkenazi burial ground in England. The ceremony, held in the consecrated cemetery grounds, was attended by religious and lay community leaders. In appearance, this historic Anglo-Jewish cemetery is a brick-walled, grassy site with trees and a scattering of small, upright stone markers and weathered chest tombs with faint inscriptions. The late Rabbi Dr Bernard Susser described it as being 'like an oasis in a world of bustle and modernity. . . . [It] radiates an atmosphere of peace, tranquillity and holiness.'[7] In his welcoming remarks, the president of the United Synagogue noted that a Jewish cemetery is called 'the house of everlasting light', and it was this theme of enduring heritage that was developed by the Chief Rabbi.

In paying tribute to the cemetery, the Chief Rabbi acknowledged the significance of this historic site 'containing the mortal remains and memory of the architects of the Anglo-Jewish community'. He metaphorically described the memorial stones of the cemetery as the 'living stones of the original Temple', the bones of the community's ancestors as 'memory and reverence for the past', and the cemetery as the 'symbolic re-creation of the original cave purchased by Abraham to bury Sarah when he was a sojourner in Israel'. He depicted the establishment of this cemetery as the foundation of the Anglo-Jewish community in Britain, thereby emphasizing that the burial of the dead instituted, secured and marked the settlement of Jews in London and lay the claim of belonging.[8] He spoke further of the instructive ideals inscribed on the memorial stones of the community's founders and emphasized that to pay tribute to their heritage was to guard their ethical bequest for the future:

> Society is a partnership between those who are dead, the living,
> and those not yet born. We are a link in the chain of the genera-
> tions. . . . Bonds of memory and obligation bind us to those
> before us to carry on their values and traditions. . . . We are the
> sacred guardians of their legacy to future generations. . . . This
> is the Jewish concept of time.

Thus, in concluding his remarks, the Chief Rabbi emphasized the role
of the present generation as the 'ligature' in the allegiance between
the dead and the unborn.[9] Cemeteries containing the dead of the past
embody, in the most literal sense, this contract between generations.

In 2002 the Greek community enunciated a similar theme of
intergenerational continuity and the implicit agreement that it is the
responsibility of the living to transmit the values of the past to their
descendants. An exhibition at the Hellenic Centre in London commemorated the foundation of the Greek Orthodox section at West
Norwood Cemetery by reviewing the significant contributions of its
benefactors and detailing the architectural importance of its listed
buildings and monuments. The site is an impressive necropolis, closely
packed with large tombs, mausoleums and mortuary chapels and
separated from the rest of the cemetery by 'its own Doric entrance and
Classical statues of the Virtues on the piers of the railings'.[10]

Norwood Cemetery contains the remains of renowned Hellenes
who in many ways laid the foundations of modern Hellas, brought
back to public awareness the Hellenic spirit, honoured their origin and
won the respect of the British public. The cathedral of Saint Sophia
and Norwood Cemetery are reminders of the determination of the
people of the Hellenic diaspora to maintain their cultural and spiritual
identity not only while in this world but in eternal life as well.[11]

In both examples, these Jewish and Greek burial grounds, containing the mortal remains of the communities' founders and prominent
members, acted as mirrors for their descendants, reflecting cultural
values, both spiritual and practical, of respectful burial and proper
living. They also articulated the social and cultural contributions each
group had made to English society and reminded the descendant
community of its forebears' status and commitments.

The annual occasion of the Bronterre O'Brian oration similarly
marks the contribution to society of this leading nineteenth-century
Chartist and Nonconformist, who is buried at Abney Park Cemetery.
Very mixed groups celebrate his Irish non-Catholic origins, along with
his political status. For instance, the oration that took place during
our fieldwork period was delivered by Arthur Scargill (a once prominent trade unionist) and attended by people from ethnic Irish, socialist

and trade union groups, and also by local people, including family groups.

These cemeteries are thus landmarks of cultural distinctiveness and also have relevance for local, urban and national history. They may also be read as political and moral statements of the value to all parties of immigration, settlement and cultural exchange and of the importance, particularly to incoming groups distant from their origins, of maintaining religious traditions. As historical and social landscapes, old cemeteries also become sites of personal consciousness and repositories of group identity and collective memory. As such, they should and sometimes do underscore the communal responsibilities of the present generation as the custodians of the group's heritage to maintain and protect other, less celebrated and now closed ethnic cemeteries against vandalism, abandonment, or sale and to pass on their legacy intact to future generations.

The same case could be made for indigenous communities whose landmark sites in London are cemeteries such as Highgate, although it is recognized that the curiosity and affection that Highgate inspires does not necessarily transfer to lesser-known sites or to less notable municipal cemeteries.[12] The idea of 'cemetery' in the public imagination is frequently dominated by images of the older, 'romantic' cemeteries that attract the most attention (Fig. 8.1). Whereas many people may express reluctance or even revulsion at the idea of visiting a 'modern' municipal cemetery as possibly too functional and austere,[13] too close to death, popular views of the churchyard and of nineteenth-century cemeteries are generally benign and indicate greater interest and engagement.

What is the particular attraction of old cemeteries that no longer witness burial? Our enquiry into whether and how cemeteries continued to have meaning and purpose long after their burial potential had been exhausted suggested that both old and new communities of cemetery users attach significance to local sites.[14] Study participants at Abney Park, for example, explained their interest in terms of a past community of users who, they believed, might provide a grounding for their own new, relatively self-conscious sense of 'community'. Members of new groups such as the first- and second-generation Muslims at Woodgrange Park Cemetery took a different perspective on a more personal – though still distant – history. When they spoke of Woodgrange as representative of all cemeteries and all the dead, they related this new, Western burial site to the burial sites in the *desh*, long sanctified by the burial of holy men and their own ancestors. Resisting a focus on the particular site of Woodgrange enabled the link with the homeland site and its ancestral holiness to be forged.

Figure 8.1.
Abney Park
Cemetery, 1997.

Returning to our earlier Jewish and Greek cemetery examples, such burial grounds of first settlement also serve as resources for group history. Jews and Greeks in London now document their past from the standpoint of their new homeland. One Bushey study participant remarked:

> The cemetery is continuity. We're scattered, our great-grand-parents came from Eastern Europe. Our grandparents are buried at Rainham and Edmonton [Federation of Synagogues cemeteries in London], my parents are at Bushey. It's an accident that we're in England. We're rooted, but rootless at the end of the day. The grave is something to come back to. I have hopes of going to Galicia for my mother's family and tracking down my roots and finding their graves. The cemetery is the whole Jewish context, content and continuity.

In another telling case, members of the Hassidic Orthodox Jewish community (a sect of Orthodox Jewry) assembled at Alderney Road Cemetery on the fast day marking the destruction of the Temple, 'when all Jews are mourners' (Fig. 8.2).[15] Their stated purpose, as the present living generation, was to visit the graves of the community's ancestors,

Figure 8.2.
Hassidic Orthodox Jews visit the graves of the founders of London's Anglo-Jewish community at Alderney Road Cemetery, 1998.

who are no longer visited by their own family descendants, and to 'demonstrate that there is still interest in old, forsaken cemeteries':

> *Tisha b'Av* is a time when people go round to the cemeteries to see what has become of our ancestors, the great men of our nation, what they started. We look at the . . . grounds to learn what their lives and congregations were like and to make sure no one desecrates the cemetery. Cemeteries keep us attached to the past.

In praying for the souls of the long deceased, these Hassidic Jews remembered the individual founders of the Anglo-Jewish community as their communal ancestors and honoured the contract between generations that Orthodox Jews be buried in perpetuity, that sacred burial lands not be used for other purposes and that their legacy be transmitted to future generations. For them, as with the more recently arrived Greek and Muslim immigrants described in the last chapter, the cemetery acts as a bridge between two worlds, this time the world of Jewish religious origins and that of English settlement, between the present, material world of the living and the future, spiritual and metaphysical afterlife of the soul.

The memorials at Abney Park, a historic site where few burials now take place, prompted comments from study participants that suggested such generational and communal contracts. Sometimes those who spoke about the cemetery as a historic site were closely related to the dead: 'I like the spot where both my parents are at rest.' Even when visitors were not connected to the dead through ties of kinship and personal memory, they drew existential inspiration from visiting: '[You] can meditate, look at the graves and the way people died, . . . and can think about it.' This historic site also offers the opportunity for another form of 'contract' between generations and across cultural divides: by living in the area and visiting the local burial ground, people can claim a sense of belonging, a relationship to place and to the community once served by the cemetery. The connection is made not through kinship but through acknowledgement of the history and the sacred purpose of the cemetery. As in the Jewish and Greek communities, the bodies of the dead at Abney Park validate the assertions of the living who declare a new place as home: 'It's new to me. . . . It reminds me of home [Ireland]. The graveyard implies freedom of spirit . . . the dead here are beyond the restrictions under which we live.' Here, through claims of communal inheritance by new geographically based cultural groups, the old cemetery was reanimated and the spirits of the adopted dead were given voice, identity and ancestral authority.

Such relational contracts across generations could be only tentatively formed, in hope rather than firm expectation, by the middle- and working-class people who buried their dead at Woodgrange Park Cemetery until after the Second World War. While conducting research at Woodgrange as a developing Muslim burial site, we recorded the observations of the English descendants who sought the graves of parents and grandparents who had been buried in the cemetery's public and purchased graves. Many said that a sense of being part of a generational chain had been reawakened when they themselves became parents. They recalled their last visits, decades earlier, when as children or teenagers they visited the graves of grandparents in a cemetery they now found hard to recognize. Their own children's interest in family origins may have been responsible for this middle generation's hesitant acknowledgement that their links with deceased family members had been fractured, partly through their own forgetfulness.[16] For those who successfully located the graves of past kin, there was a strong feeling of family identity and a resolution to maintain the renewed relationship, expressed partly through attending the grave. For most of these study participants, the course of life between a childhood entailing wartime displacement and present maturity as parents of grown children had not offered an earlier opportunity to find lost graves. Moreover, the shift between these personal memories and the beginnings of a more collective history, which we discuss below, coincided with impulses to construct generational structures as comprehensively and meaningfully as possible.

Where neither kinship nor spiritual links can be claimed between living visitors and the distant dead, the identification of graves of once famous people may open another conduit for connection between the cemetery and its contemporary population. Abney Park, following the precedent of the higher-profile Highgate and Kensal Green Cemeteries, now offers tours every few weeks in which a guide points out significant monuments and provides visitors with personal and historical background about the cemetery and its past residents. Such tours are also held annually at the City of London Cemetery, and the Friends of Woodgrange maintain a scrapbook of notable people and the many community disasters marked by monuments or by mass graves and their plaques. These tours and information about the famous dead buried in these older burial grounds raise the public profile of the cemetery and help to build support for conservation of the site as a significant repository of the community's past history.

If the idea of a 'contract' implies two knowing parties to an agreement, then we can claim only a fictive contract between those communities which, retrospectively, seek connection at Abney Park and Woodgrange Park Cemeteries and those who are buried there. And yet in both these cases the 'agreement' is accompanied by a strong sense of responsibility towards the dead. It is this commitment to acknowledge the dead that scholars such as W. Lloyd Warner and Robert Pogue Harrison argue is a basic institution that underlies all human communities: an intergenerational understanding that the living will ceremonially bury the dead and honour their memory and that their future descendents will, in turn, assume that same obligation and responsibility toward them.[17] This trans-generational contract is an acknowledgment that human beings cannot determine their own continued existence after death but must trust others to grant them an afterlife. This insight that the living are the caretakers of the memory of the dead[18] was demonstrated in organized efforts at Abney Park and Woodgrange Park Cemeteries to protect the monuments and human remains of the dead or, failing this, to preserve at least the names of the interred for remembrance. As we discuss below, such responsibilities were not assumed lightly. Fictive contracts may appear to be retrospectively constructed as past communities are brought into focus, but our study participants also alluded to a future in which they and their families or communities could also be lost to memory. Such a fearful insight may have motivated their actions in 'adopting' the dead.

Old Cemeteries as Defences against Erasure

In the 1990s, Woodgrange Park Cemetery was overgrown: brambles and knotweed obscured the graves and erased the secondary pathways. To increase income from burial fees and to make room for new Muslim interments, the present owners started to bury between existing plots and in the unused upper spaces of graves from the early to mid-twentieth-century English community. These activities entailed a gradual removal and loss of many of the cemetery's original head-stones. Although the required three-month notice of intended area clearance was posted at the cemetery and announced in the local press, such notices were seldom seen by family members, who no longer lived in the area or rarely visited the grounds. The cemetery rules plainly stated: 'Any grave abandoned for a year and a day can be cleared', and the owners applied this rule as they judged necessary. The Friends of Woodgrange, a group formed in the 1980s to defend the cemetery against radical change, were alarmed by the clearance of stones. To counter this policy of removal, they established a series of open days, four a year, to encourage members to visit the cemetery to clean the stones of overgrowth, 'to not risk losing the grave'. The committee members were present on these occasions to provide security, refresh-ments, practical help and useful tools.

Many of the grave owners at Woodgrange Park believed that the crucial balance between the domestication of the grave as home, brought about by the imposition of human order and tidiness, and nature's wilful chaos had been breached. Much of the cemetery had grown unruly, disorderly and chaotic; it had become a place of thorns and brambles 'up to the shoulders'.[19] Woodgrange Park Cemetery seemed to be 'outside the Garden'.[20] Human intervention, in the company and safety of others, was required to reclaim graves from overgrowth and obscurity. This was the objective of the four 'clear-up' days arranged annually by the Friends. At a yearly general meeting, one Friend addressed management's invited representative: 'By clear-ing the stones you have destroyed history . . . the information about names, relationships, what people did, the circumstances of their lives.'[21]

In 1993 Parliament passed the Woodgrange Park Cemetery Act. It allowed redevelopment of part of the cemetery (with generated funds to be used for cemetery refurbishment and future maintenance), though it specified that the previously buried remains from the cleared sections should be moved to a garden of remembrance. Although the remains were reburied accordingly, the garden of remembrance has yet, as of the time of this writing, to be developed. Significantly, at a

Friends of Woodgrange meeting, the group voted to fund a memorial 'for those exhumed and moved'.

The overgrowth of vegetation, the clearance of original headstones to make way for new burials and the exhumation of human remains at Woodgrange appear to have violated cultural ideals of the cemetery as the physical link between generations of once-local families and their living heirs. In trying to restrain the actions of the cemetery owner, the Friends group attempted to protect the memory of all the cemetery's dead and thus the meaning and cultural legacy of those lives. We argue that in so doing the Friends constituted themselves as the surviving heirs of the area's once vibrant English community, thereby acknowledging and accepting the intergenerational pledge not to forget.[22] In approving funds for a memorial plaque for the exhumed remains of people who were not their direct ancestors but whose 'home' and names should still be marked within the community's cemetery, the Friends were reinforcing the cultural ideal of the cemetery as a place of protection from oblivion. It is important to note that the Friends took this action in the face of rapid changes that left many convinced that in a decade's time, 'this will be a Muslim cemetery'. Erasure of the community's past was only a hair's breadth away, but was nonetheless to be resisted, at least in small measure.

Erasure was also imminent in the 1970s and 1980s for those who had been laid to rest in Abney Park Cemetery. The cemetery had fallen into dangerous dereliction, was frequented by those judged undesirable, to be avoided by the local residents. In this densely populated, inner London area, where housing shortages remain acute, the proposed reuse of cemetery space for new dwellings was in tune with current thinking that objected to burial grounds as a waste of resources: 'Land for the living' was a frequently invoked slogan. The cemetery was safeguarded by the formation of the Abney Park Trust and was preserved – but just narrowly. Although graves have been lost at Abney Park, enough stones remain to give descendants a partial appreciation of their family and community past – a historical presence strong enough to stave off total oblivion. At Woodgrange Park this claim can no longer be made with any confidence.

Old Cemeteries as Community Amenities

The chronicle of Abney Park Cemetery, though unique, resembles the histories of many other Victorian cemeteries in London and, undoubtedly, elsewhere. Abney Park Cemetery was established by Congregationalists in 1840 and is significant in cemetery history for its

commitment to meeting the burial needs of the Nonconformist middle-
and working classes, the historical importance of its monuments and
its renowned garden landscape, which combined disposal of the dead
with an arboretum of named trees, plants and shrubs. Decline and
erosion of these designed grounds began in the nineteenth century as
paths were infilled and trees cut down to make space for further
interments. Income began to dwindle when the cemetery's burial
capacity reached a critical point in the early twentieth century.

In the 1950s the lack of security and regular maintenance at Abney
Park encouraged vandalism and theft; one study participant who had
grown up near the cemetery, for example, recalled climbing over the
wall at night with teenage friends and breaking headstones. The
overgrowth of vegetation had made the interior grounds inaccessible,
while also creating an 'atmosphere of romantic decay'. In 1974, within
this milieu of picturesque ruin, abandonment and destruction, the Save
Abney Park Cemetery Association was established; and in 1979, the
London Borough of Hackney purchased the site. The Abney Park Trust
was given administrative responsibility for the cemetery and began
implementing a plan to manage the landscape and restore the monuments. Although the cemetery is classified as an 'inactive' burial
ground, half a dozen interments a year take place in family plots
purchased decades ago; and family graves, established as far back as
the 1920s, are still visited. Once located at the outer limits of the city,
Abney Park Cemetery is now encircled by a dense, multicultural, inner-
city population that it serves in new ways. It is a quiet retreat for walking, a repository of funerary art, a genealogical archive, a memorial
space and a nature reserve.[23]

The atmosphere of this historic cemetery is that of an urban woodland, and study participants contrasted its 'alive' landscape with that
of an adjacent park where nature was described as 'artificial', 'institutional', 'manicured' and 'clinical'. Visitors reported that the cemetery's
dense vegetation provided a place of seclusion and peace.[24] 'I prefer
it because of all the trees – it's enclosed, it's a really wonderful place!'
The cemetery, unlike the park, was associated with spirituality and
was seen as a place of quiet retreat, as 'God's garden'.[25] Like other
gardens, the atmosphere of Abney Park was said to encourage meditation, imagination and creativity. For some people who have family
members buried in the cemetery, it is a personal place of remembrance
to which they were taken as children and where they now visit the
graves of grandparents and great-aunts and uncles. For others, it is a
community space for local identification, involvement and concern.

A review of research on natural landscapes in urban areas, sponsored by the organization English Nature, documents many of the

reasons Abney Park is valued as a unique community resource.[26] It suggests that contact with nature, particularly areas with woodlands and paths through low vegetation – the environment of Abney Park Cemetery – provides emotional sustenance and engenders feelings of calm, serenity and restoration, as well as exhilaration. Wilderness offers an opportunity for personal engagement with nature and the possibility of a transcendental experience. Further conversations with people concerning their reasons for visiting Abney Park support this positive view of wildness and, importantly, suggest an emergent view linking nature and death that enhances this historic cemetery's importance as a unique type of urban open space. Visitors describe the site as life affirming – as a place of life in the face of death, where 'the spirits of those laid to rest' are free. Significantly, such responses propose a view of death that supports a 'green' and sustainable cemetery environment and possibly suggests the woodland ecology of Abney Park as a model for new burial landscapes that mimic natural patterns. The cycles of vegetation are unmistakable in this 'overgrown, untended' and undomesticated garden; here, nature's time is indeterminate, thereby denying the finitude of individual life. The cemetery is valued as a place of restoration, redemption and regeneration for both person and nature.

Abney Park Cemetery remains a contested site, however. Architectural historians decry the dilapidation and ruin, pointing out how the root systems of self-seeded trees have undermined graves and broken up monuments. Those who prefer the cemetery to be a romantic wilderness do not always concur with the removal of mature trees in order to preserve the monumental record. Urban ecologists claim that Abney Park supports one of the largest tracts of woodland in London,[27] and provides a habitat for birds, mammals and invertebrates; grave owners, however, are likely to complain that the dense vegetation impairs security and access to memorials.[28] While visitors are pleased with the recent improvements to the site, many of these people are new local residents who have no responsibility for a particular grave. To further restore the original designed landscape and arboretum might mean planting a specimen tree where a grave now stands; conversely, to repair a memorial might necessitate the felling of a historic tree.[29]

Comparisons of the proposed restoration of the Abney Park landscape with the restoration of the built environment, the location of the home, suggest a similar interchange between proponents for the conservation of the long-standing and those who wish to introduce the new. Throughout this book we have been guided by the metaphors used by our study participants, and have referred to the home as the image or model that the grave must echo. 'Like human dwellings, the after-life needs places to take place in.'[30] If we assert that the historic cemetery may come to represent the garden restored, what are we to say about the grave as home after the stone has been broken or the inscription erased? If the home is a private place accommodating and supporting the relationships it shelters, then the desired orderliness and propriety of these relationships should be reflected in an ideal of tidiness.

When we regard a historic cemetery such as Abney Park we see a degree of disorder that is not generally tolerated in an active site where burial continues. Although some of the cemetery visitors in our study might have appreciated the romantic wildness of a historic site and selected woodland burial for themselves, most believed that the living grave and the cemetery itself must display respect for the deceased and therefore be kept clear of such disorder. Does this distinction between the appreciated romantic wildness of a historic cemetery ('I like it wild and overgrown, rather than organized') and the expected order of an active cemetery suggest that a historic grave cannot be retained within culture but must be placed beyond it, in nature? Or does it transcend the opposition of nature and culture and suggest their integration within the environment, a merging of nature and culture and the emergence of a new cultural relationship to nature?

One City of London study participant supported the latter argument by suggesting that the cemetery was a progression of stages of the garden. Initially, the carefully tended garden in front of the stone marker was the true memorial, but over time, when family members had passed away and no one was left to tend the plot, the stone alone became the memorial – as in the older Victorian sections of the City of London Cemetery, where the gravestones had become grey with age and their gardens bare. Finally, when the cemetery was closed, then nature, in the form of a wild garden, would again become the memorial, concealing the individual graves under thick vegetation. This man's mother, however, found the inaccessibility of such an old, neglected cemetery objectionable.

The Cemetery in Nature

This brief discussion of old cemeteries in London suggests a range of views about cemetery as garden. The original Alderney Road Jewish Cemetery and the Greek section of Norwood are both walled gardens where nature is subject to human control. The untended overgrowth of Woodgrange and the deliberate removal of older memorial stones there leave the English community of descendant families feeling that the cemetery's owners have not honoured the contract to 'keep the garden'. And Abney Park is perceived by many local residents as a garden of restoration and solace where the elements of nature help visitors to reclaim their lives and acknowledge those who preceded them. Such contrasting views reflect changing ideas about nature and demonstrate different understandings of the place of human beings in nature. An additional concept of cemetery as garden in which nature is an equal partner in a sustainable relationship with the living is being initiated at the City of London Cemetery, as well as at other sites throughout England. At CLCC, the nineteenth-century ideal of the cemetery as a place of remembrance, reflection and sanctuary is being acknowledged through the conservation of its historic landscape, the employment of ecologically based management practices, the maintenance of burial as a viable option and the development of a woodland burial section.

Cemetery land is limited in London, and the City of London Cemetery has initiated a series of policies to reclaim and reuse existing burial space. Identification of unused space in old Victorian graves is proceeding, and this legal strategy of reclamation may entail new inscriptions being placed on old monuments to mark a new burial. Unlike the managerial practices adopted from time to time at Woodgrange Park Cemetery, the original memorial will not be cleared, nor its inscription erased, but it will be kept in place to preserve personal and local history as well as the historic landscape combining stone and garden. To guide this policy of reuse of graves and memorials, the cemetery is developing a landscape management plan which will guide the conservation and management of this historic site.[31]

In accord with the public's growing awareness of the heritage value of cemetery landscapes (and also to foster that awareness and appreciation), the CLCC's management plan is being developed as a 'generic model' providing guidance to other burial authorities. Many older but still active cemeteries have been similarly faced with the need to find new burial space without cramming graves into land reserved as open space, paths or gardens, thereby compromising the integrity of the historic design. With the implementation of its conservation management plan, the landscape of City of London Cemetery will physically renew its continuity with the past as historic Victorian plantings are restored and old graves are newly occupied and tended. The cemetery will thereby reaffirm its historic tradition as a place of contemplation and tranquillity as it attempts to meet the needs of a range of users: the newly bereaved who come specifically to tend graves in an area of carefully maintained memorials and gardens; longer-term users who visit family graves and spend time ambling along the tree-lined avenues and meditating among the historic monuments of the older Victorian sections; and ecologically oriented community residents who visit the cemetery as a place of nature, recreation and open green space.

To further meet the needs of these environmentally interested visitors, CLCC has developed self-guided tree and heritage memorial trails. Such educational tools encourage groups of schoolchildren and others to come to the cemetery to learn about its historic trees, flora, lichens and wildlife, just as they might visit Kew Gardens or Hampton Court to see its English Heritage-listed buildings and memorials. As Loudon suggested in the nineteenth century, it was the cemetery as historical record and botanical storehouse that made it worthy of preservation for future generations.[32] The unique funerary architecture, carved memorials and composed epithets, the tall conifers and designed grounds could make up a place of recreation, instruction and contemplation.

Mindful also of the goals of environmental sustainability and emerging concepts of cemetery design, the City of London Cemetery has created a woodland conservation area known as the Birches and has established a 'green' burial site where native trees substitute for rows of stone monuments. This type of managed woodland burial landscape, which appears to offer many of the attributes of an Abney Park, is becoming popular throughout England.[33] It presents an alternative style of interment for people who wish to be buried in a more 'natural' ecological setting. In our postal survey of those who had pre-selected woodland burial, the responders' answers revealed a strong environmental orientation and a commitment to the future by planting trees as living memorials.[34] A few had chosen to plant small trees from their home gardens, thereby linking past and future. Such responses suggest that the tree and the woodland garden are symbols of trans-generational continuity[35] – not of oblivion and erasure by nature. They are material manifestations of ritually transformative organic processes that are similar to those of the human life cycle[36] and are built on an understanding of the integration of nature and culture. As symbols of life and eternity, trees answer what W. Lloyd Warner referred to as 'the fundamental sacred problem of the graveyard: to provide suitable symbols to refer to and express man's hope for immortality'.[37] As such, trees and woodland cemeteries may hold the secrets of future burial grounds, just as weathered memorial stones and old cemeteries contain the confidences of the past.

As views linking nature and death continue to evolve, nineteenth-century cemeteries such as Abney Park and the older Victorian sections of City of London and Richmond and Sheen Cemeteries are becoming more highly valued by local communities as peaceful places that provide a welcome contrast to the metropolitan pace of life. Such sites are also valued for the 'history' visitors know they hold. People's explanations for visiting, however, focus on communities that are as imagined as they are 'real.' Abney Park and other older cemeteries offer a canvas that displays only the barest of outlines. The twenty-first-century visitor uses the historic cemetery in all the ways we have described, but they are also drawn to and try to unravel its secrets.

The Secrets of the Cemetery

All cemeteries, however, hold secrets for present-day users and visitors to decode and also to 'plant' for future generations. Success in this will always be conditional in that as contexts change, and without insights from the living, the memorial landscapes on their own can give only partial explanations. In the historic cemetery this is particularly the case; the tomb, the home that once conveyed ordered narratives of kinship and contemporary custom, has often been – literally – broken up or partially buried by vegetation. The code has in this instance been degraded; imagination must do its best. For living communities the code – the secrets – may be veiled by cultural complexity arising out of developing ethnicities. Nonetheless, there are compensatory benefits in the wildness that arise through the passage of time and in the many layers of cultural overlay. Imaginative and creative efforts to unravel the cemetery's secrets can thus be revived by changes across time and space.

For historic, inactive sites the 'disordered' garden is welcomed as more than compensation for the family and home that has been reburied under vegetation; it is the preferred explanation for the disappearance of decontextualized history. Perhaps those who visit Abney Park and describe their experiences in ways that suggest a deep and engaged connection allude to this new understanding of new meanings – of the merged relationship of nature and culture. They refute any suggestion that cemetery equates with park, not least because 'there are bodies of the dead here'. The meanings of park and cemetery lodge at different levels; those of cemetery are literally more profound. In the historic cemetery, especially when users and Friends groups have had a chance to 'tame' the wildness that grew up during a period of abandonment, the frame that holds lost secrets can be laid bare. It becomes clear, however, that we cannot enter the world of those who died and those who were present at the interment. Yet the stones, the landscape and the atmosphere convey more than enough to inspire engaged conjecture about lives past, about past deaths and about the relationship between life and death. Generations past are revived by the interests of the living, who carry their messages forward to the future. Those who visit historic cemeteries say they feel a strong pull to such sites. Even in foreign places, people apprehend enough of the cemetery code – of their own culture and that of others – to feel 'at home'. Settled groups, for example the Jewish cultures across Europe, may have adopted the local style, yet retain much of what is essential and so continues to resonate.

Where contemporary, secular cemeteries are concerned, regular visitors often perceive many of the secrets that the more casual visitor is denied. Mourners are familiar with the precise implications of the inscription and the memories it is meant to carry; they understand why the stone has its particular shape, texture and colour. These people – our study participants – gave us detailed reasons for the plantings and voiced their opinions about what a 'proper' cemetery should be like: a place for the appropriate disposal of the dead and a site for ongoing practices of commemoration, a place of individual, family and collective memory and future cultural heritage. They told us these things, and we recorded them. They also revealed that they shared this information with their children and grandchildren and with friends of the deceased. But death and its aftermath are in many ways private affairs; feelings of loss and grief may be diluted and misrepresented if shared too widely. Though cemeteries are ostensibly public places with responsibilities to the neighbouring community, they exist to obscure the terrifying fact of death through ritual practice. This is the central secret of the cemetery, circumvented and generally unspoken by most of our study participants. It is the secret that generates and shapes practice, habit and ritual on the part of mourners and of managers. It is the unstated contract among members of cemetery-visiting families that each generation will not let those of the past die, but will care for their memory just as they trust their descendants will remember them.[38] 'The cemetery is an enduring physical emblem, a substantial and visible symbol of the agreement among individuals that they will not let each other die.'[39] Cemetery users, standing at the gravesite, sometimes came close to revealing their inner and existential thoughts about the death of the other and the future loss of self, but it was evident that much could not be put into words if a degree of reincorporation[40] were to be achieved.

If this analysis holds – that the cemetery contains secrets about the deceased and the living and about trans-generational and trans-spatial connections – then we should not be surprised that many people are drawn to them. Cemeteries intrigue, they inspire and they face the visitor with contradictory meanings and existential ambiguities that alternate between clarification and obfuscation through ritual action. People's experiences of cemeteries, 'places apart', are not of the everyday. For many, not least our study participants, these sites hold a powerful and disturbing charge that is not comfortably resisted. However public and municipal they may appear, each and every cemetery is the most concentrated repository of mystery and secret that is available to modern, urban, twenty-first-century people.

Appendix 1

The *Aide-Mémoire* Used during Fieldwork

UNIVERSITY OF NORTH LONDON: CEMETERY RESEARCH PROJECT: Check list for all visitors/ all cemetery sites

1.   Cemetery site:...Researcher...

2.   Date of visit: Day............... Date.................Time; am/pm..   Weather...................

3.   Why did you come here today ?

4.   Description of group?

    Lone visitor   Couple   Friends   Siblings
    Family group   Family & friends   Other

5.   Where live ?

    London - which Borough ?...Other - where ?........................

6.   Main means of transport to come to this cemetery today?

    On foot   Tube   Private car
    Train   Bus   Other

6a.   How long did it take to get here ?..

7.   Religious/cultural /ethnic affiliation ? ....

8.   Is coming here anything like going to church/mosque/synagogue ? ....

9.   Dates of death of deceased being visited today ? (include any dates for others
                                        indicating which other cemeteries they are in)

10.   How often do you visit this cemetery ?

    Daily   Weekly   Monthly   Yearly
    Christmas   Mother's Day   Easter   Father's Day

    Other days/occasions mentioned
11   How many graves did you visit today ? (get details of relationships and where
                                        the grave(s) are located.)

12.   Visit any other cemetery/cemeteries ?
    If so, which & when ?

13. How long will you be/have you been in the cemetery today ?
     Time arrived   Time left

14. What do you do and what do you think whilst you are here?
     PROMPT FOR:

     A.   GARDENING; TALKING WITH THE DECEASED;
     B.   PRAYING;
     C.   WALKING AROUND/TALKING WITH OTHER PEOPLE;
     D.   OTHER SEASONAL ACTIVITIES;
     E.   ANYTHING ELSE;

15. What are your thoughts about an afterlife ?
     PROMPT FOR:

     A.   NOTHING HAPPENS, WE COME TO THE END OF LIFE;
     B.   OUR SOUL PASSES ON TO ANOTHER WORLD;
     C.   OUR BODIES AWAIT RESURECTION;
     D.   WE COME BACK AS SOMETHING/SOMEONE ELSE:
     E.   TRUST IN GOD/ALLIN GOD/THE PROPHET HANDS;

17. The Cemetery Landscape:
     How would you describe this Cemetery ?

     Is it like, or different to other cemeteries you know? In what ways?

     Is it anything like going to a park coming here?

18. Does the way the cemetery looks make it easier or harder for you to come here?
     PROMPT FOR VARIATION IN FEELINGS BECAUSE OF:

     A.   TIME OF YEAR
     B.   TIDINESS AND GENERAL UP-KEEP
     C.   OTHER PEOPLE AND THEIR ACTIVITIES

19. Who came, with ages and gender ?   Males   Females
                              Under 10 years   ....
                                    11 - 16   ....
                                    16 - 24   ....
                                    25 - 34   ....
                                    35 - 44   ....
                                    45 - 54   ....
                                    55 - 64   ....
                                    65 - 75   ....
                              75 and over   ....

20.   KINSHIP CHART WHERE POSSIBLE

2

Appendix 2

Forms Used for Household Surveys at Abney Park and Woodgrange Park Cemeteries

UNIVERSITY OF NORTH LONDON

CEMETERY RESEARCH PROJECT

Abney Park Neighbourhood Study

From the point of view of someone who lives or works next to the Cemetery, please would you tick the boxes to show your answers to the questions below. Please also write in any additional comments you wish to make. You can post the form back to us by folding it so the reply paid address shows. Alternatively, one of us will call to collect it and take any additional information you wish to give.

1.   How aware are you of **Abney Park Cemetery** near your premises ?

        ....

2.   Do you ever go into Abney Park Cemetery?   Yes ....   No ....

        If NO, do you watch/look into the Cemetery ever?   Yes ....   No. ....

        Comments..

        If YES:
3.   How frequently do you go into Abney Park Cemetery?

        Every day   ....
        Every week   ....   any particular day ?.....................................
        About monthly   ....
        Two or three times a year ....
        Perhaps once a year   ....
        Other (please state when)...

4.   Why do you go to Abney Park cemetery?...

        ....

5.   Who would you generally go with?

        On your own ......   With family ....   With friends ......

        Mix of family and friends ....

        Other [please say who] ....

6.   Do you know anything about the Cemetery, and of those buried there ?

                                                            Yes ......   No ......

        Comments:..

7.   Do you have any relatives/friends buried at Abney Park Cemetery?

Yes ....   No ....

Comments ....

8.   Do you visit any other cemeteries ?   Yes......   No ......

If YES: How far away are these? ....

9.   In what ways, if any, do you think that Abney Park Cemetery 'adds' to the area?

....

10.   In what ways, if any, do you think that Abney Park Cemetery 'spoils' the area?

....

11.   Does Abney Park Cemetery ever cause you uneasiness?   Yes ...... No ....

Comments ....

12.   Does Abney Park Cemetery ever cause trouble or disturbance? For example during burials, because of traffic or other reasons?

Yes .... No ....

Can't say ....

If **YES** , can you say how, when, what kind of trouble?

....

13.   Would you say that property very close to Abney Park Cemetery loses or gains in financial value ?

Loses   ....
Gains   ....
No difference ....
Don't know   ....

Why do you think that is ? ....

14.   Do you feel that having the open, green space of Abney Park Cemetery nearby is good or bad for:

a)   Your property?   Good......   Bad......

b)   The area generally?   Good......   Bad......

Comments...

15.   Would you say that:

      a)   the vegetation in the Cemetery is 'out of control' ?   Yes.....   No .....

      b)   the way the Cemetery is managed is suitable?   Yes....   No.......

      c)   the Cemetery is a place for children to visit?   Yes....   No.......

      d)   the Cemetery is a place for women to visit?   Yes....   No.......

      Comments..

16.   What do you feel is the difference between Abney Cemetery and a Park?

      ....

17.   Do you have beliefs about spirits and the dead ?   Yes........   No........

                                               Uncertain   ....

      Can you say more on this?...

      ....

18.   In what ways do you think the Cemetery could be improved ?

      ....

19.   Do you feel that any of the services or facilities in the local area should be altered/improved because of the presence of Abney Park Cemetery?

      Comments   ....

Finally, would you mind giving the following details about yourself. All information is confidential, you do not have to give your name.

20.   Are you: Male............. Female..............

21.   Which age group do you fall into ?

      15 years or under ...... 16-24 years........   25-34 years ....   35-44 years ....

      45-54 years ....   55-64 years........   65-74 years ....   75 years or over........

22.   Who else lives in your house or flat ?...

23.   Which religion, if any, do you belong to?...

24.   What is your ethnic background?...

      Thank you very much for your help.
      Dr. Doris Francis & Leonie Kellaher University of North London

Dear Householder,

May we request a few moments of your time to answer these questions about Woodgrange Park Cemetery, in your neighbourhood. Please see information leaflet enclosed for details of our research project.

Leonie Kellaher
Nick Jordan
Fred Galooba

....Fold here..

Postage
will be
paid by
licensee

Do not affix Postage Stamps if posted in
Gt Britain, Channel Islands, N Ireland
or the Isle of Man

BUSINESS REPLY SERVICE
Licence No. N.D. 2326

Centre for Environmental & Social Studies in Ageing
The University of North London
Room 403, Ladbroke House
62-66 Highbury Grove
London
N5 2BR

....Fold here..

Thank you very much, please fold and post back to us.

UNIVERSITY OF NORTH LONDON

CEMETERY RESEARCH PROJECT

Woodgrange Neighbourhood Study

From the point of view of someone who lives or works next to the Cemetery, please would you tick the boxes to show your answers to the questions below. Please also write in any additional comments you wish to make. You can post the form back to us by folding it so the reply paid address shows. Alternatively, one of us will call to collect it and take any additional information you wish to give.

1.   How aware are you of **Woodgrange Park Cemetery** near your premises ?

      ....

2.   Do you ever go into Woodgrange Cemetery?   Yes ....   No ....

      If NO, do you watch/look into the Cemetery ever?   Yes ....   No. ....

      Comments...

      If YES:
3.   How frequently do you go into Woodgrange Cemetery?

      Every day   ....
      Every week   .... any particular day ?...
      About monthly   ....
      Two or three times a year   ....
      Perhaps once a year   ....
      Other (please state when)...

4.   Why do you go to Woodgrange cemetery?...

      ....

5.   Who would you generally go with?

      On your own ......   With family ....   With friends ......

      Mix of family and friends ....

      Other [please say who] ....

6.   Do you know anything about the Cemetery and of those buried there ?

                                                       Yes ......   No ......

      Comments:..

7. Do you have any relatives/friends buried at Woodgrange Cemetery?

Yes ....   No ....

Comments ....

8. Do you visit any other cemeteries ?   Yes......   No ......

If YES: How far away are these? ....

9. In what ways, if any, do you think that Woodgrange Cemetery 'adds' to the area?

....

10. In what ways, if any, do you think that Woodgrange Cemetery 'spoils' the area?

....

11. Does Woodgrange Cemetery ever cause you uneasiness?   Yes ......   No ....

Comments ....

12. Does Woodgrange Cemetery ever cause trouble or disturbance? For example during burials, or because of traffic or for other reasons?

Yes .... No ....

Can't say ....

If **YES** , can you say how, when, what kind of trouble?

....

13. Would you say that property very close to Woodgrange Cemetery loses or gains in financial value ?

Loses   ....
Gains   ....
No difference.......
Don't know   ....

Why do you think that is ? ....

14. Do you feel that having the open, green space of Woodgrange Cemetery nearby is good or bad for:

a)   Your property?   Good......   Bad......

b)   The area generally?   Good......   Bad......

Comments...

15. Would you say that:

    a)   the vegetation in the Cemetery is 'out of control' ?   Yes.....   No .....

    b)   the way the Cemetery is managed is suitable?   Yes....   No.......

    c)   the Cemetery is a place for children to visit?   Yes....   No.......

    d)   the Cemetery is a place for women to visit?   Yes....   No.......

    Comments...

16. What do you feel is the difference between Woodgrange Cemetery and a Park?

    ....

17. Do you have beliefs about spirits and the dead ?   Yes........   No........

                                                           Uncertain ....

    Can you tell us a bit about this this?...

    ....

18. In what ways do you think the Cemetery could be improved ?

    ....

19. Do you feel that any of the services or facilities in the local area should be altered/improved because of the presence of Woodgrange Cemetery?

    Comments ....

Finally, would you mind giving the following details about yourself. All information is confidential, you do not have to give your name.

20. Are you: Male............. Female..............

21. Which age group do you fall into ?

    15 years or under ...... 16-24 years........   25-34 years ....   35-44 years ....

    45-54 years ....   55-64 years........   65-74 years ....   75 years or over........

22. Who else lives in your house or flat ?..

23. Which religion, if any, do you belong to?..

24. What is your ethnic background?..

    Thank you very much for your help.
    Dr. Doris Francis & Leonie Kellaher University of North London

Dear Householder,

May we request a few moments of your time to answer these questions about Woodgrange Park Cemetery, in your neighbourhood. Please see information leaflet enclosed for details of our research project.

Leonie Kellaher
Nick Jordan
Fred Galooba

....Fold here...

| Postage will be paid by licensee | Do not affix Postage Stamps if posted in Gt Britain, Channel Islands, N Ireland or the Isle of Man |

BUSINESS REPLY SERVICE
Licence No. N.D. 2326

Centre for Environmental & Social Studies in Ageing
The University of North London
Room 403, Ladbroke House
62-66 Highbury Grove
London
N5 2BR

2

....Fold here..

Thank you very much, please fold and post back to us.

Appendix 3

Form Used for the Woodland Burial Survey

The following letter accompanied the questionnaire and a reply-paid envelope for return of the completed document directly to the researchers at North London University.

From:

Bereavement Services
The Cemetery Office
Richardson Street
Carlisle
Cumbria

1997

Dear . . . .

WOODLAND BURIAL SURVEY

I am writing to request your help regarding the above survey, which is being organised by Dr. Doris Francis and Leonie Kellaher at the University of North London. They have already reported some of their findings on cemeteries in general and they are proving very interesting.

Woodland Burial, which began in Carlisle, has opened in over 60 locations in the U.K. This is a remarkably rapid increase, and yet very little is known about why this has occurred. This is why the assistance of people like yourselves, who have supported and fostered this very radical change in funeral practices, is being sought.

The survey is being sent to forty Woodland Grave purchasers, twenty of whom have also arranged a burial and experienced a bereavement. I am aware of the sensitive nature of the survey at such a time, and this has not been treated lightly. Even so, we are aware that only people who have been through a bereavement have the insight and knowledge based on experience. The findings will be very helpful to the City Council, who wish to manage the Woodland and develop it in a satisfactory way into the next century.

As your ownership of a woodland grave, and your address, are confidential, your details have not been released to the researchers. They have been asked by the Council to provide the enclosed envelope and contents, which the Council have agreed to pass on to you. The envelope contains a letter, details of the project, a questionnaire and a reply-paid envelope. If you feel the survey is insensitive or intrusive, please return the envelope uncompleted, and accept my apologies for approaching you. Alternatively, I would be pleased if you felt able to help, as I am positive this will improve Woodland Burial, and services to the bereaved in the coming years.

Yours sincerely

Manager, Bereavement Services

UNIVERSITY OF NORTH LONDON
CEMETERY RESEARCH PROJECT
Woodland Burials

1. Why did you – or a member of your family – select Woodland Burial?

2. Which, if any, of the following reasons were important in making a choice? Please tick all that apply and please add comments to clarify your response:

    a) family and personal concerns
    b) for religious or belief reasons
    c) financial
    d) as a particular alternative to cremation
    e) instead of burial with a headstone
    f) because of concerns about nature and the environment
    g) other reasons, please write in and continue on a separate page.

3. May we please ask you to tell us more about your choice and reasons for selecting Woodland Burial?

4. Did you choose Woodland Burial in order to create a particular type of funeral?

    Yes . . .   No. . .

    a) If YES; Can you explain further?

5. Did, or will you use a cardboard coffin/shroud/other?

    a) Please describe the type of coffin/shroud etc, if you know.

6. Is the tree itself an important feature of Woodland Burial to you?

    Yes. . .   No. . .

    a)   If YES, can you please explain further?

7. Would you wish to plant the tree yourself, or with your family, as a symbolic act?

8. Would you have chosen Woodland Burial had there not been a single tree on every grave?

9. Would you have chosen Woodland Burial if there had been one larger tree for a cluster of graves?

10. Do you ever come to the cemetery to visit the grave?

Yes. . .   No. . .

If YES:

 a) How often do you visit?
 b) How long does it take you to get to the cemetery?

If NO:

 a) If you do not visit the cemetery to visit the grave, can you say why?

11. Is there any difference in the ways you think about the Woodland Burial place from the way you would think about a traditional grave?

12. Do you visit other Cemeteries or memorial places?

Yes. . .   No. . .

 a) If YES, which ones?

13. Are other family members and/or friends connected in any way with this Woodland Burial grave?

Yes. . .   No. . .

 a) If YES, who. . .

14. Are you aware of any other family members, or others, who are finding or will find some difficulty with Woodland Burial? Can you say whether it relates to a specific aspect, e.g. the low mainte-nance, absence of a memorial etc.?

15. Carlisle Cemetery has an approach to ecology which favours working with nature. Some areas are not mown weekly to allow the native wild flowers to grow. How do you feel about this approach to Cemetery management?

16.   Many people are becoming more concerned with the environment and are using fewer chemicals, planting more native species to attract birds and insects and to encourage wild life. Do you think this changing relationship between man and nature also has a place in the Cemetery? Please explain.

Finally, would you mind giving the following details about yourself:

      a)   Please indicate any religion: e.g. Roman Catholic, etc. or if secular, Humanist, Atheist etc.

      b)   Male. . . Female. . .

      c)   Age group:

Thank you very much for your help, please use additional pages if necessary.

Appendix 4

Facsimile of a Deed from the City of London Cemetery and Crematorium

72241

CORPORATION
OF LONDON

City of London Cemetery and Crematorium

Manor Park, E12 5DQ

By virtue of the powers conferred on the Common Council of the City of London (Hereinafter called "the Common Council") under Section 214 of, and Schedule 26 to, the Local Government Act 1972 and Article 10(1) of the Local Authorities' Cemeteries Order 1977 to grant exclusive right of burial we, the Common Council in consideration of the sum of One thousand two hundred and thirty five pounds paid to us by

(hereinafter called "the GRANTEE") Do hereby grant to the GRANTEE the exclusive right of burial for the period of Seventy five years commencing on the 27th August 2004 in the City of London Cemetery and Crematorium at Manor Park, in the London Borough of Newham in the parcel of ground described in the said Cemetery and Crematorium as Square **234** Number **148332** including the right of placing a memorial thereon of the nature and in the position and under the conditions approved by the Common Council TO hold the same unto the said GRANTEE for the purpose of Burial subject to the regulations of the Common Council and any regulations now in force or which may hereafter be issued with regard to interments in the said Cemetery and Crematorium by her Majesty's Secretary of State the appropriate Minister or by the Common Council or any other competent authority.

As Witness the hand of Dr Ian E. Hussein

Director

City of London Cemetery and Crematorium

27th August 2004

WITNESS to the signature
of the said
Dr Ian E. Hussein
LO-GRN01

Appendix 5

Visiting Patterns at Four Study Sites

At the four sites where we carried out continuous qualitative fieldwork, we also undertook selective quantitative observation. This took the form of surveying the numbers and groupings of visitors to each site on ordinary days and on days that had ritual significance for the particular group that used each cemetery. The approach was to count the people in the visiting group, note their gender and estimate their approximate ages. At City of London Cemetery, where religious affiliation could not be assumed, we asked a few people for this information and also whether they were visiting a grave or the gardens of remembrance. Because this was an addition to the research originally proposed, resources were often stretched, and while these numbers give a good picture of the volume and character of visiting, we make no claims for their precision.

City of London Cemetery

The guards at City of London Cemetery keep a count of visitors passing through its main entrance each day. On Father's Day in June 1996 they estimated that some 6,000 visitors entered during the eight hours of opening. We were able to obtain information on just a small sample of these people.

Of 428 people we approached during the time the cemetery was open, 9.00 a.m. to 5.00 p.m., the great majority (83 per cent) were visiting in groups. We observed 164 groups, often in cars (96 per cent), ranging from couples to five or six people. The average group size was 3.2 persons, with an age range predominantly between 25 and 64 years. Family groups of three generations, however, were not unusual; one person in five in this sample appeared to be under 24 years, and 15 per cent appeared to be over 65. The gender balance on this Father's Day was predominantly female: 65 per cent women and 35 per cent men.

Of those prepared to give information about their frequency of visiting, most reported that they came on special days such as Christmas, Mother's Day and personal anniversaries such as the deceased's birthday. A minority of those visiting on Father's Day appeared to correspond to those who visited more routinely: weekly, monthly or several times a year.

Comparing these statistics with those collected on an 'ordinary' weekday later in the year – a Thursday in September – we see a rather different picture. The cemetery's official figures for visitors on such a day would be around 500 people. We observed 322 of these and found that fewer were in groups than was the case on Father's Day. Just over half (54 per cent) were in groups of two or three people – an average of 2.5 per group. These visitors appeared to be a decade or so older than those on Father's Day; the largest number (38 per cent) appeared to be over 65. A higher proportion of these visitors were men (46 per cent) than was the case on Father's Day. Interestingly, more of the men than the women fell into the category of older visitors; 41 per cent of men and 36 per cent of women were in the 65 years and over age group. That nearly half of ordinary day visitors were on their own suggests that visiting on a weekday had a different, perhaps more private character. Indeed, some informants admitted that they preferred to avoid the noise and agitation associated with the special days, as it disrupted their more contemplative mood.

The City of London Cemetery's records of visitor numbers throughout the year help contextualize our survey of an 'ordinary' week, April 1997, at CLCC. The official figures show that nearly 13,000 visits were made that April, giving a daily average of 705. The difference between weekdays and weekends is marked, with 580 typifying Monday to Fridays, Saturdays averaging at 796 and Sundays over a thousand (1,299). The counts for Monday, Friday, Saturday and Sunday that we were able to record reflect this hierarchy of visiting preferences. They also allow us to say a little more about the solitary and group nature of visiting on particular days. Whereas people tended to visit on their own on Mondays, Saturday visits were more likely to be of two people. These patterns were reflected at the other three sites as well, though it was not possible to deploy resources as intensively there as at the main site, CLCC.

Bushey United Jewish Cemetery

The special ritual day chosen to survey visitors at Bushey was the Sunday preceding the Day of Atonement (Yom Kippur) in September 1996. We counted 2,859 visitors between 8.30 a.m. and 5.00 p.m. that day, almost equally men and women (women 50.2 per cent, men 48.7 per cent). The largest age group appeared to be those between 45 and 65 years (40 per cent), with 31 per cent falling into the next largest category, 65 and older. Nearly half of these special-day visitors were in groups of two (48 per cent), and nearly a third visited alone (32 per cent).

Comparison of the special day with an ordinary Thursday several weeks later, in October 1996, shows much smaller numbers: 262, or less than 10 per cent of those visiting on the special day. Marginally more women visited on the weekday (52 per cent vs. 50 per cent), and the age distribution suggests that older people visited on the ordinary day, a pattern also seen at CLCC. Significantly, of the 75 visitors in the over 65 age group, the number of male visitors was 47 and the number of female visitors 28. As at CLCC, there were no very large groups – those of five or more – on the ordinary day.

New Southgate Cemetery

A Sunday in July 1997 yielded a count of 1,055 persons entering New Southgate Cemetery between 9.00 a.m. and 5.00 p.m. Of these, well over 90 per cent were in family groups of three or more generations. Most of the visitors came in cars from the local church following the Sunday service. Some family groups who were there for the memorial service of the deceased included 20 visitors or more. The age distribution of these groups ranged from 5 to over 70 years. An equal number of men and women were noted at the cemetery.

Sundays at New Southgate are exceptional days in that memorials are almost always being carried out then, and therefore unusually large numbers of people attend. On ordinary weekdays, smaller groups and solitary visitors are more common. Marginally more elderly female visitors than males visit on ordinary weekdays. Special visits at Christmas, Easter, name days and birthdays combine the annual memorial service at the church with prayers at the grave in the cemetery.

Woodgrange Park Cemetery

The special day observed at this site was the end of Ramadan in February 1997. This was a Saturday, and we observed between 8.00 a.m. and 4.00 p.m.

We counted approximately 2,012 visitors, mainly between 8.30 a.m. and 1 p.m. While half of these were in groups of four, five and six in cars, many were also on foot. Individual men and boys came in the first few hours, and women and very small children arrived towards midday and into the afternoon, usually as part of large groups of six or seven. The volume of visitors on this occasion was in marked contrast to the small trickle noted on an ordinary fieldwork day. Then, we counted possibly six or seven visitors, both Muslims and people visiting older Christian memorials, per hour, amounting to 50 or so per day, with a peak in visiting between 2.00 and 3.00 p.m., after prayers, and a concentration of male visitors at that time after Friday prayers.

Notes

Chapter 1

1. For frequently cited anthropology and archaeology volumes about mortuary rituals among non-Western peoples, see Huntington and Metcalf (1979); Humphreys and King (1981); Bloch and Parry (1982); Cederroth, Corlin and Lindstrom (1988); Damon and Wagner (1989); Chesson (2001); and Silverman and Small (2002). For more general discussions, see Goody (1974); Barley (1995); Hockey (1996); and Sheridan (2000). Among the useful individual studies of funerary behaviour in non-industrial societies, see Goody (1962); Plath (1964); Bloch (1971); Danforth (1982); Badone (1989); Kan (1989); Pardo (1989); Catedra (1992); and Parry (1994). Historians and archaeologists have also contributed stimulating research on changes in Western funerary practices and mortuary rituals; see, for example: Aries (1974; 1981); Taylor (1980); McManners (1981); Whaley (1981); Cannon (1989); Litten (1991); Llewellyn (1991); Sloane (1991); Laqueur (1996); Houlbrooke (1998); Rugg (1998); and Tarlow (1999).

With regard to studying funeral rituals and cemetery behaviour in contemporary Western, industrial society, it must be noted that cemetery research is often considered an insensitive topic and the bereaved too vulnerable a population for study. Furthermore many social scientists, like others in Western society, possibly wish to distance death and have eschewed this subject of investigation. Even in the gerontology literature, where death is a frequent topic, the place of the cemetery in the lives of the elderly – either as a site to mourn a deceased spouse and/or as a place to prepare for their own certain demise – has not been examined. However, one important exception to the lack of studies of cemeteries from the perspective of the users-mourners is the ground-breaking anthropological research of New England cemetery behaviour by Warner (1959). See also, Sudnow (1967); Clegg (1989); Prior (1989); Williams (1990); Jonker (1996); Reimers (1999); and Small (2001).

It is also necessary to note the growing number of sociologists and anthropologists who are publishing contemporary studies of death and dying. See, for example, Hockey (1990); Walter (1991, 1994, 1999); Littlewood (1992); and Clark (1993).

2. For studies of cemetery design and memorial monuments see Weaver (1915); Clegg (1984); Hunt (1984); Brooks, Elliott, Litten, Robinson, Robinson and Temple (1989); Elliott (1989); Woudstra (1989); Meller (1994); Bowdler (1996); Waterfield (1996); and Watkin (1996). See also, Etlin (1984); Jackson and Vergara (1989); Sloane (1991); and Meyer (1993).

3. Evergreens, particularly the yew in England and the cypress tree in Greece, have traditionally symbolized immortality and their presence often indicates the existence of a cemetery. In Greece, this association is so close that mention of the word 'cypress' is assumed to refer to the cemetery. For a discussion of this Greek association, see Panourgia (1995).

4. Douglas (1985).

5. For an introductory discussion of the image of the rural churchyard in English consciousness and iconography see Worpole (2003: 63-77); Draper (1929); and also Schuyler (1984: 291-304) for an analysis of the influence of Gray's Elegy, which celebrated, indeed romanticized, the beauties of England's country churchyards. However, if the churchyard did not provide an image of an appropriate burial environment to many study participants in this study, it might have been in part because it was only in rural areas that churchyards continued to be used for burial (B. Elliott, pers. com). Class issues might also have influenced images of appropriate burial places (J. Woudstra, pers. com).

Importantly, too, from the seventeenth century onward, there was a growing advocacy from persons such as Christopher Wren, John Evelyn and John Vanbrugh for burial and commemoration within a 'natural' landscape setting, rather than in an overcrowded, unwholesome churchyard. Traditionally, most memorials to the dead were displayed in churches or churchyards at the site of burial, but in the eighteenth century, landscaped estates also came to serve as sites for commemorative monuments. The Grand Tour had given many in the British upper classes an awareness of the Roman practice of burial in the open countryside, outside the city walls, rather than on sacred, urban ground. This new sensibility found expression in Yorkshire in Hawksmoor's design for the mausoleum at Castle Howard and also in Lincolnshire with the neoclassical tomb at Brocklesby Park, which evoked the image of Elysium and Arcady as seen in the paintings of Poussain and Claude. As David Coffin (1994) has pointed out, this gradual shift in the tradition of burial from urban and architectural sites to the natural landscape, to the garden, was continued in William Shenstone's placement of a funerary urn on the grounds of The Leasowes, in Alexander Pope's garden at Twickenham with its memorial obelisk and at Stowe with its triumphal columns. These concepts linking death and the garden were realized most fully in the nineteenth century with the creation of the extra-mural garden cemetery. Here it must also be noted that these early cemeteries took their inspiration from the late eighteenth-century England landscape parks where the word 'garden' then referred to an informal landscape (for a discussion of this history, see Hunt (1992). As Brent Elliott further points out, however, the development of cemeteries took place at a time when the meaning of the term 'garden' was ambiguous and shifting (for a discussion of these changes in garden aesthetics and vocabulary, see Elliott (1986). Elliott (pers. com) suggests that the public transferred these changing attributes of 'garden' from that of informal landscape to formal garden to the cemetery and thereby helped to bring the changing nineteenth-century styles of the garden into the cemetery world.

For a further discussion of the evolution of the garden cemetery, see the various writings of Curl; (1972; 1975; 1984; 1993; 1994); Brooks et al. (1989); Elliott (1989); and Bowdler (1996). Interesting, too, are the comments of nineteenth-century observers about cemeteries and churchyards; see, for example, Stone (1858) and Mrs Basil Holmes (1896).

6. For literature on the Garden of Eden in different religious and cultural traditions, see Ashton and Whyte (2001); and Manuel and Manuel (1971).

7. Thomas (1983: 236).
8. For an excellent discussion of the many myths and interpretations of the biblical story of the Garden of Eden and the theme of nature, see Merchant (2003).
9. A number of historians have traced the multilayered meanings of the English garden through time. Among these scholars are Strong (1979); Thomas (1983); Elliott (1986); Hunt and Willis (1990); Hunt (1992); Coffin (1994).
10. For a discussion of the garden, the cycles of nature and ideas of time, see Leach (1961); Paul (1984); and Francis and Hester (1995). Also see Gell (1992).
11. Webster's Third New International Dictionary (1981).
12. Oxford English Dictionary (1989, Vol. 7).
13. Harrison (2003: 37–54); Hallote (1991:38–9).
14. Hodder (1984: 51–68).
15. Azara (1999: 8-39).
16. See Meskell (2002).
17. Azara (1999:31).
18. Firth (1936).
19. Hallote (1991: 37).
20. We chose to study whole-body, earth burial for the following three reasons: (1) cremation has peaked and with the ageing population in England, the number of burials is unlikely to decrease; (2) England is a multicultural nation, and growing populations of Muslims and Afro-Caribbeans traditionally select burial and rule out cremation and (3) from our research, we found broad evidence of possible influence, usually subtle and sometimes direct, on the part of local authorities and funeral directors encouraging people to select cremation, when it might not be their real preference.
21. Halcrow Fox (1996); Environment, Transport and Regional Affairs Committee (2001; Vol. I and Vol. II).
22. Environment, Transport and Regional Affairs Committee (2001: Vol. I, xlviii). This 2001 Parliamentary Committee on Cemeteries and Burial Policy in England drew upon Davies and Shaw's (1995) regionally based study of burial and cremation preferences, as well as the London Planning Advisory Committee (LPAC) (1997) and Halcrow Fox (1996) audit of each of the London authorities responsible for burials.
23. Responsibility for most cemeteries in England involves local authorities, which range from metropolitan borough councils to city district and borough councils and the smaller administrative entities of the town and parish councils. Local authority responsibility for municipal cemeteries, as opposed to those not in public

ownership, varies enormously, from a relatively hands-off approach, limited to overseeing safety and maintenance, to more involved approaches that have led to an integrated bereavement service. Authority to bury and cremate is not restricted to local authorities, however; private companies, as well as those that fall under the heading 'not-for-profit', have had such authority since the nineteenth century. Before that, religious groups assumed the responsibility. Denominational sites such as those provided for Anglican, Jewish, Catholic and Orthodox Christian burials are likely to be among the 'not-for-profit' group. Legislative provision has been made for the local authority to assume responsibility for a site that is closed, and responsibility for some Church of England and older denominational burial sites has been transferred in this way.

24. The selection of the six research sites took account of this spectrum of characteristics as it applied to London in 1995. Location is crucial, because land availability and values differ, as do catchment areas and accessibility. Size has implications for management and organizational strategies. Denominational versus non-denominational use also influences practices, which in turn are reflected in the larger- and smaller-scale landscapes of the cemetery. Ownership – public or private (local authority, private business, religious/cultural/trust) – determines, at least partly, the aims of the cemetery, its lines of accountability, and its style of operation, as well as the level of funding available for the management and development of the site. The date of establishment has some bearing upon the level of activity a cemetery can support at the beginning of the twenty first century. Although the managers of the cemeteries chosen for research anticipated problems with shortage of space, all the sites were active at the time of the study except Abney Park, where the few burials that still took place were in plots already owned by a family. The various selection features interlock and overlap: for instance, levels of activity and inactivity, in terms of numbers of burials each year, affect decisions about emphasizing historic or ecological value in future planning for old sites.

25. The LPAC (1997) and Halcrow Fox (1996) audit of London cemeteries was not yet available when we reviewed and evaluated possible sites, so the LPAC frame of 147 London cemeteries could not be employed. However, as in the LPAC audit, the older, small, and now inactive inner city churchyards were ruled out of our frame of selection. The intention was to concentrate upon these cemeteries, opened in the nineteenth century, which continued to accommodate the dead and receive mourners at the end of the

twentieth century. New forms of burial, such as those termed 'green', 'ecological' or 'woodland', which entail the use of open land followed by tree planting, are still minority choices in London, though of increasing significance nationally. Such sites were not given prominence in the study, but they were investigated through a postal enquiry focussing on informants who were associated with the Carlisle Cemetery and its woodland burial developments. Carlisle Cemetery, opened in 1855, is a 94-acre municipal cemetery located in Cumbria, in the north-west region of England.

26. To date, little detailed information has been available about the ownership and management of these denominational cemeteries, or about their relationships with their members. This information is now acknowledged as necessary for the future planning of the ongoing needs of these groups. Furthermore, the contrasting migration and settlement patterns of these three communities – Orthodox Jewish, Greek Orthodox and Bengali Muslims – documented through the geography of their older cemetery sites – allows examination of their death customs, forged in earlier times and different places, and the mutual influences between the incoming and receiving communities over decades.

27. Brooks et al. (1989: 51); Meller (1994); and Hussein (1996).

28. For a discussion of the history of London's East End, see Cox (1994); Pewsey (1996); Palmer (2000).

29. Gardner (2002).

30. The East End population who used the City of London Cemetery is well known through the pioneer research on East End family and kin relations conducted by the Institute of Community Studies (ICS): Townsend (1957); Young and Willmott (1957); Marris (1958); Willmott and Young (1961). These studies provided us with important background information and proved helpful in interpreting our data. Interestingly, many of those studied earlier by the ICS are now dead and are the focus of the visits to graves described by some of the participants for this study. Also, many visitors to the City of London Cemetery have forbears buried at Abney Park and Woodgrange Park Cemeteries (two other research sites), thus giving additional perspectives on these very different burial grounds. Research was also conducted at Tower Hamlets Cemetery (now a nature refuge), Manor Park and St Patrick's Catholic Cemetery. All of these are geographically close to the main research site, and are known to many CLCC visitors who have deceased family members buried elsewhere.

31. Newman (1976: 17).

32. Gould and Esh (1964: 6); Wolfston (1985: 32).
33. Gould and Esh (1964: 1); Newman (1976: 1).
34. Tucker (1992).
35. In addition to Bushey Cemetery, we conducted research at other United Synagogue cemeteries: Alderney Road, opened in 1696; East Ham, opened in 1919; Willesden, opened in 1873 and Waltham Abbey, opened in 1960. This information on the founding dates of United Synagogue cemeteries was taken from the United Synagogue (1955) *Laws and Byelaws of the Burial Society*. With authorization from the West London Synagogue of British Jews, we conducted a few days of fieldwork at Edgwarebury and Golders Green Cemeteries, and with permission of Adath Yisroel Burial Society, we also did research at its cemetery at Carterhatch Lane, Enfield. We also contacted the Federation of Synagogues and the Spanish and Portuguese Jews' Congregation, but they both declined to grant permission for research at their respective cemeteries.
36. New Southgate Cemetery and Crematorium Newsletter, Summer, 2000.
37. New Southgate Cemetery and Crematorium Web page at www. newsouthgate.com.
38. We conducted some additional research in the Greek sections of Norwood Cemetery and also at Hendon Cemetery, an older burial site used before New Southgate became available
39. Gardner (2002).
40. Woodgrange Park Cemetery Act 1993, House of Lords.
41. For a history of Abney Park Cemetery, see Joyce (1994: 11–55).
42. For a discussion of the significance of Egyptian motifs in the iconography of death, see Grant (1988: 236–53).
43. Solman (1995).
44. Our analysis of these extended and detailed narratives has been made within the broader context of the many shorter accounts of visiting experiences and also alongside findings from the quantitative surveys conducted at each of the main sites.
45. During the first year of the study during the Jewish High Holidays, the superintendent at Bushey United Jewish Cemetery requested that Francis confine her conversations with visitors to the cemetery's main entrance area. Visitors there were usually eager to get to the grounds or in a hurry to leave, and although most expressed willingness to help with the research project, many conversations were truncated and conducted in haste, far from the affecting presence of the grave. For this reason, Francis instead chose to spend additional time at Willesden and East Ham Cemeteries,

where she could circulate more freely and speak with people in a more relaxed manner on the grounds. Many of the visitors to these two older cemeteries, however, were in their sixties and seventies or older, and their comments reflected a view of life, death and religion from the perspective of their years. It was not until the second year of the study that Francis received permission to talk with people on the grounds of Bushey Cemetery and was free to accompany consenting family members as they made their 'annual rounds' to the graves of kin and friends. Although a concerted effort was then made to speak with people of a variety of ages at Bushey, the entire data set reflects the conditions and research decisions made during the first year of study. It is interesting to note that recent survey work (see United Synagogue web-page) of the age profile of the United Synagogue membership indicates a high proportion of older members: in 2001, 65 per cent of the members were over fifty years of age and only 5 per cent of the total membership was under thirty. This survey data corroborates our own survey research at Bushey (see Appendix 5) and supports our belief that the research data collected for this book are representative of the age distribution of the wider United Synagogue community.

46. Neophytou conducted many interviews in Greek; she was familiar with New Southgate Cemetery before the research project began and was already acquainted with some of her study participants and their families.

47. For information about the survey research conducted at the royal parks by the Centre for Leisure and Tourism Studies of the University of North London, see Curson, Evans and Bohrer (1995); and also Curson (1997).

48. This research strategy was devised by Ian Turner, a retired superintendent of the City of London Cemetery, who generously shared it with the researchers.

49. We also asked visitors who mentioned family members who did not visit to take questionnaires to their not-visiting kin, but none were returned.

50. For the discussion about how different anthropologists have dealt with the study of death, see Fabian (1973) and Rosaldo (1984). Also see Walter (1997) for a parallel discussion about the possible differences among cultural groups in the expression of grief.

51. Bourdieu (1977).

52. Notable exceptions are the publications of various religious groups detailing prescribed mourning behaviour. Among these are: Vaporis (1977); Rabinowicz (1982); Burial Society of the

United Synagogue (1986; 1995); Goldberg (1991); Kutty (1991); Vassiliadis (1993); Churches' Group on Funeral Services at Cemeteries and Crematoria (1997); Jupp and Rogers (1997); National Funeral College (1998). Also see Walter (1990).

Also, many cemetery managers and religious leaders have a detailed understanding of cemetery behaviour and use this knowledge in policy and practice, but, unfortunately, this information has not usually been made available through publications. See, however, the writings of Lynch (1997; 1998; and 2000), which provide wonderful insight into the mortuary 'dismal trade'.

53. The contract between generations is a major theme in Harrison (2003).
54. Warner (1959: 285).
55. For a discussion of this idea, see Bloch (1971) and Miller (2001a: 13).
56. Goody (1993: 283–320).
57. For a discussion of metaphors and flowers as metaphors, see Lakoff and Johnson (1980); Fernandez (1991) and Ross (1995). For the symbolism of flowers, see Clegg (1984); and Chevalier and Gheerbrant (1998).
58. For a discussion of the healing properties of gradens, see Gerlach-Spriggs, Kaufman and Warner (1998); Tyson (1998).
59. Hecht (2001: 136).
60. Francis and Hester (1995).
61. Douglas (1985).
62. In medieval times as flowers were conceptually and symbolically linked with bones and other bodily relics, today they can serve as metaphors for the dead themselves. For a discussion of this point, see Goody and Poppi (1994: especially page 160).
63. Goody and Poppi (1994); see also Brown (1981).
64. Ware (1991: 90–110).
65. Polson and Marshall (1975: 285): 'Cremation is not practised, because burning is associated with uncleanness; Mohammed gave no authority for it; and it is believed that the soul remains in the body after death for from three to forty days.'
66. Gardner (2002).
67. Lamm (1969: 225); Raphael (1996); Jacobs (1997: 71).
68. Goldberg (1991: 382, 41:2).
69. The following notice was posted outside the Bushey Cemetery office: 'The term *SHEMOT* refers to pages from sacred books such as *Chumashim* and *Siddurim* that are no longer usable because they are old or torn, etc. Jewish law requires that *SHEMOT* be treated with due respect and therefore, they may not be thrown

away. Please place any such *SHEMOT* here so that they may be disposed of in an appropriate manner.'

70. For a useful discussion of rituals and death, see Hockey (1990); Bell (1997); and Seale (1998: 29–32).
71. See Brown (1981) and Meskell and Joyce (2003).
72. While the idea of home is an expression of the self, it also entails a connection with the physical body; see Bachelard (1969); Giddens (1991); Turner (1992, 1996); and Lock (2002).
73. For discussion of the sociology of the body see Turner (1991) and Synott (1992).
74. For attempts to develop an inclusive model of grief, see Klass (1999).

Chapter 2

1. Brooks, Elliott, Litten et al (1989); Rugg (1992); and Hussein and Rugg (2003).
2. Silverman (2002: 3). For discussions of landscapes and ideas of space and place that were used in the writing of this chapter, see: Stilgoe (1982); Foucault (1986); Cosgrove and Daniels (1988); Lefebvre (1991); Bender (1993); Cosgrove (1993); Rose (1993); Hirsch (1995); Hirsch and O'Hanlon (1995); Schama (1995); Williamson (1995); and Malpas (1999).
3. Curl (1972; 1993).
4. Gorer (1965). Psychologists and psychiatrists have tended to order the emotions and behaviours of grief into stages: Kubler-Ross (1970); phases: Parkes (1986); or tasks: Worden (1991).
5. Merchant (1986).
6. Brooks et al. (1989); Dunk and Rugg (1994).
7. Lees (2000).
8. Rugg (1997).
9. Chadwick (1843).
10. Richardson (1989).
11. Walker (1839).
12. Strang (1831); Milner (1846).
13. The idea of the outdoor tomb had already gained prestige in the eighteenth century when the very wealthy, in imitation of the Romans and the classical elegiac tradition, had chosen to be buried in a romantic, landscaped garden set in the open country-

side, rather than on sacred, urban ground. In the early nineteenth century, outdoor burial for the well-to-do was further accepted as select churchyards were chosen by important persons such as Sir John Soane, who deemed St. Giles-in-the-Fields, adjoining Old St. Pancras Church, a site suitable for the tomb memorialization of his beloved wife. See Coffin (1994); and Waterfield (1996).

14. Petrucci (1998).
15. Phrase taken from Sloane (1991: 54).
16. Brooks et al. (1989: 156).
17. Rugg (1992; 1997).
18. Meller (1994).
19. Laqueur (2002).
20. In Kensal Green Cemetery, however, the bodies of the poor, hidden in unmarked shaft graves, subsidized these middle-class burials.
21. Hussein and Rugg (2003) trace London's current burial crisis to this cemetery legislation of the 1850s. Rather than reforming policy and encompassing all burial functions under a single state department, the centuries-old tradition of parish ownership and local control was continued, resulting, they argue, in today's critical lack of burial space, uneven provision of services and inequities in cost.
22. The following material was adapted from Francis (1997).
23. On the City of London Cemetery as an intact historical landscape, see Meller (1994).
24. Phrase taken from Sloane (1991: 133).
25. Elliott (1991).
26. Moore, Mitchell and Turnbull (1977: vi.)
27. Moore, Mitchell and Turnbull (1977: vii).
28. Loudon(1981/1843). Loudon was the foremost British horticulture expert of the nineteenth century, and his many publications had a profound effect on English gardening and landscape design. See Elliott (1986); and Simo (1988) for discussions of Loudon and horticulture.
29. Loudon (1981/1843: 1).
30. Recently, as part of the conservation-management plan, the mature conifers screening the front road have been removed to 'open-up' the cemetery.
31. Foucault (1984); also see Rotenberg (1995) for an analysis of Foucault's ideas of heterotopias.
32. Warner (1959: 287).
33. Archival evidence from the 1850s suggests that Haywood adopted the catacomb design of the Lebanon Circle at Highgate Cemetery to a Gothic style suitable for the City of London Cemetery.

34. Elliott (1986); and Simo (1988).
35. Rugg (1992).
36. Taylor (1994); also see Greenhalgh and Worpole (1995).
37. Elliott (1996).
38. The identification of the Gothic style with Christian belief during the period from about the 1850s to the early twentieth century guaranteed its success as the most fitting mode for cemeteries. See a discussion by Brooks et al. (1989: 21–2); and Environment, Transport and Regional Affairs Committee (2001: Vol. 1, 204).
39. This practice continues today.
40. Warner (1959); also see Rugg (2000) for a discussion of this and other defining characteristics of a cemetery.
41. Strange (2003) discusses the pragmatic, often shared, use of third-class grave space by working-class families. Her work challenges the traditional assumption of Cannadine (1981: 187–242) that burial space held the same meaning as a site for grief, commemoration and remembrance for all social classes.
42. Strang (1831).
43. Thomas (1983); Rival (1998: 1–36).
44. Brooks et al. (1989: 14).
45. For a discussion of the history and complex nature of Victorian garden designs, see Elliott (1986).
46. As the members of the Victorian Society's committee on cemeteries noted (Brooks et al. (1989: 51): 'The character of the City of London [Cemetery] is more than the sum of its influences, and quite different from that of any predecessor. At little Ilford, the Victorian cemetery is redefined: the key factor is the enhanced scale on which it is conceived and planned. This is more than a mere function of size. Haywood's cemetery has a consistent and proportionate breath of design that sets grandly formal features – the wide principal drives, the carriage-turns about the chapels, the sunken oval of the catacombs – in a more relaxed, essentially open landscape, with long, curving paths and informally planted trees, standing alone or grouped into copses. Both rural and urban in its connotations, both personal and public, the large coherence of the City of London Cemetery was an expression of the new corporate identity taken on by the hundred and more parishes it served. At Little Ilford, the Victorians created a model for the municipal cemetery.'
47. Silverman (2002b: 167–90).
48. Stroebe, Geigen, Geigen and Stroebe (1996: 37).
49. On the nation's post-war bereavement mood, see Winter (1995).

50. For a discussion of ideas linking death and nature, see Coffin (1994).
51. For a discussion of the history of cremation, see Jupp (1990).
52. Elliott (1991).
53. Creese (1966); and Brown (1982).
54. At that time the cemetery was conducting 3,373 cremations a year. January, the busiest month, saw 29 cremations a day.
55. Winter (1995).
56. Longworth (1967).
57. The landscape designer Brenda Colvin (1970: 328) also lauded this new uniformity of design as a contrast to older-style memorial grounds, in which 'the worst effects are produced by the cult of individuality run wild . . . especially manifested in the memorials and headstones, whose lack of orderly unifying design makes eyesores of many urban cemeteries'.
58. Cemetery superintendent, F. G. Herbert, made this comment in a presentation on 'Lawn Cemeteries – Private Graves' to the Burial Board for the City of London in 1959.
59. For a discussion of paradigms of grief, see Silverman and Klass (1996: 3–27).
60. A less expensive form of private lawn grave was offered in place of communal interment. In it, the exclusive right of burial was limited to fifty years, and memorials were restricted to bronze tablets laid flush with the ground; inscriptions could be engraved on them upon payment of a fee. The area was kept flat 'to facilitate mowing and preserve the beauty of the landscape'. Within a few years, this grave lease scheme was discontinued. Management has drawn on past experience and future predictions to develop a new set of policies that provide income to maintain memorials and to cap future repair costs while managing capital assets in a sustainable fashion.
61. Cemetery superintendent F. G. Herbert made this comment in a presentation of 27 June 1950, entitled 'Lawn Section – Common Graves' to the Burial Board for the City of London.
62. For a discussion of Victorian cemetery practices, see Jalland (1996).
63. Townsend (1957: 12).
64. Miller (2001b: 107–21).
65. Miller (2001b: 113–14); Taylor (1999: 223–37).
66. Lancelot 'Capability' Brown was the designer of eighteenth-century landscape parks, the design elements of which were broad expanses of lawn with clumps or belts of trees. Brent Elliott (pers. com) suggests that the popularity of lawn cemeteries in the twentieth

century was encouraged by the publication of Stroud's (1975) study re-evaluating the informal landscapes of Capability Brown.

67. Mourners underscored this version by contrasting the lawn section with their image of the Victorian cemetery as 'morbid' and inappropriate for the realities of death in today's society: 'I always associated the Victorian idea of death with the death bed scene and the family all around. But now, when our daughter died, we were on our way and rushed into the hospital to find she had already died. But my wife was with her Nan when she died.'

68. *Collins Greek-English Dictionary*, 1980, London & Glasgow: Collins.

69. Hirschon (1989); Hart (1992).

70. Many visitors find the cemetery to their liking ('The cemetery is peaceful and pleasant, I quite like it. Most of my friends are here; I'd like to be buried here'), though others object to Bushey's huge size ('This cemetery is packed to overflowing. At the last funeral I came to, we had to walk miles').

71. Hallote (2001: 48–49) also discusses biblical references to Jewish burial under a tree.

72. For a further discussion of the place of the cemetery in Jewish life, see the manuscript for the play the *Stones of Kolin* by Herman (1996).

73. Gardner (2002: 104).

Chapter 3

1. Several theorists have put forward frameworks for grief that group the cultural mourning practices into larger patterns. One such structure advanced early in the twentieth century by van Gennep (1960/1909) and slightly modified by Meskell (2001) separates these mortuary rituals into three stages: separation and bereavement, recovery and readjustment and finally maintenance, a time of ongoing practices of commemoration when the dead may be incorporated into the world of the living. Hertz (1960/1907)) argued that the death practices of mourners also deal with the body and soul of the deceased. He saw the three principal actors in the drama of death – the corpse, the soul and the mourners – as being linked symbolically as they moved together through the rites of passage: separation, transition and incorporation. The ultimate

goal of death rituals, according to Hertz, is to effect a smooth transition from one state to another for each of the three actors in this ritual drama.

2. Before the corpse can be buried, the law requires that a medical certificate be issued, stating the cause of death. The death must also be registered within five days by the registrar of births, marriages and deaths in the sub-district in which it occurred. The certificate for disposal (referred to as the 'green form') is then issued by the registrar, giving permission for the body to be buried. No funeral can take place until this certificate has been obtained. (For cremation, additional documentation is required.) In arranging for the funeral, the undertaker needs to know whether the deceased is to be buried or cremated, where the body is to await the funeral, whether there will be a funeral service and, if so, where it will be held and who will conduct it. With a burial, it is also necessary to establish whether the dead person had already acquired the right of burial in a grave space in a cemetery. See Smale (1994).

3. A staff member is available to show mourners the various burial options and to give them a pamphlet explaining the grave owner's rights and obligations. Members of the Afro-Caribbean community, for example, usually choose the new classic grave as 'more American', and consequently their plots are clustered together within the sections where this type of grave is now offered.

4. Only the owner has the legal right to open the grave for burial; or if the deceased is the grave-owner, he/she has the right to be buried there. When a grave is purchased, it is the Right of Burial in that particular space which is acquired, rather than a land purchase. This Right of Burial entails the right to place a memorial there, or to have the grave opened for interment. The deceased cannot be the owner of a new grave, as a living owner is needed to take responsibility for the grave. The law states that without the written authority of the owner, no burial can take place in that grave; the exception is when the deceased him/herself is the owner, and then the burial can proceed. However, only written authority allows a memorial to be erected. Therefore, if the deceased is the grave owner, the title must be transferred before the headstone can be erected. These regulations can lead to 'awkward' situations, as when a CLCC widower was denied permission to be buried with his wife by her brother, the owner of the grave.

5. During the period of research, two conferences on 'Good Funeral Practice' were sponsored by the National Funerals College Project, and various publications were directed toward improving the quality of funerals in England – for example: *The Charter for the*

Bereaved was written and published in 1996/1998 by the Institute of Burial and Cremation Administration, while *The Dead Citizens Charter* was prepared in 1996 by the National Funerals College Project. The funerals we observed at the City of London Cemetery were usually conducted by ministers who had not known the deceased personally. At one ceremony, for example, the minister had visited with the family at home before the service, and his eulogy paid tribute to the major events of the deceased's life, mentioning her devotion to spouse and children, her work to help support her family and her principles and values. The minister concluded by urging the family members to seek comfort in religious belief. In a second service, the minister stumbled through a letter describing the deceased that had been handwritten by a son-in-law, and Frank Sinatra's version of the song 'I Did It My Way' was played.

6. This is also the case for those with no religious affiliation.
7. For further discussion of this idea, see Young and Cullen (1996).
8. The idea of death as an 'opportunity' is discussed by Taylor (1989a: 149–53).
9. Some mourners, however, may not yet accept the loss or its implications for their own mortality and delay selecting a stone, which could eventually mark their own grave. Equally difficult for mourners may be the task of writing an appropriate epitaph, which necessitates defining the meaning of the other and sometimes leaving a blank space for oneself. 'One side is all of Mary; the other is black, blank, for me.'
10. Also see Davies (1996) for a discussion of the significance of nature, planting and flowers in new rituals of death and memory.
11. See note 1, which explains Hertz's concept of a parallel journey of the body, soul and mourner.
12. One Jewish study participant, a member of a Liberal congregation, contrasted her feelings about Jewish cemeteries with her understanding of Church of England burials: 'There is a sense of being separate, even in death. . . . This was brought home to me in the country. I went to funerals for people who were buried in the local church grounds. They were near home, it was right, it had a human scale. The cemetery was tended by people who knew each other and the people buried there. There was a sense of extension, that the living years were extended after death. They were still in the local community where you belong. But as for Jews, we have to be separate. We have to travel long distances to vast, anonymous, ugly, uncaring burial grounds. The land does not care if it receives us. We are just an object after life. There is no sense of

belonging at all. It's anonymity, almost brutality. There's a shrug-your-shoulders indifference about big cemeteries. Also, there's a sense of being given permission by the country we live in; we are given permission to be buried in our own particular type of cemeteries. For others, it's their right; they do not have this sense of segregation. You can be buried where you like.'

13. A Jewish grave must be located among other Jewish graves or on grounds bought by a Jewish organization, and burial rights must be permanent. The United Synagogue owns its own burial land and conducts its own rites of burial.

14. All members of the *Chevrah* must be observant Jews. At the annual meeting of the Ladies' *Chevrah Kadisha*, the women were welcomed by the head of the United Synagogue with these words of praise, which illustrate their position of honour within the community: 'The women who do this work do a *mitvah* (good deed) which is beautiful; they stand on the interface of this and the next world . . . they are like the mother who brings a baby into this world. They, too, stand on the interface of the other and this world. They are also a source of comfort, solace and support. They are one of the great jewels of the United Synagogue, and their task is sacred and beautiful.' In discussing her work as head as the Women's *Chevra*, the leader commented: 'People can't say "thank you", that is the beauty in it. For some, it is the first time they have had respect – some women have had very hard lives and this is the first time they were shown respect.'

15. Any hair on the comb or a plaster (band-aid) with blood is buried with the body. Any part of the body that was there in life is buried with the corpse. If, for example, the person had had a limb amputated, it would be buried with him or her. The body, in its complete state, expresses faith in the possibility of future physical resurrection.

16. The shroud consists of six garments for women and seven for men, see Sheridan (2000: 80). The arms are laid at the side and the hands are not clenched, the position of the body at death signifying a Jewish burial.

17. Rabinowicz (1982: 34–7) explains that the mourners stand when this rite is performed, as 'all sorrow should be met standing upright'. Lamm (1969: 38–44) further suggests that this rite may serve as a substitute for the 'custom of tearing the flesh and the hair which symbolizes the loss of one's own flesh and blood in sympathy for the deceased'; and that this rite also confronts the mourner with the finality of separation, expressed on his/her own clothes and on his/her own person.

18. Kaddish does not mention death, but rather praises God and concentrates on life. Kaddish 'helps the soul move one step further'; it is recited daily in the synagogue during the mourning period, at *Yiskor* services and on the anniversary of the day of death.

19. Walter (2001) suggests that these ritual practices are small rites of incorporation within a larger encompassing ritual of liminality and incorporation.

20. During this time, some daughters regularly attend Saturday Sabbath services at the synagogue and silently join the recitation of Kaddish.

21. One United Synagogue rabbi, in discussing people who come to the cemetery regularly, further elucidated Orthodox Jewish ideas about frequent grave visiting: 'People who come to the cemetery often are those who cannot let go, they make the grave a shrine; to come every week is too much, it is not healthy. What is here? The physical remains only, the spiritual part, the spirit and the memories are at home and with you all the time.'

22. Sliw (1995).

23. Vaporis (1977).

24. In many municipal burial grounds, the installation and erection of crosses in the Orthodox style is permitted so long as existing guidelines and procedures are followed. According to one Greek study participant at the City of London Cemetery, it was fairly easy to obtain permission to install an Orthodox cross and glass box-holder for her father's grave. In a counter-example, however, the Greek Orthodox priest at Brighton's Orthodox church explained how he had to dismantle the Orthodox memorial cross at his son's grave because it contravened the lawn cemetery's strict rules regarding memorial stones.

25. According to Orthodox doctrine the human body must be buried complete and in its natural state. Therefore embalming is prohibited on theological grounds. In addition, such chemical procedures delay the natural decomposition of the body. For practical and hygiene purposes, however, these religious requirements are rarely adhered to and few study participants were aware of the Orthodox theological position.

26. 'Tying the deceased's hands and feet resembles and symbolizes Christ's crucifixion; untying them is the metaphoric dissolution of the deceased's earthly bonds with family and kin.' See Vassiliadis (1993: 98); du Boulay (1974); Dubisch (1989: 189–200); and Danforth (1982).

27. Vaporis (1977).

28. Vassiliadis (1993: 99).
29. Traditionally it was considered a sign of authentic feeling to show strong emotions at the funeral, and there were social expectations for close relatives of the deceased to do so.
30. Vassiliadis (1993: 99).
31. Genesis 3:19.
32. Vassiliadis (1993: 99).
33. Gardner (2002: 196).
34. Gardner (2002: 191).
35. See CRC Report (1975: 7): 'Although the first generation may take the body of an older person to the country of origin . . . this will not necessarily be the case for the second generation, which means that the need for special local facilities for Muslims will increase.'
36. See Khan Patel (2000: 2) on mental preparation for death.
37. Polson and Marshall (1975: 284).
38. See Khan Patel (2000: 3) on the Virtues of preparing the deceased.
39. Bowker (1990: 106).
40. Haleem (1995).
41. Brookwood Cemetery at Woking is described in a CRC Policy Paper on Muslim Burials (1975: 7) as 'One example is Woking Cemetery in Surrey. . . . This is expensive for Muslims in terms of the price and the distance in travelling to the burial and visiting.'

Chapter 4

1. The data for this chapter are taken from research done at the City of London, Bushey United Jewish and New Southgate Cemeteries; research on the Muslim users of Woodgrange concentrated on other topics, as the study participants visiting the site were mainly males, whose focus was often outside the home.
2. For some, the home may be the only place of mourning and memory, suggesting that certain cemeteries may not invite or may even discourage remembrance rituals at the grave.
3. Lawrence (1987) has put forward the idea that home involves mutually defining transactions between personal and social identity, the material world of domestic space and the non-physical world of ideas and symbols. In his study, home is viewed as inseparable from the self: it is an embodiment of the essence of the self and self-identity

and is an extension of the inner self. In other analyses, such as those of Cooper (1976; see also Marcus 1997), home provides a mirror for the self, and so, allows each individual to register a solid manifestation of who he or she is. Home is also a symbol of the self and one's self-identity. The home becomes a symbol for what is unrepresentable: It is the intimate interior of the self viewed from within, the public exterior of the self we display to others and a reflection of how we wish to be viewed by others. It is through such connections that the grave becomes the home of the deceased, the place for the regeneration of the identity of the occupant. It is because the past home is so closely identified with the deceased that this metaphorical pathway of relational connection can be forged between home and cemetery. For further studies on the meaning of home, see Hayward (1975); Lawrence (1982); Altman and Werner (1985); Werner, Altman and Oxley (1985); Werner (1987); and Sixsmith and Sixsmith (1990).

4. Kellett (1982).
5. Thomas (1983: 228).
6. Kellett (1982: 109).
7. Kellett (1982: 114).
8. Hoyles (1994: 1); and Porter (1995).
9. Chevalier (1998: 47–71).
10. Chevalier (1998: 50)
11. Csikszentmihalyi and Rochberg-Halton (1981); and Rubinstein (1987; 1989; 1990).
12. Rubinstein and Parmelee (1992: 140).
13. Birdwell-Pheasant and Lawrence-Zuniga (1999: 6).
14. Both parlour and cemetery are sacred places of transformative power associated with rites of passage. See Taylor (1999). The parlour is a room set apart from daily life, reserved for special occasions and formal entertaining and where the body of the deceased lay until the funeral; so, too, is the cemetery a unique space of ritual.
15. As one Jewish daughter explained: 'At the *shivah* last year for an aunt-in-law who died over age ninety, I met neighbours who knew my father growing up. An old lady of ninety-six told me I had my father's eyes. In London, everyone who knew him growing up was either all dead or I did not know them. It was wonderful to hear this, and then to have the picture of my father's mother [which is now kept on the sideboard. "When I look at my father's mother, I see my own eyes and my father's eyes – we are facially similar and are the same as his mother's."] My own mother had a difficult relationship with her mother-in-law, but I have come to understand

the situation better and to give a new explanation; I have come to know her better.' The inheritance of family photographs, sometimes only seen and acquired after the parent dies, thus may work to build a sense of family identification with generations of the past. 'I feel I am getting to know her more as she is here on my sideboard; my youngest daughter was named for her.'

16. Danforth (1982: 133), writing about mortuary practices in rural Greece, suggested that the cemetery becomes a 'second home'. 'Not only is the grave a kind of house or home for the deceased, it is also . . . a second home for the bereaved woman who spends so much time there visiting and caring for her dead relatives.'

17. Hirschon (1989: 208).

18. Dubisch (1989: 189–200); Hirschon (1989: 217); and Seremetakis (1991).

19. Dubisch (1989); Seremetakis (1991).

20. Finch and Hayes (1994).

21. For a discussion of this idea, see Weiss (1997: 169–70).

22. Mines and Weiss (1997).

23. For a discussion of a similar idea, see Hallam and Hockey (2001).

24. Hecht (2001: 123); for a discussion of the added meanings of home for older persons, see Lawton (1986) and Rowles (1993).

25. Taylor (1999: 224). For a discussion of the changing interpretation of the significance of environments, rooms and things, see Taylor's whole article, pages 223–37.

26. Lawrence (1987); Rubinstein (1987; 1989; 1990).

27. Bott (1957).

28. Rubinstein (1986a; 1986b) also discusses how elderly, widowed men construct their days.

29. As will be discussed in Chapter 6, many widowers saw their cemetery grave visiting and tending as an extension of the caregiving activities they performed before the death of their spouses.

30. When he was alive, this particular man also tended his wife's parents' grave.

31. See Rubinstein and Parmelee (1992), and also Rubinstein (1987; 1989; 1990).

32. Here the garden, like the home, becomes a domain of creative investment and personal and family expression.

33. Lawson (1910: 123); Hart (1992: 138); Panourgia (1995: 181).

34. Panourgia (1995: 181).

35. Rapport and Dawson (1998).

36. Bourdieu (1977)

37. Halbwachs (1992).

Chapter 5

1. Merewether (1993).
2. Here we suggest that landscape, like architecture, is experienced through the senses, that it arrives through the body, through the physical act of moving in and around the space.
3. Bernstein (1973); Bloch (1976).
4. The cemetery is a sanctified place and it is forbidden to eat or drink there, to pasture animals, gather grass or plants, or to sit or lean on a monument.
5. It is customary for many members of the United Synagogue to visit the cemetery on the Sunday preceding the Day of Atonement, although any time during the month of *Elul* is appropriate for this annual visit to the graves of one's parents. Holidays are determined by the Jewish calendar, which differs from the civil calendar and so do not fall on the same day each year. In addition to the annual visit at the time of the Jewish New Year, cemetery visits are also made on the day of the *Yortseit*, the Hebrew anniversary of death.
6. Although many people used similar phrases in talking about the 'meaning' of their annual visit, their uniform answers masked a wide spectrum of emotions, meanings and feelings reflecting the psychological disposition of the visitor, the nature and length of the relationship with the deceased, whether the deceased was a parent, spouse, or child, the age of the deceased at death and the age of the mourner. All of these variables are needed in order to interpret the response concerning the meaning of the visit. As one visitor remarked at the grave of his father, who had died in 1941: 'After fifty years, it is not grief but respect and memories.'
7. As one woman, who had lost both her 42-year-old husband and her 80-year-old mother replied when asked why she had come to the cemetery to visit her mother's grave: 'Do you want me to tell you the formal answer, or why I really came? Well, I really come because my father would be upset. Personally, I get nothing out of coming here; it has nothing to do with the person.'
8. Thus the date of this annual *Yortseit* visit is different for every family.
9. The time of the Jewish New Year is dictated by the religious calendar and falls during the Hebrew month of *Elul*, which comes at a different time each year from the civil calendar. To enable the elderly and others without private transport to visit Bushey for the High Holidays, the United Synagogue provides coach service on two consecutive Sundays before Yom Kippur.
10. Personal communication from *Dayan* Binstock.

11. On Yom Kippur, prayers of atonement and redemption are recited both for the dead and the living. 'Yom Kippur is a time when life can be seen as if it were not there anymore.' At this time, a person should write his or her own epitaph, and men may choose to wear a *kittel*, their future shroud, clothing the living body in the garment of death on the Day of Atonement. Burial grounds emphasize, as well, the fragility of life.

12. Raphael (1996: 333–4). The Jewish mystical tradition concerning the intercessionary powers of the souls of the departed is most fully expressed at London's Enfield Cemetery (Adath Yisroel Cemetery), where Hassidic Jews visit the sepulchre of Rabbi Schulim Moskovitz, the Rebbe of Shatz, as well as the tombs of other holy men whose powers of intercession are believed to be strong. Visitors are instructed to light candles to alert the rabbi's soul that they are there to ask for assistance and influence; in return, the supplicant is expected to improve his or her standard of Jewishness. For accounts of Eastern European cemeteries and death rituals, see Zborowski and Herzog (1952); Kugelmass and Boyarin (1983); and Roskies and Roskies (1975).

13. King (1999:150); for a further discussion of the complex relationship between acts of remembering and forgetting and the role of commemorative artefacts – particularly monuments – also see Forty (1999); Rowlands (1999); and Kuchler (1999). See Miller (1998) for a useful introduction to material culture studies.

14. When asked why she was so distraught that a scroll from another memorial, removed for a second burial, had been inadvertently left on her mother's stone, a woman replied, 'I felt like my mother had been desecrated.'

15. Notes for 'Gathering Stones: A Video Installation' by Alan Berliner, from the exhibition entitled *Jewish Artists: On the Edge*, College of Santa Fe, Santa Fe, New Mexico, 4–30 June 2000.

16. Some United Synagogue members find that placing stones on the grave stains the memorial. 'I do not want stones, which discolour the grave, really, it marks the grave.' Some families, therefore, place their stones at the base of the grave rather than on top; others put a layer of plastic under the pebbles to prevent their leaving blemishes and yet other families have discarded the custom altogether.

17. One woman described her need to bring flowers to her mother's grave at Willesden, an older United Synagogue cemetery: 'When I visit my mother's grave, first I look to see if everything is in order, to see if the stone is clean, that there are no odd bits, if it is not damaged or broken. Second, the inscription – if the lettering is

clear; I take automobile paint and touch them up if they need it. Then I empty the vase and bring fresh flowers, but only for my mother. She had the vase built in. To take flowers helps me – it gives me something to focus on when I first get there. I need to do something, to be active. I need to make a contribution of some sort, so I clean the stone and place fresh flowers, but I do not know the meaning of these acts.'

18. 'Perpetual care', as grave maintenance is called, is usually paid in advance.

19. For articulation of this viewpoint, see Gorer (1965) and Winter (1995).

20. This phrase was used by King (1999: 161) to describe the Cenotaph in Whitehall, but it can also be applied to the memorial stones in the lawn section at CLCC.

21. The following is an example of the verse texts we observed on tombstones: "Who plucked this flower?

> I, said the Master
> The Gardener held his peace
> We miss her smile her cheery way
> We miss the things she used to say
> and when Old Time's we oft recall
> It's then we miss her most of all

Such epitaphs, however, are rejected for those who die before their prime and who require something 'bright and trendy'.

22. When a significant burial occurs, a number of families use this occasion to refurbish an earlier memorial: 'It's bringing them back to consciousness.'

23. For a discussion of working-class attitudes toward the funeral and the grave, see Strange (2003) and Laqueur (1983).

24. Meskell (2001: 36).

25. Hallam and Hockey (2001: 47–76) note that this dynamic interplay of longevity and transience is frequently a component of mortuary rituals and remembering.

26. Hunt (1994; 1997).

27. This seems to be in line with the case made by Argenti (1999: 21–52) when he describes the ephemeral monuments which initiate long-term memorial activity among a Cameroon people.

28. Mead (1934); Warner (1959: 346).

29. Some mourners, however, believe that their cemetery gardening is directed by the deceased, whose wishes they merely implement.

30. Plastic flowers have found their way into the grave garden, where visitors exploit their durability. Used in the same way as fresh

flowers, plastic flowers extend the period of use, serve as substitutes when mourners are unable to visit, can be used during bad weather and are not as 'depressing' to see as dead flowers that have been left too long on the grave. Some people prefer silk flowers, which they intersperse with fresh ones to keep the floral display looking attractive until the next visit. In the hierarchy of the cemetery's flower culture, fresh cut flowers are valued over plastic ones, silk flowers are esteemed more highly than plastic, but less highly than fresh, and artificial have earned a useful place when purchased with care and forethought and kept clean and attractive. For a pictorial essay on various styles of floral tributes see Weston (1969).

31. In preparation for their routine visits, users keep their cemetery gardening tools, usually a hand fork, trowel, secateurs, perhaps an edging tool, gloves, scissors, plastic bottle, clippers, a cloth and some Miracle Grow in an old leather/canvas bag, which they always bring with them to the cemetery. 'I keep it just for coming here.' The order of the tasks varies slightly from individual to individual, family-to-family, but includes removing unsightly weeds and invasive grass 'that choke the flowers and kill off the plants', throwing away the dead flowers, cleaning out the flower urns, washing or wiping down the stone, laying out the cut flowers on the florist paper, cutting the stems and arranging the new, fresh flowers in the urns with fresh water and possibly saying a prayer.

32. The public dimension of the grave is further illustrated by the comments of a woman and her son: 'Dad always said, "I look alright in the front, but what about the back?" We like to see the back and we clean the weeds behind the stone.'

33. Butler (1963).

34. For a historical discussion of various views of heaven, see McDannell and Lang (1988).

35. Though we did not specifically focus our research on the meaning of interred cremated remains, observation and conversations with mourners suggested that the 'presence' of the deceased may also be identified with the ashes interred in a marked plot. For example, one woman whose husband was cremated came daily to the cemetery during the first few months and would lie down next to the grave 'to be close to him'.

36. A few mourners at Bushey seem to share this identification of the stone with the presence of the deceased. As one woman said when asked why she had come to the cemetery that day: 'I've come for my mother's stone; I've come for my mother.' Others at Bushey, however, deny any association between the stone and the person:

'The stone means nothing, it has nothing to do with the person who died. He's not there.' Still others at Bushey find the stone cold, hard and unappealing and wish to have no tactile contact with it.

37. This planting code reflects the culturally shared East End values of tidiness and respect for a neighbour's property; 'Untended conifers impinge on other's graves.' 'Even rose bushes can be a problem, with leaves falling on a neighbour's grave and bird droppings.'

38. Christmas can be an exception when some graves are elaborately decorated.

39. The Greek custom of gardening in pots may have had its origin in a cult of Adonis, who, in Greek mythology, represents the yearly cycle of death and rebirth. Following his death, Adonis was permitted by Zeus to spend half the year with the goddess Aphrodite after spending half the year in the underworld with Persephone. In ancient Athens at midsummer, women would gather on rooftops around a statue of Adonis, singing death laments for him and ceremonially sowing fennel, lettuce, barley and wheat seeds in flowerpots. The seeds were never watered after they germinated, so they quickly died. The swift death of the plants echoed the untimely, but inevitable death of the beautiful youth Adonis. By the beginning of the common era, these small cultic rituals had become great public festivals. In literature (e.g. Shakespeare, Spencer, Milton), Adonis gardens became symbolic of short-lived pleasures. In Greece, gardening in pots grew in popularity over many centuries. See Keeling (1990).

40. Warner (1959: 285).

Chapter 6

1. Firth, Hubert and Forge (1970: 157); see Schneider (1968) for a cultural analysis of American kinship done at roughly the same period. Firth and Schneider shared an interest in the kinship systems of modern, western societies and had planned a comparative study of kinship in Britain and the United States.

2. This chapter has drawn on verbal interviews to examine the nature of the conversations survivors hold with the deceased at the grave-site and is meant to complement the analysis of non-verbal behav-

iour emphasized in chapters 3 and 5, particularly for the City of London Cemetery site. Please also see chapter 7 for a discussion of Greek Orthodox and Muslim groups, as well as articles by Francis, Kellaher and Lee (1997), and Francis, Kellaher and Neophytou (2000, 2001). Significantly, these data taken from verbal interviews with cemetery study participants do not support the views of modern death advanced by Baudrillard (1993) or Bauman (1992). Rather they suggest a different interpretation of the meaning of death and spirituality in contemporary society and support the documentation of popular rituals, such as cemetery-based memorial practices, as providing insights into the dynamic and creative nature of contemporary religious life. See also Klass, Silverman and Nickman (1996) and Walter (1996) for a discussion of the modern meaning of death and the dead in the lives of surviving family members.

3. Bott (1957: 221); Firth et al. (1970: 452–3); Francis (1984).

4. See Bouquet (1993: 193) who critiques this idea and offers an alternative interpretation that challenges the theoretical and methodological underpinnings of classic British kinship studies. Also see Needham (1962).

5. Unlike some African societies, in which ancestors were feared because of the vengeance they might wreak on their descendants if their wishes were not attended (Fortes, 1959; Goody, 1976), in London cemeteries, the deceased whose graves people visited were seen as benign and not a source of harm. Mourners chose to come to the cemetery not out of apprehension or intimidation but because they wished to maintain contact with specific kin. For another analysis of the impact of the spirit world on the living, see Vitebsky (1993).

6. It is important to note, however, that not all participants had access to or knowledge of the locations of their parents' graves. The locations of unmarked common graves had usually been forgotten or in some cemeteries were inaccessible under untamed vegetation. 'My father is too far to the back; it is overgrown. . . . I keep my grandmother's grave cut and pruned.' Also, older persons who had immigrated to England were often unable to visit the distant graves of parents who were buried in the homeland, had perished in the Holocaust, or were lost during the 1974 Turkish invasion of Cyprus. The lighting of memorial candles, church and synagogue prayers of remembrance during which the names of the deceased were recited and annual services for Holocaust victims and the Greek Cypriot 'missing' provided links of memory. For Greek Cypriots, the dead whose bodies lie in northern Cyprus have been

metaphorically relocated and symbolically united with kin at New Southgate through the construction of a cenotaph. Shared loss is part of the cemetery experience for many Jews as they walk past the Holocaust memorial positioned at the entrance to Bushey United Jewish Cemetery.

7. This information was obtained from interviews and non-visitor surveys. Also, when asked about the possible alternative commemorative activities she thought the people who do not come to the cemetery to grieve might use, one woman told of her friend who 'goes to her church, where her mother's name is in the book. She goes every week – it is where her mother used to go. She has more memories of her mother being there, than here [in the cemetery].'

8. Personal communication from Alan Crane, a member of cemetery office staff.

9. In this section we concentrate on the oldest members (75 and older) of our elderly category, which includes people who are 65 and up.

10. It was expected in all groups studied, that the parent would have made financial arrangements, either through an insurance scheme, synagogue dues or savings to pay for their own burial expenses and the cost of the stone. As one City of London couple explained about her parents who had no insurance: 'They always said: "Just bury me in the back garden," which leaves the burden on us.'

11. Some people had to take two or three buses, and the trip might take over two hours.

12. Toward the end of the period of fieldwork, cemetery policy disallowed this practice.

13. See Seremetakis (1994) for a discussion of the multi-sensed nature of remembering past experiences.

14. These comments were made during a cemetery visit on the day before Mothering Sunday and were perhaps prompted by the holiday.

15. Trips to the cemetery for middle-aged mourners were sometimes also a way of grieving for a pattern of life lost. In one telling example, a 58-year old daughter and her husband moved from their home in the East End area to Essex after the wife's mother died. The couple had lived 200 yards from the old lady and took care of her daily. While they lived in the East End, one son visited in the morning and then came for lunch, but now this traditional way of life had ended. Monthly visits to the cemetery commemorated both the mother's death and the absent pleasures of a customary life pattern. And for isolated Bushey members still

living in once-Jewish areas, the annual cemetery visit commemorates a different type of life in the past. Also the trip to the cemetery was for many a stimulus to memory – visitors think as they travel to the cemetery and memories and thoughts continue long afterward.

16. However, with the death of the connecting relative the link to these old burial grounds may be broken. The cemetery recedes further in time, the physical distance needed to travel to the burial ground being paralleled by the social distance of the ancestral generation.

17. Research on visiting patters conducting during the Christmas season in 1996 revealed that during the month of December visits were made to graves dating as far back as 1921, while in the month of June, more visits were made to recent graves. June visitors tended to visit weekly, while those in December came less often, mostly on special occasions.

18. Our research suggests that in order for grave locations not to be lost, it is necessary to keep a written record of the cemetery, location and number of the grave for each deceased kin member. Some families write these as notations in a family Bible or prayer book; some pass down inherited photographs of the memorials, which, if no other information is available, are sometimes used to trace the location of graves. If parents and grandparents were buried close by each other, there was a greater likelihood that both sets of graves would be visited. One Jewish woman took advantage of this possibility and gave her adult children plots in the same small cemetery where she had reserved a space. Her daughter remarked: 'She organized us all to be in one place, and so when our children visited us, they would also visit her.'

19. See Durkheim (1965/1915) on the societal nature of religious experience.

20. The guards at City of London Cemetery are the 'front line', the first staff members that visitors see as they enter the cemetery gates. Guards also take turns 'walking the grounds', patrolling the cemetery to make sure everything is safe and in order. As they do, or as they sit accessibly in the gatehouse, some 'regulars' stop to 'have a chat'. For many such visitors, this may be the only human contact they enjoy that day. 'We're someone to talk to, we never turn them away.' The guards also do a bit of informal bereavement counselling. They listen to stories about the death of the deceased, refrain from making judgements about the grieving behaviour they witness or hear about and encourage people 'to remember the good times'. Although each guard holds personal views on what constitutes an appropriate number of cemetery visits, they

nonetheless reassure those who come daily. A guard told one widow, for example, 'I've just been down to see Jimmy and I told him you'll be coming soon.' Another confirmed to a widower in his eighties, 'My Dad's just the same, he keeps the house just like Mum left it.' The tins of biscuits and occasional notes of appreciation to the superintendent thanking the 'fellows who work on the gate for looking after me' let the guards know that people appreciate what they do.

21. Stroebe and Schut (1999); also see Schut, Geigen, Geigen and Stroebe (1997: 63–72); and Stroebe (1998). In this context, it is also interesting to consider Walter's 1997 discussion of the norms for public expression of grief among different ethnic and class-based groups in the British Isles, and to compare his findings with the observed behaviour of study participants at different cemetery sites.

22. This family's practices recall those of the Yoruba of Nigeria, who have a high rate of twinning. If one twin dies, an effigy figure is carved which the mother keeps like a real child, feeding it, rubbing its body with sacred colour and dancing with it and the live twin together in her wrapper. See Houlberg (1973).

23. Jecker and Schneiderman (1994).

24. We were only able to gather data on a few cases of gay relationships, too small a group to permit generalization.

25. Although study participants generously shared information with us, many were reluctant to tell us their exact age and/or year of birth. Most preferred, instead, to place themselves in a broad age category: 24 and under; 25–44; 45–64; 65 and over. Thus we were not able to do more close-grained analysis of generational differences in relation to cemetery visiting patterns and their possible evolution and change. For a model of this research, see Richardson (1984).

26. For further discussion of the relationship between individual and social memory, see Halbwachs (1992/1941); Connerton (1989); Radstone (2000); and Climo and Cattell (2002).

Chapter 7

1. Kenna (1976).

2. For an informed discussion of the theoretical issues surrounding the concept of 'diaspora', see Anthias (1988).

3. Stevens-Arroyo (1998).
4. Gardner (2002).
5. Bhabha (1993); Brah (1996).
6. Fortier (2000).
7. Fortier (2000: 157).
8. Jonker (1996).
9. Hickman (2000).
10. For unmarried or childless people, the decision to repatriate or to be buried in the place of settlement will rest upon estimations as to where their significant attachments were located, as well as upon cost factors.
11. Brah (1996).
12. See chapters 1 and 7 on historical cemetery sites.
13. Susser (1997: 13).
14. This practice continued at the City of London until the 1950s.
15. LPAC (1997).
16. Perpetuity more often than not actually means forty to sixty years. Also see Environment, Transport and Regional Affairs Committee (2001, Vols. I and II).
17. Personal communication with both Mr Michael Harris, Heritage Task Group, Board of Deputies of British Jews, and with Dr Sharman Kadish, Project Director, Survey of the Jewish Built Heritage in the UK and Ireland; Environment, Transport and Regional Affairs Committee (2001: Vol. II: 33).
18. Similarly for the Greek Orthodox the earth containing baptized human remains is essentially anointed and thus automatically consecrated.
19. Soil is brought to London from Cyprus by the management at New Southgate cemetery. This recent practice appears only to be offered at New Southgate Cemetery.
20. Temporary wooden markers on new Muslim graves sometimes gave the address in London where the deceased had lived before death, but this identification appeared to reflect a need to provide an administrative identity or perhaps an alternative form of notification of the death to those who might have known the deceased and wished to contact the family.
21. Chapple (2000).
22. Interview with the management of New Southgate Cemetery.
23. Horowitz (1984).
24. See Baumann (2000); Rapport and Dawson (1998).
25. Boyarin (1994: 1–37); see also Francis, Kellaher and Neophytou (2002: 100–10).

Chapter 8

1. Pred (1984: 6).
2. This idea receives support in the writings of Harrison (2003) and Worpole (2003), but is largely rejected by anthropologist Warner (1959) and historian Sloane (1991).
3. See, for example, the significant studies by Curl (1972); Etlin (1984); Hunt (1984); and Brooks, Elliott, Litten, Robinson, Robinson and Temple (1989).
4. The fate of English cemeteries in the 1950s through the early 1980s is thoroughly analysed by Dunk and Rugg (1994). Furthermore, the shortage of burial space has often led to the use of land not originally designed to accommodate interments. These areas include land directly adjacent to paths and/or the paths themselves, areas between graves and areas that were originally part of the cemetery's decorative landscaping, such as gardens or clumps of trees that have been removed to make way for more graves.
5. Reinforcement was further provided by English Heritage listing of historic cemeteries and by the Heritage Lottery Fund allocating grants for cemetery restoration, by the creation of Friends groups linked to specific cemetery sites and by environmentalists who recognized that old cemeteries were valuable sites of ecological biodiversity and urban green space.
6. Susser (1997); Theodoropoulou-Polychroniadis, http: //www. stsophia.org (uk/greeksection)
7. Susser (1997: 18).
8. Harrison (2003: 24–5).
9. The use of the term 'ligature' is from Harrison (2003: ix).
10. Brooks et al. (1989: 156).
11. http: //www.stsophia.org (uk/greeksection)
12. For a discussion of the argument that all cemeteries have unique value to their local communities, see Dunk and Rugg (1994: 89).
13. For an expression of this view, see Worpole (2003: 56).
14. The same is true for other cemeteries of the same periods in regional locations – for example, Sheffield, Liverpool, Glasgow and Bristol, to name only four nineteenth-century cemeteries.
15. Goldberg (1991: 26, n.19).
16. Forgetting can be a strategy to make 'space' for a focus on matters that are current and more pressing than those in the past. For a discussion of this idea, see Rowlands (2000: 137).
17. Warner (1959); Harrison (2003).
18. Harrison (2003: 137).

19. As one Friend noted, 'Neglect means we cannot find and maintain the graves.'
20. Merchant (2003: 55).
21. Quotation recorded during the 1996 Annual General Meeting of the Woodgrange Friends. Subsequently, however, the owners co-operated in having the records microfiched. They have also proposed that eventually the records will be deposited in a local archive.
22. In some cases, this action also reaffirmed and strengthened their personal ties with their own deceased kin, whose graves may occasionally have been allowed to fall into neglect.
23. Joyce (1994); LPAC (1997).
24. Our survey of visitors to Abney Park included the questions, 'Why did you come to Abney instead of [another] park?' and 'What is the difference between Abney and a park?'
25. In contrast, parks were associated with activity, as places where 'there are too many dogs and people'.
26. Rohde and Kendle (1994). This review of research was sponsored by English Nature, the statutory body that champions the con-servation and enhancement of the wildlife and natural features of England.
27. Environment, Transport and Regional Affairs Committee (2001: Vol. II: 138).
28. As one man described his monthly trips to Abney Park to visit the communal grave of his father who died thirty years ago: 'It's more a nature reserve, wild; I climb over the brambles and bushes to get to the grave and clear around and put flowers there. . . . '
29. Such decisions require a balanced approach prepared by man-agers, in partnership with interested bodies, and are only now beginning to be realized in a number of historic cemeteries.
30. Harrison (2003: 51).
31. With funding from the Heritage Lottery Fund in 2003, CLCC, as an active cemetery, is engaged in an extensive study to assess how its many and varied sections should be managed so that conserva-tion and development are balanced.
32. Loudon (1981/1843: 13).
33. Clayden (2003: 22–5).
34. For a copy of this survey, sent to those who had pre-selected to be buried in the woodland burial areas at Carlisle Cemetery in Cumbria, see Appendix 4. Survey respondents referred to the Carlisle woodland burial as 'a place of hope, of beginning', 'a peaceful retreat of harmony and healing', 'a wildlife habitat managed with a minimum of human interference' and 'a way to

give something back'. Responders also described death as a 'natural process' and compared woodland burial to the 'ecologically harmful pollutants of cremation', the 'fuss of a stone' or the 'dead, sterile' landscapes of traditional burial grounds. They also spoke of visiting such woodland sites and taking pleasure in their initiation and maturation.

35. Rival (1998: 1–36). For other studies of the symbolism of trees, see Daniels (1988); Harrison (1993); Constant (1994); Schama (1995); Gough (1996); Clayden (2003); and Clayden and Woudstra (2003).
36. Bloch (1998: 39–55).
37. Warner (1959: 285), quoted in Francaviglia (1971: 502).
38. Harrison (2003).
39. Warner (1959: 285).
40. van Gennep (1960/1909).

References

Altman, I. and Werner, C. (eds) (1985), *Home Environments: Human Behavior and Environment*, New York: Plenum.

Anthias, F. (1998), 'Evaluating "Diaspora": Beyond Ethnicity?', *Sociology*, 32(3): 557–80.

—— and Lloyd, C. (eds), (2002*), Rethinking Anti-racisms: From Theory to Practice*, Routledge: London and New York.

Argenti, N. (1999), 'Ephemeral Monuments, Memory and Royal Sempiternity in a Grassfields Kingdom', in A. Forty and S. Kuchler (eds), *The Art of Forgetting*, Oxford: Berg.

Aries, P. (1974), *Western Attitudes toward Death: From the Middle Ages to the Present*, Baltimore: Johns Hopkins University Press.

—— (1981), *The Hour of Our Death*, London: Allen Lane.

Ashton, J. and Whyte, T. (2001), *The Quest for Paradise: Visions of Heaven and Eternity in the World's Myths and Religions*, New York: HarperCollins.

Azara, P. (1999), 'The House and the Dead', in M. Gili (ed.), *The Last House*, Barcelona: Editorial Gastavo Gili.

Bachelard, G. (1969), *The Poetics of Space*, Boston: Beacon Press.

Badone, E. (1989), *The Appointed Hour: Death, Worldview, and Social Change in Brittany*, Berkeley: University of California Press.

Barley, N. (1995), *Grave Matters*, New York: Henry Holt and Company.

Baudrillard, J. (1993), *Symbolic Exchange and Death*, London: Sage.

Bauman, Z. (1992), *Mortality, Immortality and Other Life Strategies*, Oxford: Polity.

Baumann, G. (1996), '*Contesting Culture', Discourses of Identity in Multi-ethnic London*, Cambridge: Cambridge University Press.

Bell, C. (1997), *Ritual: Perspectives and Dimensions*, Oxford: Oxford University Press.

Bender, B. (ed.) (1993), *Landscape: Politics and Perspectives*, Oxford: Berg.

Bernstein, B. (1973), *Class, Codes and Control*, London: Paladin.

Bhabha, H. (1994), *The Location of Culture*, London and New York: Routledge.

Birdwell-Pheasant, D. and Lawrence-Zuniga, D. (1999), 'Introduction: Houses and Families in Europe', in D. Birdwell-Pheasant and D. Lawrence-Zuniga (eds), *House Life: Space, Place and Family in Europe*, Oxford: Berg.

Bloch, M. (1971), *Placing the Dead: Tombs, Ancestral Villages, and Kinship Organisation in Madagascar*, New York: Seminar Press.

—— (1976) 'The Past and the Present in the Present', Malinowski Memorial Lecture, *Man,* 12: 278–92.

—— (1998), 'Why Trees, Too, Are Good to Think With: Towards an Anthropology of the Meaning of Life', in L. Rival (ed.), *The Social Life of Trees*, Oxford: Berg.

—— and Parry, J. (eds) (1982), *Death and the Regeneration of Life*, Cambridge: Cambridge University Press.

Bott, E. (1957), *Family and Social Network: Roles, Norms, and External Relationships in Ordinary Urban Families*, New York: The Free Press.

Bouquet, M. (1993), *Reclaiming English Kinship*, Manchester: Manchester University Press.

Bourdieu, P. (1977), *Outline of the Theory of Practice*, Cambridge: Cambridge University Press.

Bowdler, R. (1996), 'Et in Arcadia Ego: The Neoclassical Tomb 1760-1840', in G. Waterfield (ed.), *Soane and Death*, London: Dulwich Picture Gallery.

Bowker, J. (1990), *The Meanings of Death*, Cambridge: Cambridge University Press.

Boyarin, J. (1994), 'Space, Time, and the Politics of Memory', in J. Boyarin (ed.), *Remapping Memory: The Politics of TimeSpace*, Minneapolis: University of Minnesota Press.

Brah, A. (1996), *Cartographies of Diaspora. Contesting Identities,* London and New York: Routledge.

Brooks, C., Elliott, B., Litten, J., Robinson, E., Robinson, R. and Temple, P. (1989), *Mortal Remains: The History and Present State of the Victorian and Edwardian Cemetery*, Exeter: Wheaton.

Brown, J. (1982), *Gardens of a Golden Afternoon*, London: Allen Lane.

Brown, P. (1981), *The Cult of the Saints: Its Rise and Function in Latin Christianity*, Chicago: University of Chicago Press.

Burial Society of the United Synagogue (1986), *Notes for the Guidance of Mourners and the Composition of Tombstone Inscriptions*, London: Burial Society of the United Synagogue.

—— (1995), *Services for Use at the Cemetery*, London: Burial Society of the United Synagogue.

Butler, R. N. (1963), 'The Life Review: An Interpretation of Reminiscence in the Aged', *Psychiatry, Journal for the Study of Interpersonal Processes*, 26(1): 65–76.

Cannadine, D. (1981), 'War and Death, Grief and Mourning in Modern Britain', in J. Whaley (ed.), *Mirrors of Mortality: Studies in the Social History of Death*, New York: St Martin's Press.

Cannon, A. (1989), 'The Historical Dimension in Mortuary Expressions of Status and Sentiment', *Current Anthropology*, 30(4): 437–58.

Catedra, M. (1992), *This World, Other Worlds: Sickness, Suicide, Death and the After Life Among the Vaquerios de Altzada of Spain*, Chicago: University of Chicago Press.

Cederroth, S., Corlin, C. and Lindstrom, J. (eds) (1988), *On the Meaning of Death: Essays On Mortuary Rituals and Eschatological Beliefs*, Stockholm: Almqvist & Wiksell International.

Chadwick, E. (1843), *A Supplementary Report on the Results of a Special Enquiry into the Practice of Interment in Towns*, London: W. Clowes & Sons for HMSO.

Chapple, R. (2000), 'Statistical Analysis and Preliminary Classification of Gravestones from Craughwell, Co. Galway', *Journal of Galway Archaeological and Historical Society*, 52: 155–72.

Chesson, M. S. (ed.) (2001), *Social Memory, Identity, and Death: Anthropological Perspectives on Mortuary Rituals*, Archaeological Papers of the American Anthropological Association, No. 10, Arlington, VA: American Anthropological Association.

Chevalier, J. and Gheerbrant, A. (1996), *A Dictionary of Symbols*, London: Penguin.

Chevalier, S. (1998), 'From Woolen Carpet to Grass Carpet: Bridging House and Garden in an English Suburb', in D. Miller (ed.), *Material Cultures: Why Some Things Matter*, Chicago: University of Chicago Press.

Churches' Group on Funeral Services at Cemeteries and Crematoria (1997), *Guidelines for Best Practice of Clergy at Funerals*, London: The Churches' Group on Funerals.

Clark, D. (ed.) (1993), *The Sociology of Death*, Oxford: Blackwell.

Clayden, A. (2003), 'Down in the Woods', *Landscape Design*, No. 322: 22–5.

—— and Woudstra, J. (2003), 'Some European Approaches to Twentieth-Century Cemetery Design: Continental Solutions for British Dilemmas', *Mortality*, 8(2): 189–208.

Clegg, F. (1984), 'Problems of Symbolism in Cemetery Monuments', *Journal of Garden History*, 4(3): 307–15.

—— (1989), 'Cemeteries for the Living', *Landscape Design*, No. 184: 15–17.

Climo, J. J. and Cattell, M. G. (eds) (2002), *Social Memory and History: Anthropological Perspectives*, Walnut Creek, CA: AltaMira Press.

Coffin, D. (1994), *The English Garden: Meditation and Memorial*, Princeton: Princeton University Press.

Cohn-Sherbok, D. and Lewis, C. (eds) (1995), *Beyond Death: Theological and Philosophical Reflections on Life after Death*, London: Macmillan.

Colvin, B. (1970), *Land and Landscape: Evolution, Design and Control*, London: John Murray.

Community Relations Commission (CRC) (1975), *Observations on Muslim Burials – A Policy Paper*, London: The Institute of Burial and Cremation Administration.

Connerton, P. (1989), *How Societies Remember*, Cambridge: Cambridge University Press.

Constant, C. (1994), *The Woodland Cemetery: Toward a Spiritual Landscape*, Stockholm: Byggforlaget.

Cooper, C. (1976), 'The House as Symbol of the Self', in H. M. Proshansky, W. H. Ittelson and L. G. Rivlin (eds), *Environmental Psychology: People and their Physical Settings*, New York: Holt, Rinehart & Winston.

Cosgrove, D. (1993), 'Landscapes and Myths, Gods and Humans', in B. Bender (ed.), *Landscape: Politics and Perspectives*, Oxford: Berg.

—— and Daniels, S. (eds) (1988), *The Iconography of Landscape*, Cambridge: Cambridge University Press.

Cox, J. (1994), *London's East End: Life and Traditions*, London: Weidenfeld & Nicolson.

Creese, W. L. (1966), *The Search for Environment*, New Haven: Yale University Press.

Csikszentmihalyi, M. and Rochberg-Halton, E. (1981), *The Meaning of Things: Domestic Symbols and the Self*, Cambridge: Cambridge University Press.

Curl, J. S. (1972), *A Victorian Celebration of Death*, Newton Abbot: David and Charles.

—— (1975), 'The Architecture and Planning of the Nineteenth-Century Cemetery', *Garden History*, 4(3): 13–41.

—— (1984), 'The Design of Early British Cemeteries', *Journal of Garden History*, 4(3): 223–54.

—— (1993), *A Celebration of Death*, London: Batsford.

—— (1994), 'Young's "Night Thoughts" and the Origins of the Garden Cemetery', *Journal of Garden History*, 14(2): 92–118.

Curson, T. (1997), *Survey of Islington Parks*, London: Centre for Leisure and Tourism Studies (CELTS), University of North London Press.

——, Evans, G. and Bohrer, J. (1995), *Market Research Survey of People Using the Royal Parks*, Annual Report 1994, London: Centre for Leisure and Tourism Studies (CELTS), University of North London Press.

Damon, F. and Wagner, R. (eds) (1989), *Death Rituals and Life in the Societies of the Kula Ring*, DeKalb: Northern Illinois University Press.

Danforth, L. M. (1982), *The Death Rituals of Rural Greece*, Princeton: Princeton University Press.

Daniels, S. (1988), 'The Political Iconography of Woodland in Later Georgian England' in D. Cosgrove and S. Daniels (eds), *The Iconography of Landscape*, Cambridge: Cambridge University Press.

Davies, D. (1996), 'The Sacred Crematorium', *Mortality*, 1(1): 83–94.

—— and Shaw, A. (1995), *Reusing Old Graves: A Report on Popular British Attitudes*, Crayford, Kent: Shaw and Sons.

Douglas, M. (1985), *Purity and Danger: an Analysis of the Concepts of Pollution and Taboo*, London: Boston and Henley: Ark Paperbacks.

Draper, J. W. (1967/1929), *The Funeral Elegy and the Rise of English Romanticism*, London: Frank Cass.

Dubisch, J. (1989), 'Death and Social Change in Greece', *Anthropological Quarterly*, 62(4): 189–200.

du Boulay, J. (1974), *Portrait of a Greek Mountain Village*, Oxford: Clarendon Press.

Dunk, J. and Rugg, J. (1994), *The Management of Old Cemetery Land: Now, and the Future: A Report of the University of York Cemetery Research Group*, Crayford, Kent: Shaw & Sons.

Durkheim, E. (1965/1915), *The Elementary Forms of the Religious Life*, New York: The Free Press.

Elliott, B. (1986), *Victorian Gardens*, London: B. T. Batsford Ltd.

—— (1989), 'The Landscape of the English Cemetery', *Landscape Design*, 184: 13–14.

—— (1991), 'Notes on the City of London Cemetery', Unpublished Manuscript.

—— (1996), 'The Cemetery Movement – Planning and Design', Paper presented at the *London Cemeteries And Churchyards – A Dying Legacy?* Conference, organized by the London Historic Parks and Gardens Trust, 1 November 1996.

Environment, Transport and Regional Affairs Committee (2001), *Eighth Report: Cemeteries, Vol. I. Report and Proceedings of the Committee, Together with Minutes of Evidence Taken Before the Environment Sub-Committee*, London: The Stationery Office Ltd.

282 References

—— (2001), *Eighth Report: Cemeteries, Vol. II. Memoranda Relating to the Inquiry Submitted to the Environment Sub-Committee*, London: The Stationery Office Ltd.

Etlin, R. (1984), *The Architecture of Death: The Transformation of the Cemetery in Eighteenth-Century Paris*, Cambridge: MIT Press.

Fabian, J. (1973), 'How Others Die – Reflections on the Anthropology of Death', in A. Mack (ed.), *Death in American Experience*, New York: Schocken Books.

Fernandez, J. (1970), 'Persuasions and Performances: Of the Beast in Every Body . . . And the Metaphors of Everyman', in C. Geertz (ed.), *Myth, Symbol and Culture*, London: Hutchinson.

—— (ed.) (1991), *Beyond Metaphor – The Theory of Tropes in Anthropology*, Stanford: Stanford University Press.

Finch, J. and Hayes, L. (1994), 'Inheritance, Death and the Concept of the Home', *Sociology*, 28(2): 417-433.

Firth, R. (1936), *We, the Tikopia: a Sociological Study of Kinship in Primitive Polynesia*, London: G. Allen & Unwin Ltd.

——, Hubert, J., and Forge, A. (1969), *Families and Their Relatives*, New York: Humanities Press.

Fortes, M. (1959), *Oedipus and Job in West African Religion*, Cambridge: Cambridge University Press.

Fortier, A. M. (2000), *Migrant Belongings: Memory, Space, Identity*, Oxford: Berg.

Forty, A. (1999), 'Introduction', in A. Forty and S. Kuchler (eds), *The Art of Forgetting*, Oxford: Berg.

Foucault, M. (1986), 'Of Other Spaces', *Diacritics*, Spring: 22–7.

Francaviglia, R. V. (1997), 'The Cemetery as an Evolving Cultural Landscape', *Annals* (Association of American Geographers), 61(2): 501–9.

Francis, D. (1984), *Will You Still Need Me, Will You Still Feed Me, When I'm 84?* Bloomington: Indiana University Press.

—— (1997), *A Cemetery for Posterity: The Conservation of the Landscape of the City of London Cemetery*, Unpublished Thesis, London: Architectural Association.

——, Kellaher, L. and Lee, C. (1997), 'Talking to People in Cemeteries', *Journal of the Institute of Burial and Cremation Administration*, 65(1): 14–25.

—— Neophytou G. (1998), 'Cemeteries: Use and Re-Use: The Visitors' Perspective', *Journal of the Institute of Burial and Cremation Administration*, 66(4): 8–19.

—— (2000), 'Sustaining Cemeteries: The User Perspective', *Mortality*, 5(1): 34–52.

——, and (2001), 'The Cemetery: The Evidence of Continuing Bonds', in J. Hockey, J. Katz and N. Small (eds), *Grief, Mourning and Death Ritual*, Buckingham: Open University Press.

—— (2002), 'The Cemetery: A Site for the Construction of Memory, Identity, and Ethnicity', in J. J. Climo and M. G. Cattell (eds), *Social Memory and History: Anthropological Perspectives*, Walnut Creek, CA: AltaMira.

Francis, M. and Hester, R. T. (1995), *The Meaning of Gardens*, Cambridge, MA: MIT Press.

Gardner, K. (2002), *Age, Narrative & Migration: The Life Course and 'Life Histories' of Bengali Elders*, Oxford: Berg.

Gell, A. (1992), *The Anthropology of Time: Cultural Constructions of Maps and Images*, Oxford: Berg.

Gerlach-Spriggs, N., Kaufman, R. E. and Warner, S. B. (1998), *Restorative Gardens: The Healing Landscape*, New Haven: Yale University Press.

Giddens, A. (1991), *Modernity and Self-Identity: Self and Society in the Late Modern Age*, Cambridge: Polity Press.

Goldberg, C. B. (1991), *Mourning in Halachah*, The Artscroll Halachah Series, Brooklyn, NY: Mesorah Publications Ltd.

Goody, J. (1962), *Death, Property and the Ancestors*, Stanford: Stanford University Press.

—— (1974), 'Death and the Interpretation of Culture: A Bibliographic Overview', in D. E. Stannard (ed.), *Death in America*, Philadelphia: University of Pennsylvania Press.

—— (1976), 'Aging in Nonindustrial Societies', in R. H. Binstock and E. Shanas (eds), *Handbook of Aging and the Social Sciences*, New York: Van Nostrand Reinhold.

—— (1993), *The Culture of Flowers*, Cambridge: Cambridge University Press.

—— and Poppi, C. (1994), 'Flowers and Bones: Approaches to the Dead in Anglo-American and Italian Cemeteries', *Comparative Studies in Society and History*, 36(1): 146–75.

Gorer, G. (1965), *Death, Grief, and Mourning in Contemporary Britain*, London: Cresset Press.

Gough, P. (1996), 'Conifers and Commemoration – the Politics and Protocol of Planting', *Landscape Research*, 21(1): 73–87.

Gould, J. and Esh, S. (eds) (1964), *Jewish Life in Modern Britain*, London: Routledge & Kegan Paul.

Grant, E. (1988), 'The Sphinx in the North: Egyptian Influences on Landscape, Architecture and Interior Design in Eighteenth- and Nineteenth-century Scotland' in D. Cosgrove and S. Daniels (eds), *The Iconography of Landscape*, Cambridge: Cambridge University Press.

Greenhalgh, L. and Worpole, K. (1995), *Park Life – Urban Parks and Social Renewal*, London: Comedia in Association with Demos.

Halbwachs, M. (1992/1941 and 1952), *On Collective Memory*, Chicago: University of Chicago Press.

Halcrow Fox, in Association with the Cemetery Research Group, University of York and the Landscape Partnership (1996), *Burial Space Needs in London: Final Report*, London: London Planning Advisory Committee, Corporation of London, Confederation of Burial Authorities.

Haleem, A. (1995), 'Life and Beyond in the Qur'an', in D. Cohn-Sherbok and C. Lewis (eds), *Beyond Death – Theological and Philosophical Reflections on Life after Death,* London: Macmillan.

Hallam, E. and Hockey, J. (2001), *Death, Memory and Material Culture*, Oxford: Berg.

Hallote, R. S. (2001), *Death, Burial, and Afterlife in the Biblical World: How the Israelites and their Neighbors Treated the Dead*, Chicago: Ivan R. Dee.

Harrison, R. P. (1993), *Forests: The Shadow of Civilization*, Chicago: University of Chicago Press.

—— (2003), *The Dominion of the Dead*, Chicago: University of Chicago Press.

Hart, L. K. (1992), *Time, Religion and Social Experience in Rural Greece*, Boston: Rowman and Littlefield.

Hayward, D. G. (1975), 'Home as an Environmental and Psychological Concept', *Landscape*, 20: 2–9.

Hecht, A. (2001), 'Home Sweet Home: Tangible Memories of an Uprooted Childhood', in D. Miller (ed.), *Home Possessions – Material Culture behind Closed Doors*, Oxford: Berg.

Herman, J. (1996), *Stones of Kolin: A Bohemian Jewish Rhapsody*, Unpublished Theatre Script.

Hertz, R. (1960/1907), *Death and the Right Hand*, London: Cohen & West.

Hickman, M. J. (2000), 'Reconstructing Deconstructing "Race": British Political Discourses about the Irish in Britain', *Ethnic and Racial Studies*, 21(2): 288–307.

Hirsch, E. (1995), 'Landscape: Between Place and Space', in E. Hirsch and M. O'Hanlon (eds), *The Anthropology of Landscape*, Oxford: Clarendon Press.

—— and O'Hanlon, M. (eds) (1995), *The Anthropology of Landscape*, Oxford: Clarendon Press.

Hirschon, R. (1989), *Heirs of the Greek Catastrophe: The Social Life of Asia Minor Refugees in Piraeus*, Oxford: Clarendon Press.

Hockey, J. (1990), *Experiences of Death: An Anthropological Account*, Edinburgh: Edinburgh University Press.

—— (1996), 'The View from the West: Reading the Anthropology of non-Western Death Ritual', in G. Howarth and P. Jupp (eds), *Contemporary Issues in the Sociology of Death, Dying and Disposal*, Basingstoke: Macmillan.

Hodder, I. (1984), 'Burials, Houses, Women and Men in the European Neolithic', in D. Miller and C. Tilley (eds), *Ideology and Power in Prehistory*, Cambridge: Cambridge University Press.

Holmes, Mrs Basil (1896),*The London Burial Grounds: Notes on their History from the Earliest Times to the Present Day*, London: T. Fisher Unwin.

Horowitz, I. L. (1984), 'Genocide and the Reconstruction of Social Theory: Observations on the Exclusivity of Collective Death', *Armenian Review*, 37(19): 1–21.

Houlberg, M. H. (1973), 'Ibeji Images of the Yoruba', *African Arts*, 7(1): 20–7.

Houlbrooke, R. (1998), *Death, Religion, and the Family in England, 1480–1750*, Oxford: Clarendon Press.

Hoyles, M. (1994), *Lost Connections and New Directions: The Private Garden and the Public Park*, London: Comedia in Association with Demos.

Humphreys, S. and King, H. (eds) (1981), *Mortality and Immortality: The Anthropology and Archaeology of Death*, New York: Academic Press.

Hunt, J. D. (1984), 'A Garden and a Grave', *Journal of Garden History*, 4(3): 209–10.

—— (1992), *Gardens and the Picturesque: Studies in the History of Landscape Architecture*, Cambridge: MIT Press.

—— (1994), '"Come Into the Garden, Maud": Garden Art as a Privileged Mode of Commemoration and Identity', Unpublished paper, *Dumbarton Oaks Colloquium: Places of Commemoration. The Search for Identity and Landscape Design*, Washington, DC, 19–20 May 1994.

—— (1997), '"Come Into the Garden, Maud": Garden Art as a Privileged Mode of Commemoration and Identity', in J. Wolschke-Bulmahn (ed.), *Places of Commemoration. The Search for Identity and Landscape Design*, Dumbarton Oaks Colloquium on the History of Landscape Architecture 19, Washington, DC.

—— and Willis, P. (eds) (1990), *The Genius of the Place: The English Landscape Garden 1620–1820*, Cambridge, MA: MIT Press.

Huntington, R. and Metcalf, P. (1979), *Celebration of Death: The Anthropology of Mortality Ritual*, Cambridge: Cambridge University Press.

Hussein, I. (1996), 'Blueprint for the Management of Cemeteries', *Journal of the Institute of Burial and Cremation Administration*, 64: 38–45.

—— and Rugg, J. (2003), 'Managing London's Dead: A Case of Strategic Policy Failure', *Mortality*, 8(2): 209–21.

Institute of Burial and Cremation Administration (1996), *Charter for the Bereaved*, Grantham, Lincolnshire: IBCA.

Jackson, K. T. and Vergara, C. J. (1989), *Silent Cities*, Princeton: Princeton Architectural Press.

Jacobs, L. (1997), 'The Body in Jewish Worship: Three Rituals Examined', in S. Coakley (ed.), *Religion and the Body*, Cambridge: Cambridge University Press.

Jalland, P. (1996), *Death in the Victorian Family*, Oxford: Oxford University Press.

Jecker, N. S. and Schneiderman, L. J. (1994), 'Is Dying Young Worse Than Dying Old?', *The Gerontologist*, 34(1): 66–72.

Jonker, G. (1996), 'The Knife's Edge: Muslim Burial in the Diaspora', *Mortality*, 1(1): 27–44.

Joyce, P. (1994), *A Guide to Abney Park Cemetery*, London: Abney Park Cemetery Trust.

Jupp, P. (1990), *From Dust to Ashes: the Replacement of Burial by Cremation in England 1840–1967*, London: The Congregational Memorial Hall Trust.

—— and Rogers, T. (1997), *Interpreting Death: Christian Theology and Pastoral Practice*, London: Cassell.

Kan, S. (1989), *Symbolic Immortality: The Tlingit Potlatch of the Nineteenth Century*, Washington, DC: Smithsonian Institution Press.

Keeling, J. (1990), *The Terracotta Gardener: Creative Ideas from Leading Gardeners*, London: Headline.

Kellett, J. E. (1982), 'The Private Garden in England and Wales', *Landscape Planning*, 9: 105–23.

Kenna, M. (1976), 'Houses, Fields and Graves: Property and Ritual Obligation on a Greek Island, *Ethnology*, 15: 21–34.

Khan Patel, S. (2000), *Notes on Death, Dying and Care for the (Muslim) Elderly: Prepared by Sikander Khan Patel for the Balham Mosque*, London: Tooting Islamic Centre.

King, A. (1999), 'Remembering and Forgetting in the Public Memorials of the Great War', in A. Forty and S. Kuchler (eds), *The Art of Forgetting*, Oxford: Berg.

Klass, D. (1999), 'Developing a Cross-cultural Model of Grief: The State of the Field', *Omega*, 39(3): 153–78.

——, Silverman, P. R. and Nickman, S. L. (eds) (1996), *Continuing Bonds: New Understandings of Grief*, London: Taylor & Francis.

Kubler-Ross, E. (1970), *On Death and Dying*, London: Sage.

Kuchler, S. (1999), 'The Place of Memory', in A. Forty and S. Kuchler (eds), *The Art of Forgetting*, Oxford: Berg.

Kugelmass, J. and Boyarin, J. (1983), *From a Ruined Garden: The Memorial Books of Polish Jewry*, Bloomington: Indiana University Press.

Kutty, A. (1991), *Islamic Funeral Rites and Practices*, Toronto: Islamic Foundation of Toronto.

Lakoff, G. and Johnson, M. (1980), *Metaphors We Live By*, Chicago: University of Chicago Press.

Lamm, M. (1969), *The Jewish Way in Death and Mourning*, New York: Jonathan David Publishers.

Laqueur, T. W. (1983), 'Bodies, Death, and Pauper Funerals', *Representations*, 1: 109–31.

—— (1996), 'Names, Bodies, and the Anxiety of Erasure', in T. R. Schatzki and W. Natter (eds), *The Social and Political Body*, New York: Guilford.

—— (2002), 'Spaces of the Dead', in C. Jones and D. Wahrman (eds), *The Age of Cultural Revolutions: Britain and France, 1750–1820*, Berkeley: University of California Press.

Lawrence, R. J. (1982), 'Domestic Space and Society: A Cross-Cultural Study', *Comparative Studies in Society and History*, 24: 104–30.

—— (1987), 'What Makes a House a Home?', *Environment and Behavior*, 19(2): 154–68.

Lawson, J. C. (1910), *Modern Greek Folklore and Ancient Greek Religion: a Study in Survivals*, Cambridge: Cambridge University Press.

Lawton, M. P. (1986), *Environment and Aging*, Albany, NY: Center for the Study of Aging.

Leach, E. R. (1961), 'Two Essays Concerning the Symbolic Representation of Time', *Rethinking Anthropology*, London: Athlone Press.

Lees, H. (2000), *English Churchyard Memorials*, Stroud: Trafalgar Square.

Lefebvre, H. (1991), *The Production of Space,* Oxford: Blackwell.

Litten, J. (1991), *The English Way of Death: The Common Funeral Since 1450*, London: Robert Hale.

Littlewood, J. (1992), *Aspects of Grief: Bereavement in Adult Life*, London: Tavistock/Routledge.

Llewellyn, N. (1991), *The Art of Death*, London: Reaktion.

Lock, M. (2002), *Twice Dead*, Berkeley: University of California Press.

London Planning Advisory Committee (1997), *Planning for Burial Space in London: Policies for Sustainable Cemeteries in the New Millennium*, London: LPAC.

Longworth, P. (1967), *The Unending Vigil*, London: Constable & Company.

Loudon, J. C. (1981/1843), *On the Laying Out, Planting, and Managing of Cemeteries And on the Improvement of Churchyards*, Redhill, Surrey: Ivelet Books Ltd.

Lynch, T. (1997), *The Undertaking: Life Studies from the Dismal Trade*, London: Jonathan Cape.

—— (1998), *Still Life in Milford*, New York: W.W. Norton & Company Ltd.

—— (2000), *Bodies in Motion and At Rest*, New York: W.W. Norton & Company Ltd.

Malpas, J. E. (1999), *Place and Experience: A Philosophical Topography*, Cambridge: Cambridge University Press.

Manuel, F. E. and Manuel, F. P. (1971), 'Sketch for a Natural History of Paradise', in C. Geertz (ed.), *Myth, Symbol, and Culture*, New York: W.W. Norton & Company, Inc.

Marcus, C. C. (1997), *House as a Mirror of Self: Exploring the Deeper Meaning of Home*, Berkeley, CA: Conari Press.

Marris, P. (1958), *Widows and their Families*, London: Routledge & Kegan Paul.

McDannell, C. and Lang, B. (1988), *Heaven*, New Haven: Yale University Press.

McManners, J. (1981), *Death and the Enlightenment: Changing Attitudes to Death Among Christians and Unbelievers in Eighteenth-Century France*, Oxford: Clarendon Press.

Mead, G. H. (1934), *Mind, Self and Society*, Chicago: University of Chicago Press.

Meller, H. (1994), *London Cemeteries: an Illustrated Guide and Gazetteer*, London: Scolar Press.

Merchant, C. (1986), 'Restoration and Reunion with Nature', *Restoration & Management*, 4(2): 68–70.

—— (2003), *Reinventing Eden: The Fate of Nature in Western Culture*, New York: Routledge.

Merewether, C. (1993), 'Community and Continuity: Naming Violence in the Work of Doris Salcedo', *Third Text*, 24: 35–44.

Meskell, L. (2001), 'The Egyptian Ways of Death', in M. S. Chesson (ed.), *Social Memory, Identity and Death: Anthropological Perspectives on Mortuary Rituals*, Archaeological Papers of the American Anthropological Association, No. 10, Arlington, VA: American Anthropological Association.

—— (2002), *Private Life in New Kingdom Egypt*, Princeton: Princeton University Press.

—— and Joyce, R. (2003), *Embodied Lives: Figuring Ancient Maya and Egyptian Experience*, London: Routledge.

Meyer, R. E. (ed.) (1993), *Ethnicity and the American Cemetery*, Bowling Green: Bowling Green State University Popular Press.

Miller, D. (ed.) (1998), *Material Cultures: Why Some Things Matter*, Chicago: University of Chicago Press.

—— (2001a), 'Behind Closed Doors', in D. Miller (ed.), *Home Possessions: Material Culture behind Closed Doors*, Oxford: Berg.

—— (2001b), 'Possessions', in D. Miller (ed.), *Home Possessions: Material Culture behind Closed Doors*, Oxford: Berg.

Milner, G. (1846), *On Cemetery Burial: or Sepulture Ancient and Modern*, Hull: W. R. Goddard.

Mines, D. P. and Weiss, B. (1997), 'Materializations of Memory: The Substance of Remembering and Forgetting: Introduction', *Anthropological Quarterly*, 70(4): 161–3.

Moore, C. W., Mitchell, W. J. and Turnbull, W. (1997), *The Poetics of Gardens*, Cambridge: MIT Press.

National Funerals College (1998), *The Dead Citizens Charter: The Complete Edition*, Stamford, Lincolnshire: The National Funerals College.

Needham, R. (1962), *Structure and Sentiment*, Chicago: University of Chicago Press.

Newman, A. (1976), *The United Synagogue 1870–1970*, London: Routledge & Kegan Paul.

Oxford English Dictionary (1989), Oxford: Oxford University Press, Vol. 7.

Palmer, A. (2000), *The East End: Four Centuries of London Life*, London: John Murray.

Panourgia, N. (1995), *Fragments of Death, Fables of Identity: An Athenian Anthropography*, Madison: University of Wisconsin Press.

Pardo, I. (1989), 'Life, Death and Ambiguity in the Social Dynamics of Inner Naples', *Man*, 24(1): 103–23.

Parkes, C. M. (1986), *Bereavement: Studies of Grief in Adult Life*, London: Tavistock.

Parry, J. (1994), *Death in Banares*, Cambridge: Cambridge University Press.

Paul, M. (1984), 'A Note on the Garden-Cemetery in Cliges by Chretien de Troyes', *Journal of Garden History*, 4(3): 305–6.

Petrucci, A. (1998), *Writing the Dead*, Stanford: Stanford University Press.

Pewsey, S. (1996), *Britain in Old Photographs: East Ham*, Phoenix Mill: Sutton Publishing Ltd.

Plath, D. W. (1964), 'Where the Family of God is the Family: The Role of the Dead in Japanese Households', *American Anthropologist*, 64: 300–17.

Polson, C. J. and Marshall, T. K. (1975), *The Disposal of the Dead*, London: English University Press Ltd.

Porter, H. (1995), 'Flower Power', *The Guardian Friday Review*, 23 June: 2–4.

Pred, A. (1984), *Place, Practice and Structure*, Cambridge: Polity Press.

Prior, L. (1989), *The Social Organisation of Death: Medical Discourse and Social Practices in Belfast*, London: Macmillan.

Rabinowicz, H. (1982), *A Guide to Life: Jewish Laws and Customs of Mourning*, London: Jewish Chronicle Publications.

Radstone, S. (ed.) (2000), *Memory and Methodology*, Oxford: Berg.

Raphael, S. P. (1996), *Jewish Views of the Afterlife*, Northvale, NJ: Jason Aronson, Inc.

Rapport, N. and Dawson, A. (1998), 'Opening a Debate', in N. Rapport and A. Dawson (eds), *Migrants of Identity: Perceptions of Home in a World of Movement*, Oxford: Berg.

Richardson, R. (1984), 'Old People's Attitudes to Death in the Twentieth Century', *Society for the Social History of Medicine Bulletin*, 34: 48–51.

—— (1989), *Death, Dissection and the Destitute*, London: Penguin.

Rival, L. (1998), 'Trees, from Symbols of Life and Regeneration to Political Artefacts', in L. Rival (ed.), *The Social Life of Trees,* Oxford: Berg.

Rohde, C. L. E. and Kendle, A. D. (1994), *Human Well-being, Natural Landscapes and Wildlife in Urban Areas: A Review*, Reading: University of Reading for English Nature.

Rosaldo, R. (1984), 'Grief and a Headhunter's Rage: On the Cultural Force of Emotions', in E. Bruner and V. Turner (eds), *The Anthropology of Experience*, Chicago: University of Chicago Press.

Rose, G. (1993), *Feminism and Geography: The Limits of Geographical Knowledge*, Cambridge: Polity Press.

Roskies, D. K. and Roskies, D. G. (1975), *The Shtetl Book*, New York: Ktav Purlishing House, Inc.

Ross, S. (1998), *What Gardens Mean*, Chicago: University of Chicago Press.

Rotenberg, R. (1995), *Landscape and Power in Vienna*, Baltimore: The Johns Hopkins University Press.

Rowlands, M. (1999), 'Remembering to Forget: Sublimation as Sacrifice in War Memorials', in A. Forty and S. Kuchler (eds), *The Art of Forgetting*, Oxford: Berg.

Rowles, G. (1993), 'Evolving Images of Place in Aging and "Aging in Place"', *Generations*, 17(2): 65–70.

Rubinstein, R. L. (1986a), *Singular Paths: Old Men Living Alone*, New York: Columbia University Press.

—— (1986b), 'The Construction of a Day by Elderly Widowers', *International Journal of Aging and Human Development*, 23: 161–73.

—— (1987), 'The Significance of Personal Objects to Older People', *Journal of Aging Studies*, 1(3): 226–38.

—— (1989), 'The Home Environments of Older People: A Description of Psychosocial Processes Linking Person to Place', *Journal of Gerontology*, 44(2): 545–53.

—— (1990), 'Personal Identity and Environmental Meaning in Later Life', *Journal of Aging Studies*, 4(2): 131–47.

—— and Parmelee, P. A. (1992), 'Attachment to Place and the Representation of the Life Course by the Elderly', in I. Altman and S. M. Low (eds), *Place Attachment*, New York: Plenum Press.

Rugg, J. (1992), *The Emergence of Cemetery Companies in Britain 1820–53*, University of Stirling, Unpublished Ph.D. Thesis.

—— (1997), 'The Origins and Progress of Cemetery Establishment in Britain', in P. C. Jupp and G. Howarth (eds), *The Changing Face of Death: Historical Accounts of Death and Disposal*, New York: St Martin's Press.

—— (1998), 'A Few Remarks on Modem Sepulture: Current Trends and New Directions in Cemetery Research', *Mortality*, 3(2): 111–28.

—— (2000), 'Defining the Place of Burial: What Makes a Cemetery a Cemetery?', *Mortality*, 5(3): 259–76.

Schama, S. (1995), *Landscape and Memory*, London: HarperCollins.

Schneider, D.M. (1968), *American Kinship: A Cultural Account*, Engle-
  wood Cliffs, NJ: Prentice-Hall.
Schut, H. A., Stroebe, M. S., van den Bout, J. and de Keijser, J. (1997),
  'Intervention for the Bereaved: Gender Differences in the Efficacy of
  Two Counselling Programmes', *British Journal of Clinical Psychology*,
  36: 63–72.
Schuyler, D. (1984), 'The Evolution of the Anglo-American Rural Ceme-
  tery: Landscape Architecture as Social and Cultural History', *Journal
  of Garden History*, 4(3): 291–304.
Seale, C. (1998), *Constructing Death: The Sociology of Dying and
  Bereavement*, Cambridge: Cambridge University Press.
Seremetakis, C. N. (1991), *The Last Word: Women, Death, and Divina-
  tion in Inner Mani*, Chicago: University of Chicago Press.
—— (ed.) (1994), *The Senses Still: Perception and Memory as Material
  Culture in Modernity*, Chicago: University of Chicago Press.
Sheridan, A. (2000), *Heaven and Hell and Other Worlds of the Dead*,
  Edinburgh: NMS Publishing Ltd.
Silverman, H. (2002a), 'Introduction: The Space and Place of Death', in
  H. Silverman and D. B. Small (eds), *The Space and Place of Death*,
  Archaeological Papers of the American Anthropological Association,
  No. 11, Arlington, VA: American Anthropological Association.
—— (2002b), 'Narratives of Identity and History in Modern Cemeteries
  of Lima, Peru', in H. Silverman and D.B. Small (eds), *The Space and
  Place of Death*, Archaeological Papers of the American Anthropo-
  logical Association, No. 11, Arlington, VA: American Anthropological
  Association.
—— and Small, D. B. (eds) (2002), *The Space and Place of Death*,
  Archaeological Papers of the American Anthropological Association,
  No. 11, Arlington, VA: American Anthropological Association.
Silverman, P. and Klass, D. (1996), 'Introduction: What's the Problem?',
  in D. Klass, P. R. Silverman and S. L. Nickman (eds), *Continuing Bonds:
  New Understandings of Grief*, Washington, DC: Taylor and Francis.
Simo, M. L. (1988), *Loudon and the Landscape*, New Haven: Yale
  University Press.
Sixsmith, J. and Sixsmith, A. (1990), 'Places in Transition: the Impact of
  Life Events on the Experience of Home', in T. Putnam and C. Newton
  (eds), *Household Choices*, Middlesex Polytechnic: Futures Publishers
  Ltd.
Sliw, Y. (1995), 'The Cathartic Effect of Ritual in Death and Dying in the
  Jewish Community', Unpublished Paper presented at The Social Con-
  text of Death, Dying and Disposal 2nd International Conference, Uni-
  versity of Sussex.
Sloane, D. C. (1991), *The Last Great Necessity: Cemeteries in American
  History*, Baltimore, MD: The Johns Hopkins University Press.

Smale, D. A. (1994), *Davies' Law of Burial, Cremation and Exhumation,* Crayford, Kent: Shaw & Sons.

Small, N. (2001), 'Theories of Grief: A Critical Review', in J. Hockey, J. Katz, and N. Small (eds), *Grief, Mourning and Death Ritual,* Buckingham: Open University Press.

Solman, D. (1995), *Loddiges of Hackney: the Largest Hothouse in the World,* London: The Hackney Society.

Stevens-Arroyo, A. M. (1998), 'Syncretic Sociology: Toward a Cross-Disciplinary Study of Religion', *Sociology of Religion,* 59(3): 217–36.

Stilgoe, J. R. (1982), *Common Landscapes of America, 1580–1845,* New Haven: Yale University Press.

Stone, E. (1858), *God's Acre: or, Historical Notices Relating to Churchyards,* London: J. W. Parker and Sons.

Strang, J. (1831), *Necropolis Glasguensis with Observations on Ancient and Modern Tombs and Sepulture,* Glasgow: Atkinson & Co.

Strange, J.-M. (2003), '"Tho' Lost to Sight, To Memory Dear": Pragmatism, Sentimentality and Working-class Attitudes towards the Grave, c. 1875–1914', *Mortality,* 8(2): 144–59.

Stroebe, M. S. (1998), 'New Directions in Bereavement Research: Exploration of Gender Differences', *Palliative Medicine,* 12: 5–12.

—— and Schut, H. (1999), 'The Dual Process Model of Coping with Bereavement: Rationale and Description', *Death Studies,* 23: 197–224.

——, Gergen, M., Gergen, K. and Stroebe, W. (1996), 'Broken Hearts or Broken Bonds?', in D. Klass, P. R. Silverman and S. L. Nickman (eds), *Continuing Bonds: New Understandings of Grief,* Washington, DC: Taylor and Francis.

Strong, R. (1979), *The Renaissance Garden in England,* London: Thames & Hudson Ltd.

Stroud, D. (1975), *Capability Brown,* London: Faber & Faber.

Sudnow, D. (1967), *Passing On: The Social Organization of Dying,* Englewood Cliffs: Prentice-Hall, Inc.

Susser, B. (ed.) (1997), *Alderney Road Jewish Cemetery, London E1, 1697–1853: Anglo-Jewry's Oldest Ashkenazi Cemetery,* London: United Synagogue Publications Ltd, in association with The Working Party on Jewish Monuments in the UK & Ireland.

Synott, A. (1992), 'Tomb, Temple, Machine and Self: the Social Construction of the Body', *The British Journal of Sociology,* 43(1): 79–110.

Tarlow, S. (1999), *Bereavement and Commemoration: The Archaeology of Mortality,* Oxford: Blackwell.

Taylor, H. A. (1994), *Age and Order. The Public Park as a Metaphor for a Civilised Society,* London: Comedia in Association with Demos.

Taylor, L. J. (1980), 'Symbolic Death: An Anthropological View of Mourning Ritual in the Nineteenth Century', in M. Pike and J. Armstrong (eds), *A Time to Mourn: Expressions of Grief in Nineteenth-Century America,* Stonybrook, NY: The Museums at Stonybrook.

—— (1989a), 'Introduction: The Uses of Death in Europe', *Anthropological Quarterly*, 62(4): 149–54.

—— (1989b), 'Bas InEirinn: Cultural Constructions of Death in Ireland', *Anthropological Quarterly*, 62(4): 175–87.

—— (1999), 'Re-entering the West Room: On the Power of Domestic Spaces', in D. Birdwell-Pheasant and D. Lawrence-Zuniga (eds), *House Life: Space, Place and Family in Europe*, Oxford: Berg.

Thomas, K. (1983), *Man and the Natural World: Changing Attitudes in England 1500–1800*, London: Penguin Books Ltd.

Townsend, P. (1957), *The Family Life of Old People: An Inquiry in East London*, London: Routledge & Kegan Paul.

Tucker, C. (1992), 'Jewish Marriages and Divorces in England until 1940', *Genealogists' Magazine*, Part I: 173–85; Part II: 277–86.

Turner, B. S. (1992), *Regulating Bodies, Essays in Medical Sociology*, London: Routledge.

—— (1996), *The Body and Society: Explorations in Social Theory*, London: Sage.

Turner, S. (1991), *Religion and Social Theory*, London: Sage.

Tyson, M. M. (1998), *The Healing Landscape: Therapeutic Outdoor Environments*, New York: McGraw-Hill.

United Synagogue (1955), *Laws and Byelaws of the Burial Society*, London: Woburn House.

van Gennep, A. (1960/1908), *The Rites of Passage*, Chicago: University of Chicago Press.

Vaporis, N. M. (1977), *An Orthodox Prayer Book*, Brookline, MA: Holly Cross Orthodox Press.

Vassiliadis, N. P. (1993), *The Mystery of Death*, Athens: The Orthodox Brotherhood of Theologians 'The Saviour'.

Vitebsky, P. (1993), *Dialogues With the Dead*, Cambridge: Cambridge University Press.

Walker, G. (1839), *Gatherings from Graveyards*, London: Longman & Co.

Walter, T. (1990), *Funerals and How to Improve Them*, London: Hodder & Stoughton.

—— (1991), 'Modern Death: Taboo or Not Taboo?', *Sociology*, 25(2): 293–310.

—— (1994), *The Revival of Death*, London: Routledge.

—— (1996), 'A New Model of Grief: Bereavement and Biography', *Mortality*, 1(1): 7–25.

—— (1997), 'Emotional Reserve and the English Way of Grief', in K. Charmaz, G. Howarth and A. Kellahear (eds), *The Unknown Country: Experiences of Death in Australia, Britain and the USA*, London: Macmillan.

—— (1999), *On Bereavement: The Culture of Grief*, Buckingham: Open University Press.

Ware, T. (1991), *The Orthodox Church*, London: Penguin Books.

Warner, W. L. (1959), *The Living and the Dead*, Chicago: University of Chicago Press.

Waterfield, G. (ed.) (1996), *Soane and Death*, Dulwich Picture Gallery.

Watkin, D. (1996), 'Monuments and Mausolea in the Age of Enlightenment', in G. Waterfield (ed.), *Soane and Death*, London: Dulwich Picture Gallery.

Weaver, L. (1915), *Memorials and Monuments*, London: Country Life.

Webster's Third New International Dictionary of the English Language (1981), Springfield, MA: G & C Merrian and Co.

Werner, C. (1987), 'Home Interiors: A Time and Place for Interpersonal Relationships', *Environment and Behavior*, 19(2): 169–79.

——, Altman, I. and Oxley, D. (1985), 'Temporal Aspects of Home: A Transactional Analysis', in I. Altman and C. Werner (eds), *Home Environments*, New York: Plenum.

Weiss, B. (1997), 'Forgetting Your Dead: Alienable and Inalienable Objects in Northwest Tanzania', *Anthropological Quarterly*, 70(4): 164–72.

Weston, J. (1969), *In Remembrance. A Book of Floral Tributes Executed by Jane Weston and Photographed by Marion Street*, London: Mark Weston, Four Seasons Flowers.

Whaley, J. (ed.) (1981), *Mirrors of Mortality: Studies in the Social History of Death*, London: Europa Publications.

Williams, R. (1990), *A Protestant Legacy*, Oxford: Clarendon Press.

Williamson, T. (1995), *Polite Landscapes*, Baltimore: The Johns Hopkins University Press.

Willmott, P. and Young, M. (1961), *Family and Class in a London Suburb*, London: Routledge & Kegan Paul.

Winter, J. (1995), *Sites of Memory, Sites of Mourning: The Great War in European Cultural History*, Cambridge: Cambridge University Press.

Wolfston, P. S. (1985), *Greater London Cemeteries and Crematoria*, London: Society of Genealogists.

Worden, J. W. (1991), *Grief Counselling and Grief Therapy: A Handbook for the Mental Health Practitioner*, London: Routledge.

Worpole, K. (2003), *Last Landscapes: The Architecture of the Cemetery in the West*, London: Reaktion Books.

Woudstra, J. (1989), 'The European Cemetery', *Landscape Design*, No. 184: 19–22.

Young, M. and Cullen, L. (1996), *A Good Death*, London: Routledge.

—— and Willmott, P. (1957), *Family and Kinship in East London*, London: Routledge & Kegan Paul.

Zborowski, M. and Herzog, E. (1952), *Life is With People: The Culture Of the Shtetl*, New York: Schocken.

Index